Sunset TRAVEL GUIDE TO Southeast Asia

Lane Publishing Co. · Menlo Park, California

Acknowledgments

The countries of Southeast Asia offer a stimulating array of discoveries for the traveler, each country providing travel experiences uniquely its own. Together they compress into one rather concentrated area a multitude of fascinating sights and activities.

Research for this travel guide was expedited in many helpful ways by the following individuals and organizations:

For assistance in travel arrangements, special thanks are due James Caputo, Vice President, Americas, Philippine Airlines; Donald Broadley, Manager North America, Malaysian Airline Systems; and Claus Jensen, Manager North America, Thai Airways International.

Many persons helped in the collection of information, manuscript checking, and providing photographs. We especially wish to acknowledge the assistance and cooperation of the following: the editorial staff of *Sunset* Magazine, especially Jeff Phillips, Mary Ann Reese, and Linda Anusasananan; the editors of *Pacific Travel News*, especially James Gebbie and Phyllis Elving; the Pacific Area Travel Association; free lance writer Mary Benton Smith, for much of the original research; and travel writer Robin Dannhorn of Bangkok, for assistance in checking the manuscript.

For assistance on individual countries, we would like to thank the following people:

For the Philippines: the Ministry of Tourism, especially The Honorable Jose D. Aspiras, Minister; and Dante U. Calma.

For Indonesia: the office of Directorate General of Tourism; the staff of the Indonesian Consulate-General, San Francisco; the staff of the Indonesian Tourist Promotion Board, San Francisco; Jack and Dorothy Fields; David and Susan Lampton; A. C. Wawo-Runtu of Garuda Indonesian Airways; and Bonor L. Sinaga.

For Malaysia: the Tourist Development Corporation of Malaysia; the staff of the Sabah Tourist Association; the staff of the Sarawak Tourist Association; and the Malaysian Tourist Information Office, San Francisco.

For Singapore: the Singapore Tourist Promotion Board, especially Morgan Lawrence, North American Manager; and Avis Rent a Car.

For Thailand: the Tourism Authority of Thailand, especially Visit Srinava, Chief of Publicity and Advertising Division; and Asripon Nachiengtung, Director, Los Angeles.

For Burma: Tourist Burma, Hotel and Trade Corporation; Burma Airways; and Diethelm Travel, Bangkok.

Special note: At the time the material on Cambodia, Laos, and Vietnam was written for the first printing of this book, the war in Vietnam had ended, and peaceful reconstruction of these countries appeared to be underway. With the subsequent takeover of these countries by Communist forces, they were closed to normal tourism. The information on Indochina has been retained in this book (with some necessary editing) because the history and traditions of these countries form a vital part of the composite of Southeast Asia.

Supervising Editor: Cornelia Fogle

Research and Text: Lawrence A. Clancy

Special Consultant: Frederic M. Rea, Editor & Publisher, Pacific Travel News

Design: JoAnn Masaoka

Cartography: Roberta Edwards, Doris Marsh

Cover: Volcanoes, coconut palms, and rice fields—universal elements of the Southeast Asian landscape—were photographed by Jack Fields on the Indonesian island of Bali with Mount Agung in the background.

Editor, Sunset Books: David E. Clark

Fourth Printing April 1980

Copyright © 1975, 1968, Lane Publishing Co., Menlo Park, California. Second Edition. World rights reserved. No part of this publication may be reproduced by any mechanical, photographic, or electronic process, nor may it be stored in a retrieval system, transmitted, or otherwise copied for public or private use without prior written permission from the publisher. Library of Congress No. 74-20024. ISBN 0-376-06763-2.
Lithographed in the United States.

Contents

Introduction 4
Philippines 14
Indonesia 44
Malaysia 74
Singapore 102
Thailand 124
Burma 152
Indochina 166
Suggested Reading List 174

Special Features

Exploring Southeast Asia by cruise ship 11
Preparing lechon becomes a Filipino family fiesta 19
The Philippine jeepney 25
Shooting the rapids at Pagsanjan Falls 29
Cockfighting—a Filipino passion 32
Morion Festival—a Holy Week tradition 38
Batik, Indonesia's national cloth 50
Seeing the Java countryside by rail 54
Dramatic dances relate Balinese epics 65
Minangkabau villages celebrate an ancient legend 68
Malaysia's hill stations—cool retreats from lowland heat 78
Giant top spinning—a rural Malaysian sport 85
The Sultanate of Brunei—oil-rich and independent 90
To see the Sabah countryside, charter a rail car 97
Sir Stamford Raffles—foresighted shaper of Singapore 107
Singapore's night markets—open-air bazaars 112
Across the harbor from Singapore—unspoiled Sentosa Island 116
Thai-style boxing, a national sport 130
In Surin... Thailand's elephant roundup 138
Escape to the Samui Islands 143
Tribesmen of Thailand's northern hills 147
Gold foil for Buddha 160

Village farmers *harvest rice by hand* **(top)** *in a Southeast Asian padi. Buddhist priest* **(right)** *leads a Viskha Puja ceremony. Colorfully dressed Balinese women* **(far right)** *parade to a festival, offerings of fruit and vegetables balanced on their heads.*

Southeast Asia

A cosmopolitan crossroads of cultures

Stretching more than 3,000 miles—from the southeast corner of the Asian mainland out over the island-studded Indian Ocean and South China Sea—Southeast Asia is one of the world's most diverse regions. This community of nations offers a fascinating panorama of varied geography, ethnic groups, and cultures.

The mainland portion of this tropical wonderland includes Burma, Thailand, Cambodia, Laos, and Vietnam.

Extending southward from the mainland is the Malay Peninsula, occupied primarily by Malaysia, with Singapore forming an exclamation point at its southern tip. The rest of the area is fragmented into thousands of islands comprising Indonesia, and the Philippines.

An exotic land

For centuries this intriguing region has lured travelers, drawn by tales of the rich spice islands, the jeweled spires of Thailand, Burma's golden pagodas, the archeological treasures of ancient Angkor and Pagan, the incomparable Philippine rice terraces, the fabled isle of Bali, and the romance of such cities as Singapore and Mandalay.

Populating Southeast Asia are some 300 million people, about 30 million of them clustered in the nine capital cities. Most of the inhabitants, almost 90 percent, live outside the cities — on the lush farmlands cut by winding rivers, along the sparsely settled fringes of tropical rain forests, in tiny settlements in the mountainous highlands, or in coastal stilt villages built above shallow muddy waters.

Since World War II, the world has called this area Southeast Asia, but for centuries it was known in other terms. To the Indians it was the island kingdoms of Sumatra and Java, the Indianized states of Southeast Asia. To the Chinese it was

INTRODUCTION 5

Nanyang, or southern ocean. To the British, French, and Dutch, it was "Farther India," "French Indochina," and the "Dutch East Indies."

Shaped by violent earth forces

Until some 300 million years ago, most of Southeast Asia was beneath the sea. Then the mainland rose out of the water, part of a colossal continent which included today's Europe and Africa. During the next 200 million years, this huge land mass underwent constant changes. Violent upheavals occurred in the earth's crust. Volcanoes erupted, and mountains pushed above the landscape. Then the wind and rain went to work, grinding down the mountains until the land surface became a vast, featureless plain, cut by broad and shallow rivers.

About 25 million years ago, the earth's crust once again began to churn and heave, thrusting up gigantic mountain ranges. The Alps rose in Europe, and the Himalayas appeared between India and China. Hundreds of volcanoes, curved in a giant arc from Burma south through the Indonesian archipelago and then north through the Philippines, began spitting out black basalt lava. Their eruptions brought destruction, but they also deposited mineral-rich ashes over territory destined to become some of the richest agricultural land in the world.

The melting of the polar ice cap, some 10,000 to 20,000 years ago, caused the oceans to rise, covering vast areas of coastal lowlands. Parts of Southeast

SOUTHEAST ASIA

Asia went underwater, forming the Sunda Shelf, the largest continental shelf in the world. Its warm waters make up large portions of the South China, Java, Celebes, and Sulu seas, and the Gulf of Thailand. Higher land areas remained above sea level, forming the thousands of islands of Indonesia and the Philippines.

The area is still a center of much volcanic activity, with 10 active volcanoes in the Philippines and 77 in Indonesia.

Rain and heat regulate daily life

Equatorial heat and the seasonal ebb and flow of monsoon winds and life-giving rains regulate the life rhythm of Southeast Asia's people, plants, and animals. Rainfall exceeds 80 inches a year in most areas, reaching 150 to 200 inches annually in others. The region's temperature varies only a few degrees throughout the year from a mean of about 80° F. These conditions, combined with the rich volcanic soil, create a superabundance of plant and animal life and help to support some of the world's densest populations.

Some of the rain is seasonal; twice a year, torrential rainstorms are driven across the land by the monsoon winds. Dry land and parched forests turn green and lush almost overnight. Rivers swell to overflowing, spilling their silt-laden waters over the flat lowlands. In other areas, rain falls consistently throughout the year, creating jungly rain forests so dense in some areas that they mark the limit of civilization.

The heavy rainfall creates countless rivers and streams, most of them small, a few large—such as the Irrawaddy in Burma, the Chao Phraya in Thailand, and the Mekong, which flows through several countries.

Tropical plants and animals

Over the millenniums, Southeast Asia has been graced by warm sunshine, plentiful rain, and gentle winds. Its lands and waters teem with an endless array of plant and animal life. Naturalists estimate that the area contains more than 1,500 vertebrates and possibly as many as 200,000 invertebrates. The varieties of plant life are too staggering in number to record.

Tropical forests cover much of the land; a single acre may provide growing space for 50 different types of trees, ranging from great teak forests to stands of ironwood, mahogany, and mangrove. Rubber trees—introduced from Brazil—grow on the vast plantations, making Southeast Asia the greatest rubber-growing area in the world. Hillsides support cultivated plantations of tea plants, pepper bushes, and tapioca plants. The bamboo tree, common throughout the area, supplies the most important building material; bamboo is used for houses, furniture, and utensils.

Southeast Asia is the natural habitat of the orangutan, huge lizards, and mammals that fly. Here, too, are tigers, leopards, panthers, rhinoceroses, and pythons. The waters of the Sunda Shelf provide a plentiful food supply for seemingly endless varieties of fish. Rivers, deltas, and coastal mud flats support millions of crabs.

Rice, the sacred staple

Rice is the basic food in Southeast Asia, and the shallow, flooded *padis* (rice fields) are the most striking element of the landscape.

On the plains, the rice fields stretch for miles, separated by dikes and connected by an ingenious network of irrigation waterways. On the face of the land, the rice fields create endless geometric patterns broken only by occasional villages or meandering streams.

In mountainous areas, rice is cultivated in terraces that climb in a series of giant, free-form steps from valley almost to crest. Masterpieces of engineering, they are among the wonders of the world.

The pervading rice culture lends a timeless quality to the region; since antiquity it has provided the people's major sustenance. Fields are tilled by heavily yoked water buffalo; seed is scattered into muddy planting beds; seedlings are set out in the shallow water of growing beds by straw-hatted women who wade ankle deep in the water; ripe grain is harvested by hand.

In the fields, shrines are built to protect growing grain against the displeasure of spirit gods. Religious rites are celebrated in the villages to insure a good crop, and festivals thank the gods for the bounty. This agricultural cycle has changed little in the last thousand years.

Transplanting rice seedlings *to irrigated padis is a laborious task for entire families several times a year, but the padis yield hardy plants.*

INTRODUCTION 7

Moorish-style *railway administration building, modern vehicles, and a turbaned Indian pushing a bicycle dramatize Kuala Lumpur's cultural mix.*

Burning incense sticks *engulf worshipers in aromatic clouds at Chinese temple. Many houses of worship in Southeast Asia are open to visitors.*

Over the centuries, the small, isolated villages in the padis, with their houses of bamboo topped by palm leaf roofs, have become the region's most important social and economic units. Villagers work together not only to grow and harvest the crop but also to raise animals, grow vegetables, develop handicrafts, and celebrate secular and religious events.

A cultural crossroads

Nowhere else on earth does man exist in such a diversity of races as he does in Southeast Asia. In central Java, anthropologists have found fossilized remains of the Java man, who dates back some 500,000 years. He was succeeded by later races of men in various stages of development.

Embraced by oceans on three sides and bounded by mountains to the north, Southeast Asia's original inhabitants existed for thousands of years in splendid isolation.

But as waves of migration came from the north and west and as man became more mobile and more acquisitive, most of that isolation disappeared. The area became a cosmopolitan crossroads, and today the population is a grand mix of cultures.

A mingling of ethnic groups

Tribes of Negritos found in the Philippines and Malaysia are considered representative of some of the earlier inhabitants. But most of the people of Southeast Asia are Mongoloids of various types who migrated south from mainland Asia before the Caucasoids arrived from India.

Each successive wave of people added to the existing cultures; yet each group retained its own identity. You'll recognize Indians by their facial characteristics and sometimes by their dress—notably the men's turbans and the women's saris. The Chinese number in the millions, most of them residing in city Chinatowns throughout the area.

Among the indigenous people, you'll find remarkable similarities. The Malaysian looks very much like his neighbor in Thailand, Burma, or the Philippines. A wide variety of racial groups are represented—largest of which are the Burmans, Thais, and Malays.

In Malaysia and Indonesia you'll find Arabs. And, of course, each country has small concentrations—principally in the cities—of Englishmen, Europeans, and Americans.

The customs, life styles, and attitudes developed in Southeast Asia during these centuries of migrations can be seen today: the cultivation of rice fields, the domestication of the ox and the water buffalo, the communal village, the irrigation system for cultivating rice, the belief in ancestral spirits and gods of the soil, and the placement of shrines in rice fields, on hillsides, and atop mountains.

The multiplicity of racial groups in the area has

Boat builder *on Malaysia's east coast utilizes bowlike instrument to power his ancient hand drill.*

Stilt houses, *shaded by palm trees, are found throughout the region. Children often run to greet visitors.*

encouraged a multitude of languages. Though English is commonly spoken in the cities, each country has its own national language, often a second language, as well as numerous local dialects.

Great religions dominate everyday life

In Southeast Asia religion is pervasive. In the cities you see striking temples, mosques, and churches. In the countryside, most villages surround a temple or local shrine; in the fields, shrines are erected to the gods of fertility. Often religion dominates the social life as well, and many colorful festivals are primarily religious celebrations.

Buddhism and Islam are the area's dominant religions, followed by Hinduism and Christianity. In the Philippines, Christianity is the primary religion; you'll find Christian churches in most of the main cities of the region as well.

Most of the Chinese are Buddhists. Animism and ancestor worship are still practiced by some of the primitive, isolated tribes, and some animistic influences have been mixed with the practices of Buddhist, Muslim, Hindu, and Christian faiths.

A legacy of ancient empires

Archeological discoveries in Southeast Asia have revealed the existence of ancient cultures and great empires. These empires experienced their greatest growth and development from 600 to 1,200 A.D., and their structures rank among the finest architectural achievements of man: temples built by the Chams south of Hue in Vietnam, the matchless wonders of the Khmer rulers in Angkor in Cambodia and at Pimai in Thailand, and the great Hindu and Buddhist temples in central Java and Pagan in Burma.

Outside influences bring new ideas

Beginning about the first and second centuries A.D., several waves of new ideas and concepts swept into Southeast Asia, aiding and modifying its development. The first wave came from India, the second from China, and the final surge from the colonial powers.

Indian culture. The region's most important cultural influences came from India. The major religions—Buddhism, Hinduism, and Islam—and the concept of kinship and statesmanship are based on Indian models. Indians also brought their literature and arts, the classical dance, and even language. This took place gradually, as ideas were spread by Indian merchants and priests.

The town of Pagan in northern Burma became a great center of Buddhism from 1084 to 1113 A.D. From this point, the religion expanded eastward to other Southeast Asian countries.

Islam was first introduced in northern Sumatra in the late 13th century, but its major growth came two centuries later when Malacca became a trading center and Islam spread throughout the Malay Peninsula. Today, you can find Muslims and their mosques in Sumatra and Java in Indonesia and in Malaysia, Singapore, and the southern Philippines.

China's contribution. Southeast Asia is geographically situated between India and China, yet China's influence seems slight compared to that of India.

INTRODUCTION 9

Reclining Buddha *looms over visitors at Ayutthaya, a former capital of Thailand. Area is rich in well-preserved, ancient ruins.*

The Chinese influence was most important in Vietnam, where many elements of China's culture were adopted—including Chinese Buddhism, Confucianism, and Taoism—but not the language.

Elsewhere on the Indochina peninsula, Chinese business and commercial activities strongly influenced the development of trade. Chinese influences also appear in the region's decorative arts, especially the ceramics of Thailand in the 13th and 14th centuries.

One of China's greatest contributions to all of Southeast Asia was its people. Throughout the region, the Chinese play an important economic role. Chinese temples and Chinatowns are found in most of the area's major cities.

Colonial influences. When the western powers arrived in Southeast Asia in the 16th century, the area had long been a cultural and commercial crossroads for the Indians, Chinese, and Arabs. For the next 400 years, European powers—Portuguese, Spanish, British, Dutch, and French—dominated various parts of the region.

Western influence, characterized by commercial and trading enterprises, began with the arrival of the Portuguese at Malacca in 1511 and the Spanish in the Philippines ten years later. The influence of the Europeans grew until by 1870 almost all of Southeast Asia was under their control. The Dutch dominated Indonesia; the British controlled Burma, Penang, Malacca, and Singapore; and the French extended their influence over Indochina.

Though the colonial period involved much economic exploitation, it also had lasting benefits—particularly the unifying of some countries.

It also brought major population shifts from the countryside to the new cities, added Chinese and Indian minorities to overcrowded areas, and tended to make the native population outsiders in the major cities in their own countries.

Cities built to endure. The greatest change resulting from European influence occurred in the region's cities.

The ancient empires of Southeast Asia considered cities ceremonial or symbolic centers, but the strength of the empire remained in the countryside with the scattered villages and rice farmers who fed the ruler's slaves and soldiers. When the empires fell, the cities disappeared.

In Europe, though, cities provided the focal point for survival and for the development of culture. Consequently, the colonial powers built most of the major cities of Southeast Asia. They tacked them onto the rural landscape as river-mouth settlements or beside harbors along the major shipping routes. The European-built cities were constructed to endure as power centers.

Today, wherever you travel in Southeast Asia, you'll see this legacy. Singapore's city center, with its colonial buildings, resembles a British township. You'll notice many British-inspired buildings in Rangoon and Penang. French architecture and cuisine appear in Laos, Cambodia, and southern Vietnam. In Indonesia's capital of Jakarta, you'll see the Dutch buildings and canals fashioned after those in the old country. Filipino architecture reminds many travelers of the gracious architecture of Spain.

The convulsions of change

Today, all of the Southeast Asian countries are independent nations, seeking new destinies, in some cases undergoing economic, social, and political upheaval.

Change is very much in evidence. You see it in the cities—new buildings, broad new streets, industrial growth, new housing to take the place of shacks. You hear more about it from the people—new schools, better medical care, more food, more purchasing power. It's stimulating to be on the scene and experience in some small way the shaping of these new nations.

The traveler in Southeast Asia

Modern transportation has made this exciting region easily accessible to the traveler. International airlines and cruise ships transport visitors to the major cities; popular tours follow the established sightseeing routes. Hotels, restaurants, and other tourist facilities in the big cities and resorts rank with the world's best.

You can visit the cities in comfort, get around with ease, and, if you wish, eat almost without changing your diet. Yet the travel experience is still colossal. You'll see things, do things, and encounter other cultures in one of the most exotic and fascinating parts of the world.

Off the principal routes, you'll find Southeast Asia to be an almost virgin travel land. Elephant roundups, bull races, colorful markets, train rides through rain forests, tribal craftsmen, island hideaways, spectacular river trips, festive celebrations—an almost endless list of discoveries awaits the curious traveler. In some of the more out-of-the-way places, you may be pleasantly surprised to discover comfortable accommodations, good food and drink, and companionship of congenial people.

Festivals and events

Lively and colorful celebrations are a continuing part of the scene throughout Southeast Asia. Festivals follow the agricultural cycle, the rhythm of the seasons, and the phases of the moon. Each ethnic and religious group observes its own special events, and every pagoda and temple celebrates its share of holy days.

Buddhist families mark the ordination of boys as monks. The birthday of Prophet Mohammed is honored as a national holiday in Muslim areas. For the Hindus, Thaipusam is a time of public penance. These and many other festivals are celebrated throughout the region.

In addition, each country commemorates special days exclusively its own—based on local mythology, political events, or religious peculiarities. You will find information about some of these events at the end of each chapter.

Below are some of the festivals and events celebrated in a similar manner in several Southeast Asian countries. The same festival may fall on different dates in different countries. Some events are based on the lunar calendar, with dates changing from year to year. In planning your trip, check with the appropriate government tourist office for a current calendar of events.

The rhythm of the seasons

In Asia, agricultural festivals have been celebrated for generations; most of them follow the cycle of the rice harvest. Though modern high-yield rice strains and other agricultural advances have moderated the festivals' significance, traditional communications with the gods are still observed.

Rice planting. In late April or early May, village and regional festivals celebrate the new rice season and invoke the patronage of the spirits.

Exploring Southeast Asia by cruise ship

Sightseeing by cruise ship in the island-dotted waterways of Southeast Asia is one of the great adventure trips in the world of travel. Recently, a number of ships have begun operating passenger cruises in the area. Some visit the popular tourist ports. Others anchor off remote islands that are otherwise inaccessible but have tremendous appeal. You visit villages and see cultures that have existed in near isolation for centuries, places where tourists are a rarity.

The ships do most of their sailing at night, putting into port early in the morning and offering some excellent shore excursions for the passengers. Most of the voyages are made in sheltered waters. The straits through which they sail are busy seaways with a fascinating parade of ships and fishing craft.

Among the companies offering sightseeing cruises in Southeast Asian waters are these:

Holland American Cruises' *Prinsendam* sails from Singapore. After putting in at Penang in Malaysia, it makes a stimulating series of Indonesian stops: Belawan (seaport for Medan), Sibolga, and Padang on Sumatra; Nias Island off the coast of Sumatra; Jakarta, Semarang, and Cilacap on Java; and Padang Bay off Bali.

Dominion Far East Line's *Marco Polo* runs 6 and 7-week cruises out of Australia to ports in the Orient and Southeast Asia. The cruises include stops in the Philippines, Papua New Guinea, Singapore, the Solomon Islands, Malaysia, Indonesia, and Thailand.

The *Doña Montserrat*, operated by the Negros Navigation Company, sails from Manila through Philippine waters with stops at Corregidor, Zamboanga, Cebu, Iloilo, Romblon, Sicogon Island, and Ambil Island.

Other lines that send their cruise ships occasionally into these waters include P&O Australia, Sitmar Cruises, Lindblad Travel, American President Lines, Cunard Lines, Norwegian America Lines, Royal Viking Lines, Society Expeditions Cruises, and Straits Lines out of Singapore. Ask your travel agent for details.

Cruise ship *anchors off a remote island so passengers can make a day trip ashore.*

Buddhists *pay respect with flower offerings, then use joss sticks to foretell their future.*

Carrying *lighted candles, devout Buddhists assemble at temple. Visitors are welcome at many events.*

Firewalking ceremony *highlights the Malaysian celebration of the Chinese Festival of the Nine Emperor Gods in Kuala Lumpur.*

Ploughing and rice planting ceremonies include prayers for a good crop, music, dancing, and other fair activities.

Life giving rains. Since the success of the rice crop is largely dependent on the annual rains, special festivals are held to encourage the rain and to give thanks for it.

Folk dancing accompanies celebrations in Malaysia. At festivals in Burma, Thailand, and Singapore, enthusiastic participants douse everyone with water.

Buddhist festivals

Because millions of Southeast Asia's inhabitants follow the precepts of Gautama Buddha, many celebrations revolve around Buddhism's ancient ceremonies.

Ordination of monks. When rice seedlings are transplanted in July, young boys are ordained as Buddhist monks in Burma and Thailand. Young monks serve in this capacity for three months, until the rice harvest begins in October.

This initiation to manhood, re-enacting Buddha's great departure, is similar to the Christian confirmation or Jewish bar mitzvah.

Buddhist Lent. The Buddhist Lenten period begins with the rains in April or May and continues through the rainy season. During this period those who are followers of Buddha are expected to be devout, and Buddhist monks spend their time meditating in the *wats*.

In September or October, the end of the Lenten period is celebrated with the Festival of Lights in Thailand, Burma, Singapore, and Indonesia. For three nights all the lights burn. This includes candles, oil lamps, and electric bulbs. The celebrants dance and release masses of fire balloons—a spectacular event to see.

Celebration of Lord Buddha. After the rains begin in May, Buddhist celebrations commemorate the birth, enlightenment, and death of Lord Buddha.

Lantern processions and religious rites are celebrated at major temples in Indonesia, Malaysia, Burma, Thailand, and Singapore.

Muslim festivals

In those parts of Southeast Asia where Islam is practiced, Mohammed's birthday and the Muslim holy days mark the calendar.

The fasting period. The Muslim fasting month, Ramadan, occurs during the ninth month of the Muslim year. Malaysia, Indonesia, and the southern Philippines celebrate the end of fasting with a day of mass prayers in the mosques, feasting, and the giving of gifts.

Mohammed's birthday. The birthday of Prophet Mohammed is usually celebrated in April. It is called Maolod en Nabi in the Philippines and Mauloddan Nabi in Malaysia, where it's a national holiday. All of Indonesia honors Mohammed's birth as Grebeg Maulud.

Pilgrimage to Mecca. Every follower of Islam wants to make a *haji*, or pilgrimage, to Mecca at least once in his lifetime. Annually, Muslims in Malaysia, Singapore, the Philippines, and Indonesia celebrate their haji with the Hari Raya Haji. Followers who have made the pilgrimage gather at the principal mosques to rejoice.

Hindu festivals

The origins of Hinduism go back more than 4,000 years and embrace dozens of sects. So pervasive is this religion that, in regions where Hinduism is practiced, its rituals become part of everyday life for its followers. Many daily activities—prayers, food offerings, bathing—are part of a year-round religious observance.

Two of the great Hindu epic dramas—the Ramayana and the Mahabharata—are performed in whole or in part in Indonesia, Singapore, and parts of Malaysia. Many Balinese dances and celebrations are based on the colorful, emotional Hindu observances.

Birthday of Lord Subramaniam. Hindu devotees in Bali, Malaysia, and Singapore honor the birthday of Lord Subramaniam in late January or early February with the festival of Thaipusam. Worshippers line the route, chanting and wailing prayers. Thousands of devotees, some bearing religious images, join the procession as it passes through the streets. Many penitents carry ornately decorated *kavadis*, wooden frames pinned to the back and chest by long metal skewers.

Festival of Lights. Usually held in early November, Deepavali—the Hindu Festival of Lights—marks the victory of Lord Krishna over a mythical king. On the night of the festival, all Hindu homes are lighted with oil lamps or candles. You can see this observance in Singapore, Penang, and Bali.

Chinese celebrations

Wherever you go in Southeast Asia, you find enclaves of Chinese who continue to celebrate their traditional holidays. Among major events are Chinese New Year (in January or February), Cheng Beng, similar to All Soul's Day (in early April), the Birthday of the Goddess of Mercy and the Festival of Seven Sisters (both in August), the Moon Cake Festival (usually about mid-September), and the Festival of the Nine Emperor Gods (late October). Of these, Chinese New Year (known as "Tet" in some countries) and the Moon Cake Festival are most interesting to the visitor.

Chinese New Year. The New Year gets off to a noisy start with three days of festivities—exploding firecrackers, colorful dragon parades, feasting, and visits to Chinese temples. During this period of great goodwill, Chinese decorate their homes and worshippers wear their most colorful clothing when visiting the temples.

Moon Cake Festival. Legends relate that Mongol overlords were overthrown by Chinese who hid messages in moon cakes. During the Moon Cake Festival, Chinatown shops are filled with boxes of moon cakes, and the shop fronts are decorated with colorful paper lanterns of every size and description.

During Thaipusam, *penitents demonstrate their faith by carrying* kavadis, *their spikes piercing back and chest. Metal spike skewers the man's cheeks.*

Banaue *rice terraces* **(top)**, *carved from steep hillsides, are more than 2,000 years old. Fishing boats and military ships dock in southern seaport of Zamboanga. Villagers stop for a chat* **(far right)** *outside a* sarisari *store near town of Iloilo.*

Philippines

A fascinating blend of Spain and Asia

Though it is part of Southeast Asia the Philippines is in many ways the most untypical of the Southeast Asian nations. Filipinos appear to belong to the Malayan race, but they have Spanish names. Although they speak indigenous dialects, almost everyone also speaks English, and many speak Spanish. The great religions of Asia are in evidence, though most of the population is Christian. The countryside resembles other parts of Southeast Asia, yet its landscapes include cloud-capped volcanic peaks and pine-clad highlands. Manila, its major city, combines some trademarks of big Asian cities with modern thoroughfares and suburbs.

Filipinos possess an uncommon warmth, along with a courtesy, pride, and politeness derived from their Asian and Spanish heritages. The women enjoy an independence and a place in the community unparalleled in Southeast Asia.

Scenically, the Philippines offers an incredible variety—from cosmopolitan Manila—the capital—to villages on stilts; from superb examples of baroque architecture in ancient cathedrals to red-domed mosques set in peaceful palm groves; from tiny islands bordered by dazzling white sand beaches to towering volcanoes topped with clouds; from tiny farm lands to the overpowering rice terraces covering whole mountain sides and dating back some 2,000 years.

Upon arrival (and when you depart) you'll hear one universal expression: *Mabuhay* (pronounced ma-BOO-hai). Strictly translated, it means "long live"—but the word also has come to mean "welcome," "farewell," "good luck," and "God speed."

The Philippines—then and now

Lying about six hundred miles off Asia's southeastern coast, the 7,107 islands of the Philippine archipelago are widely scattered through the blue waters

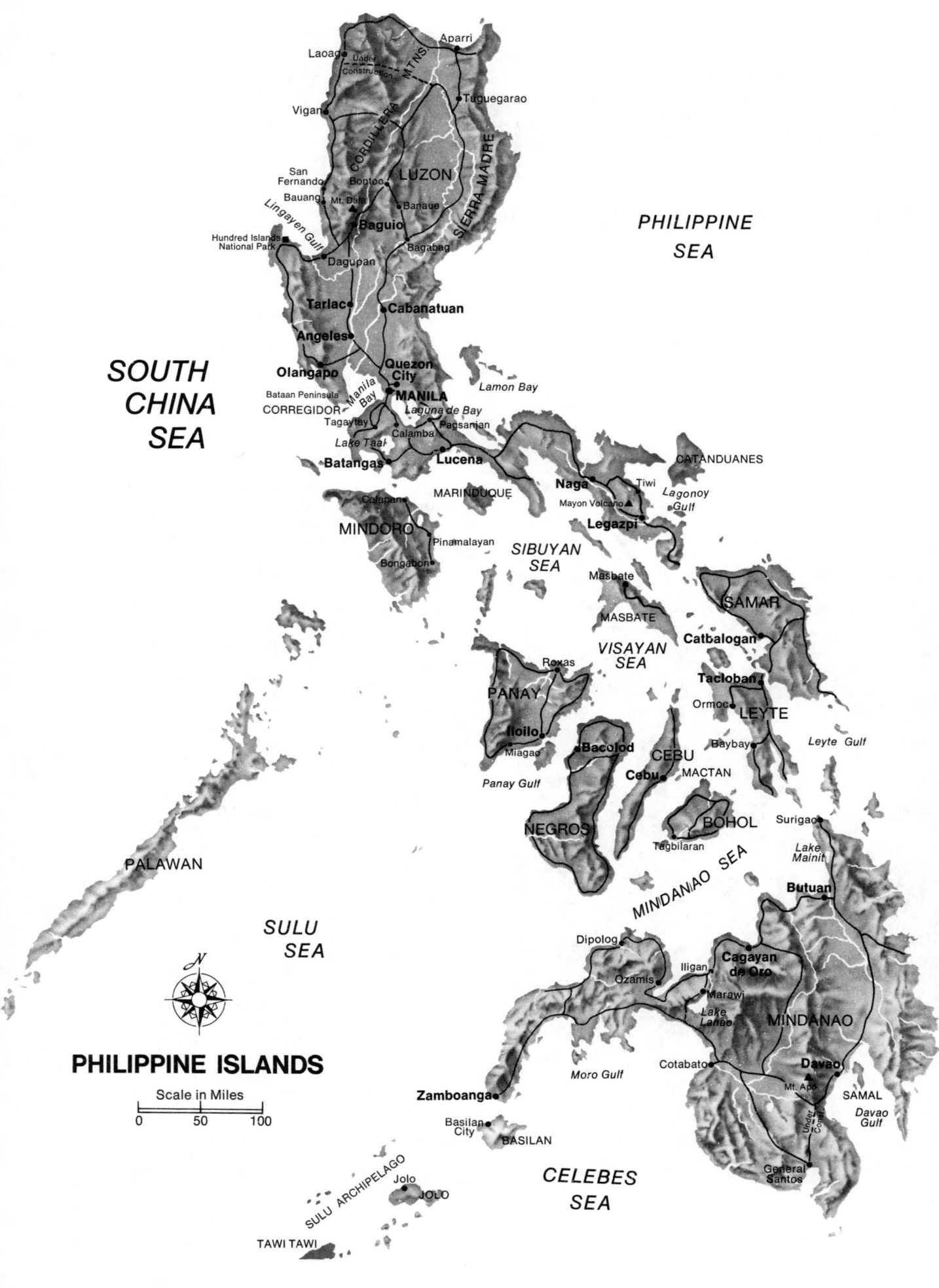

of the South China Sea. Northernmost are the rocky Batan Islands, only 100 miles south of Taiwan. Lying 1,150 miles to the south are the islands of the Sulu Archipelago, just a few degrees north of the equator; Tawi-Tawi Island, in the Sulu Sea, is only 14 miles east of the island of Borneo.

A nation of islands

Most of the Philippines are high islands of volcanic origin—the exposed summits of a partly submerged mountain mass once connected to the Asian mainland. Coral overlays some of the low islands. Some tiny atolls disappear beneath high tides. More than half are unnamed.

The islands are divided into three main groups: Luzon in the north; Visayan Islands in a central cluster; and Mindanao and the Sulu Archipelago in the south. Manila, the capital, is located on Luzon.

Mountain ranges traverse most of the larger islands, with Mount Apo (9,690 feet) on Mindanao topping all other peaks. The larger islands are also characterized by wide coastal plains, natural harbors, extensive valleys, mineral and hot springs, and volcanoes (10 are still active). Mount Taal, one of the lowest volcanoes in the world, erupted as recently as 1971. Manila Bay, nearly circled by a curving, 120-mile shoreline, is the finest harbor in the Far East. In the Pacific Ocean off the coast of Mindanao, the ocean depth drops to 34,578 feet in the Mindanao Deep.

An ancient history

Archeologists have found evidence that prehistoric tribes occupied the Philippines long ago, when its land mass was still attached to the Asian mainland. However, the first inhabitants generally are considered to be the primitive Negritos (small Negroes), descendants of whom still live in the forests of the major islands. These pygmylike people trace their origins back some 25,000 years to the great migration of Stone Age people from Asia.

Waves of immigrants. Next came Indonesians ("island Indians") from Sumatra and Java, who eventually became the hill people of the Mountain Province and of central and eastern Mindanao. Soon the seafaring Malays began to cross the South China Sea in a tremendous movement beginning about 200 B.C. and continuing until the 16th century. As the Malays settled along the coastal plains and in the valleys, the earlier arrivals were displaced and permanently driven into the high mountain ranges. Chinese and Arab traders were early visitors in the island ports, but it was not until about 700 A.D. that the Chinese began to settle in the islands.

Western influences. In 1521 Ferdinand Magellan, the Portuguese navigator, landed at a tiny, uninhabited island in the Leyte Gulf off the coast of Samar. He claimed the islands for Spain and celebrated the first Roman Catholic mass. After planting the cross of Magellan at the already thriving port of Cebu, Magellan and several of his men were killed by Chief Lapu Lapu on Mactan Island in a conflict over Christianization of local tribesmen.

Bringing the cross and the sword, Miguel Lopez de Legazpi and his band of conquistadores arrived in 1565 to establish the islands as a Spanish colony. They named the islands Las Felipinas after Philip II of Spain. These first colonizers found people living in tribal units, with a script, laws, their own culture, and a thriving trade with neighboring countries. Establishing the first capital of Las Felipinas at Cebu City, the conquistadores spent the next seven years conquering the islands. They finally overpowered the Muslim tribesmen and took Manila Bay.

Independence movement. During the 333 years of Spanish rule, more than a hundred revolts were organized by the Filipinos. Finally, in 1896 the colony was rocked by widespread insurrection following the execution of Dr. Jose Rizal, a Filipino author, scholar, and revolutionary leader who sought reform in government and religion. After unsuccessful efforts to establish a republic, insurgents led by General Emilio Aguinaldo joined American forces in the Spanish-American war. Commodore George Dewey defeated the Spanish navy in Manila Bay on May 1, 1898; and Filipino and American ground forces captured the city of Manila. The Treaty of Paris awarded the United States control of the Philippines—a great disappointment to the Filipinos, who expected complete independence.

Immediately, hostilities broke out between the Americans and Filipinos. On January 23, 1899, the First Philippine Republic was inaugurated with General Aguinaldo as its president. A year later Aguinaldo was captured; in trying to avoid further strife, he swore allegiance to the United States, officially ending the armed resistance. Peace, however, did not come until 1902, when the United States began laying the foundations for Philippine independence and self-government.

During World War II Japanese troops occupied the country until it was liberated by U.S. forces under General Douglas MacArthur. During the war years, Filipino and American forces fought side by side during some of the heaviest battles in the Pacific. Although devastated by war, the country began to rebuild in 1945.

Complete independence—promised in an earlier U.S. plan—came on July 4, 1946, with Manuel A. Roxas assuming office as the first president of the Republic of the Philippines.

Government in transition

The Philippines is a constitutional republic with an executive department headed by an elected president and vice president, a congress composed of 24 senators and 98 representatives, and a judicial system. However, in 1972 President Ferdinand E. Marcos declared martial law in response to urban and rural security disturbances and Islamic separatist movements on Mindanao and the Sulu Archipelago.

Assisted by a handful of technocrats, President Marcos presently rules with the aid of the Supreme Court, provincial governors, municipal and city mayors, and *barrio* (village) captains.

The 1935 Philippines' constitution—patterned after the U.S. constitution—is based on the belief that all government authority emanates from the people; a new constitution—more responsive to the goals of a modern Filipino nation—was adopted in 1973.

Since martial law was imposed in 1972, both Filipinos and foreigners find travel safer and more attractive.

But the red carpet is out, and the government is actively seeking visitors. Entry-exit procedures have been smoothed, and usually you are whisked through any military checkpoints.

Tropical plants and animals

Centuries of volcanic activity have given the Philippines rich soil yielding varied plant growth. Tropical evergreen rain forests cover much of the land. Forests of pine grow in the mountains; the lower slopes are covered with bamboo, coconut palm, and banyan trees. Botanists estimate some 10,000 varieties of plants and ferns; orchid species alone number about a thousand. Chief agricultural products are rice, sugar, abaca, coconuts, tobacco, corn, vegetables, and a great variety of fruits—pineapples, bananas, mangoes, and citrus fruits.

Filipino wedding party *pauses in the courtyard of San Agustin church in Manila, oldest in the Philippines. Groom is wearing the* barong tagalog.

Among hundreds of varieties of birds and animals found in the islands are the rare monkey-eating eagle and the short-horned tamarao (small buffalo), found only on Mindoro Island. Domesticated water buffaloes *(carabao)* are evident throughout the islands. The Philippines have an abundance of fish and mollusk life; and the seas—especially the warm, shallow waters on the western side of the islands—yield oysters and other edible shellfish.

The Filipino people

The people of the Philippines reflect a blending of historical influences of Asia and the West. Most of the 40 million island inhabitants are Asians, predominantly of Malay origin. Yet they are the most Westernized people of all Southeast Asia. Most of them speak English, wear Western clothes, play Western music, drive Western and Japanese cars, and have the courtly manners and friendly hospitality of old Spain.

Many old-time Filipino families trace their ancestry back to Spain; additional influences came from Europe, America, Indonesia, India, China, Mexico, and Japan.

Despite general similarity in appearance, the Filipinos belong to some 55 distinct ethnic groups, many retaining particular dress, religions, customs, and dialects.

Largest of these minority cultural groups are the Filipino Muslims from Mindanao and the Sulu Archipelago. Spanish colonizers called all Muslims "Moros" (for Moors), however the name is not commonly used today. Other groups include the Ifugao tribesmen, who built the rice terraces in northern Luzon; the Badjaos or sea gypsies, who spend most of their lives afloat on the Sulu Sea; and the Negritos, a dark race of pygmies from central Luzon.

Tagalog language. From among 87 different Filipino languages and dialects, the government chose the Tagalog dialect as the basis for the national and official tongue—which they call Filipino.

In the schools, English is the medium of instruction. Spanish is a social language, spoken mainly by the older generation. Countrywide, the estimated literacy rate is about 75 percent.

Religion. Roman Catholicism, a heritage from the Spanish conquerors, is the religion of about 90 percent of the Filipinos, making the Philippines the only Christian nation in Southeast Asia or the Orient. Other religious groups are the Aglipayans (independent Catholics), Protestants, Buddhists, and Muslims.

Popular sports. Baseball, basketball, volleyball, tennis, boxing, and jai alai dominate Philippine spectator sports. The native ball game *sipa*, played with a wicker ball, demands fancy footwork. Filipinos are avid golfers, and the country has a number of good courses. Polo enthusiasts play at the exclusive Manila Polo Club. Cockfighting is a weekend and holiday sport in the suburbs.

Preparing lechon becomes a family fiesta

One of the tastiest and most indispensable of Filipino dishes is *lechon*, a suckling pig roasted over live coals. Once reserved for family fiestas and public banquets, succulent lechon now appears on the menus of better restaurants as well.

Around the Philippine archipelago, the preparation of lechon becomes an all-day affair. Family and friends enjoy music and dancing as they take part in turning the roasting pig over the fire.

Stuffed with tamarind leaves to preserve its shape and lend a slightly tart flavor, lechon is skewered on a bamboo pole. Suspended between hot coals, it takes four hours to roast. When the outside begins to turn brown and crisp, the roast is basted with lard.

Finally, accompanied by a liver sauce and a host of spices, the crisp and golden lechon appears on the banquet table, garnished with an apple, banana, or other seasonal fruit.

Roasting lechon *turns golden brown under the watchful eyes of this family of cooks.*

Planning your trip

Situated some 7,000 air miles west of the United States, the Philippines are about 15 hours from California by air. The time difference between the west coast of the U.S. and the Philippines is 15 hours. When it is 9 A.M. Sunday in Manila, it's 6 P.M. Saturday in San Francisco.

Some two dozen international airlines—including Philippine Airlines—serve the Philippines on flights from Europe, Southeast Asia, Australia, the Orient, the Middle East, and the United States. Several steamship companies maintain regular service —both passenger freighters and cruise ships—from the United States' west coast to Philippine ports.

Jeepneys and taxis

Traveling by air is the best (and sometimes only) way to get around the Philippines, but you can see parts of Luzon and Panay Island by rail and bus. Several steamship companies operate inter-island service. Public bus lines operate in many areas of the Philippines, and tour operators run air conditioned coaches to tourist destinations.

In Manila and most other cities, you can hire a metered taxi or hail a cruising jeepney—a brightly painted 10-passenger converted jeep. In rural areas the Ford Fiera van is replacing the colorful jeepney. Many people in the barrios own a tricycle (a three-wheeled motorcycle with a sidecar) carrying three people. Rental cars with chauffeurs and U-drive cars are also available. Traffic in the Philippines keeps to the right, but drivers tend to ignore the center line and travel at high speeds. For trips into the countryside, it would be a good idea to hire a car and driver. In some parts of Manila you can still hire a colorful *calesa* (horse-drawn buggy) for short rides.

The hotel scene

Greater Manila has many luxury and first-class international hotels where hospitality—for which the Filipinos are famous—is very evident. At tourist destinations such as Baguio, Zamboanga, Davao, and Cebu, you'll find very comfortable resort-type hotels that provide restaurants, nightclubs, tour services, and shops; many have swimming pools and health clubs. Hotel rates are subject to a 10 percent service charge and a 10 percent government tax. Medical clinics, staffed with doctor and nurse, are mandatory in all hotels of more than 100 rooms.

Food and drink

With its distinct cultural heritage, the Philippines has a diverse and fascinating cuisine. Tastefully blending eastern and western cuisines, the country's hotels and restaurants offer Filipino, Chinese, Spanish, Japanese, Swiss, French, Italian, and American dishes.

Among local dishes you might try *adobo*, a spicy dish of chicken or pork (or both), and *lechon* (see above). Rice and corn, the two staple crops in the islands, frequently appear in soups or side dishes. No meal is complete without some of the plentiful and luscious local fruits—papayas, mangoes, lanzones, bananas, pineapples, coconuts—or some of the bountiful harvest of shrimp, oysters, crab, or fresh and salt-water fish, such as *lapu-lapu*.

Popular native brews (first made by tribesmen before the arrival of the Spaniards) are *tuba*, a coconut sap wine; *lambanog*, juice extracted from nipa palm flowers; *tapuy*, wine made from rice; *duhat*, wine made from blackberries; *kasoy*, wine made from cashews; and *basi*, wine made from sugar cane. For exotic non-alcoholic drinks, try *calamansi* juice or papaya punch. The favorite beer is the locally brewed San Miguel brand.

Entertainment

The Filipinos are the musicians and entertainers of Asia. You'll find their bands, singers, and specialty acts in most of the best hotels and nightclubs in the entertainment capitals of Southeast Asia and the Orient.

In recent years new interest has sparked a revival of Philippine folk music, dances, and costumes representing the various provinces, as well as the country's Spanish heritage.

The most popular and well-known Filipino dance is the *tinikling:* men hold two bamboo poles and click-clack them in time to the music, while dancers move in and out of the poles at an ever faster pace.

Entertainment is scheduled regularly in hotels and nightclubs, as well as in the Cultural Center and adjacent 10,000-seat Folk Arts Theatre.

Shopping in the Philippines

Shopping in the Greater Manila area resembles shopping in suburban North America. You'll find dozens of hotel arcades, shopping centers, department stores, tiny boutiques, dressmakers, and shoe stores. You'll find dozens of small shops in Manila's Ermita district (along A. Mabini and M. H. del Pilar streets), in the busy Escolta area, under the Quezon Bridge in Quiapo, at Makati Commercial Center, and at the Nayong Pilipino. At tourist destinations outside the city, you can browse and shop in local markets and numerous souvenir stalls.

Interesting handicrafts include woodcarvings, Igorot-woven fabrics, embroidered *jusi* and *pina* cloth articles, handcrafted jewelry, toy *vintas* (Moro sailboats), baskets, Philippine pearls, abaca rugs and bags, woven mats and shoes, shellcraft, and Muslim brassware.

Historic Manila

Manila, the largest city in the Philippines, is located in the southwestern part of the island of Luzon, at the eastern end of Manila Bay. Spreading out over a broad plain (the largest lowland in the country), the city is cut by the Pasig River, separating the old section of the city (Intramuros) on its south bank from the new section on the north bank.

The present city of Manila dates back to 1571, when Spanish conquistadores chose the site of a very small kingdom known as May-nilad for their settlement. The Spanish built their walled city, called Intramuros, where the river flowed into Manila Bay. Streets of the settlement were laid out straight and parallel to one another, with the blocks nearly uniform in size.

A bustling, modern city

Cosmopolitan Manila, a city of three million people, mixes skyscrapers, flower-filled plazas, ancient ruins, mushrooming suburbs, and fiestas. Its main waterfront thoroughfare, parklike Roxas Boulevard, follows the curving shoreline of the bay. Manila International Airport is some 12 miles south of the city. Most visitors travel along this pleasant parkway (known as the tourist belt) to reach hotels facing the bay and clustered near Rizal Park (the Luneta). United Nations Avenue links the waterfront with the central district.

Arterial highways rim the city and lead north to Quezon City, and southeast to the modern suburb of Makati. Greater Manila consists of four cities—Manila, Pasay, Quezon, and Caloocan—and 13 towns, with a combined population of more than four million.

Manila hums and sputters to the sound of brightly-painted jeepneys, lined up bumper to bumper in traffic. With honking horns, they mix with taxis, trucks, and cars, moving along the clean streets at a frantic pace.

On Sunday morning along Roxas Boulevard, it appears that the entire Manila population is out walking, swimming in the bay, or buying fish at the market on the beach. Out on sealike Manila Bay, the colorful sails of Muslim vintas add a festive

Handicraft shops *abound in downtown Manila and in hotels. Wood carvings, woven handbags and baskets, unique Filipino fabrics are popular.*

Relaxing beside the pool *at the Manila Hilton, travelers can swim, sunbathe, or sip tropical drinks at the palm-thatched snack bar. Many Manila hotels have swimming pools and health rooms.*

Patterned sidewalk *adds a distinctive touch to tree-lined Ayala Avenue, which cuts through the Makati section of Manila. High-rise office buildings, stores, and shops line the street.*

touch. Ships from around the world ride at anchor, awaiting their turn at dockside.

Early evening brings people out to view the flaming sunset over Manila Bay. Along city streets you'll see flickering candle flames, set atop whitewashed stone walls to advertise the wares of youthful cigarette vendors.

Manila's hotels

A dramatic increase in tourist arrivals in recent years has caused a scramble of new hotel construction, with the result that Manila's previous "big four" international-class hotels—the Hilton, Hyatt, Inter-Continental, and Philippine Village — have been joined by a host of new hotels.

In the downtown area, a completely reconstructed Manila Hotel, the Century Park Sheraton, and the Mirador have joined the Hilton Hotel. Along Roxas Boulevard, the Hyatt is joined by the Holiday Inn, the Philippine Plaza, Regent of Manila, and the Silahis International. In the Makati area, the Inter-Continental Manila has new neighbors—the Manila Garden, Manila Mandarin, and Manila Peninsula hotels.

Manila now has more than 40 hotels containing nearly 15,000 rooms, offering a wide range in size, quality, and price.

Dining fare

In Manila you can try a different cuisine every night of the week. Most of the large hotels have restaurants serving a variety of western, Filipino, and other Asian foods.

Outside the hotels, the dining scene seems to be one of continual expansion, with a number of good, small restaurants opening in the city. Since restaurants constantly shift in character and quality, ask for local recommendations or consult current city guidebooks.

If you wish to sample local Filipino dishes, here are some restaurants you might try:

• Aristocrat, on Roxas Boulevard or E. de los Santos Ave., Cubao, Quezon City, serves Filipino cuisine.
• Jade Vine, 537 United Nations Avenue, Manila, is well located with a good choice of Filipino foods.
• Bungalow Restaurant, 1510 San Marcelino, Manila; 100 Buenida Avenue, Ermita.
• Sulo Restaurant, Makati Commercial Center, Makati, offers Filipino folk dancing and singing, along with Filipino food.
• Turo-Turo sa Nayon (the Nayong Pilipino Village Restaurant), Manila International Airport Ave., serves specialties and native delicacies from various regions of the Philippines.

When you prefer something other than Filipino cooking, you'll find dozens of good places in Manila. Excellent continental cuisine is available at the Prince Albert Rotisserie in the Inter-Continental, the Rotisserie at the Manila Hilton, or Hugo's Grill at the Hyatt Regency.

For purely Spanish dishes, dine at the Alba on M. Y. Orosa in Manila or the Patio de Alba at 8751 Paseo de Roxas, Makati. The latter features a Spanish musical combo nightly.

If you prefer French cuisine and enjoy formal dress, try the Au Bon Vivant, 1133 L. Guerrero St., Manila, or at the Makati Commercial Center. They serve only French cuisine, with many of the ingredients imported from France.

For Indonesian food, visit the Batik Inn, Guadalupe, Makati; it is one of several restaurants serving Indonesian food in the Philippines and features nightly entertainment.

The best place for Chinese dishes in Manila is Chinatown, the area behind the Escolta, across the Pasig River. You can enjoy a mini-banquet at many restaurants along Ongpin, Chinatown's main street.

Night life

In Manila you will find cocktail lounges, piano bars, hotel discotheques and nightclubs, and numerous hostess bars. The Metro Manila Casino is located at the Philippine Village Hotel. Tourists must bring their passports for admittance.

All the major hotels have discotheques. Among the best are 1571 at the Manila Hilton, the Circuit at the Hyatt, the Where Else at the Inter-Continental Manila, the Stargaser Lounge at the Silahis, and the discos at the Manila Hotel, Century Park Sheraton, and Philippine Village.

Many of the entertainment spots in Manila are not exactly "traditional" in character to visitors from the western world—ranging from exotically named massage parlors to the "day and night" clubs strung out along Roxas Boulevard and M. H. del Pilar which parallels it. Catering primarily to male clientele are a dozen clubs featuring live bands, dancing, and a bevy of beautiful hostesses for company, and restaurants featuring lunchtime fashion shows.

Another type of evening entertainment is available at Manila's jai alai fronton on Taft Avenue. Billed as the world's fastest sport, jai alai is played daily from 4 to 11 P.M.

Folk dances and music

In recent years the Filipino people have shown renewed interest in preserving their folk dances. Best known of several excellent dance troupes is the Bayanihan Dance Company. Folk dance performances are presented at the Sulo Restaurant and the Plaza in the Makati Commercial Center, and at the Alta Vista Restaurant and the Hotel Filipinas in the downtown area. The Top of the Hilton offers a show interplaying dances, fashions, and slide presentations of Filipino festivals.

A different and unusual group is the Pangkat Kawayan (Singing Bamboos), a group of school-age orphans who play bamboo musical instruments.

Handicraft shopping

Manila's best buys are Philippine handicrafts (see page 20). Large stores and specialty shops in the Makati and Ermita districts sell the *barong tagalog*, a loose-fitting embroidered shirt for men, made of diaphanous cloth woven from pineapple fibers. The barong has become the national shirt of the Philippines and can be worn in place of a suit and tie. Women's butterfly-sleeved *ternos* usually are made to order by Filipino dressmakers, who have outlets in many hotels and shops.

Most large stores in Manila are one-price, but don't hesitate to bargain in small shops.

Sightseeing in Manila

The city of Manila is a cluster of districts—Ermita, Santa Cruz, Quiapo, Escolta, and Binondo—all fanning out from the city center. None of the districts is far from the heart of the city, yet each has a distinct character and interesting landmarks.

A downtown walking tour

You can visit many of the sights in Manila on a two-hour walking tour starting from Rizal Park.

Rizal Park (Luneta), on filled land facing Manila Bay, is an elliptically-shaped park combining flower

Manila Hotel, *one of the city's classic hotels, has been recently renovated and a new tower added. It faces Rizal Park.*

Underground dungeons in Manila's Fort Santiago meant death by drowning for prisoners of Spanish and Japanese.

Schoolchildren play ball on the grassy lawn inside the walls of historic old Fort Santiago.

gardens, green lawns, fountains, monuments, playgrounds, a circular roller skating rink, promenades, and a mixture of buildings in varying styles. The memorial park honors Dr. Jose Rizal, the Philippines' national hero. At the park's west end, a monument marks the spot where the young revolutionary was executed by the Spaniards in 1896. His remains are buried there, and members of the Armed Forces of the Philippines keep vigil.

Rizal Park is probably the best place in Manila to go people-watching by day or night (it's well lit and patrolled). At the first light of dawn, young and old stroll through the park on their way to work; others take their morning exercise roller skating on the circular concrete rink. Hundreds of people visit the park during their lunch hour—and on Sundays thousands of families come to promenade or to be entertained. You can join the Filipinos on a bench or go strolling in the park's Chinese and Japanese gardens. At lunchtime, eat at a sidewalk cafe.

Along the edges of Rizal Park are some of the important government buildings: the Philippine Congress, the Finance Building, and the Tourism Department Building.

Intramuros, a five-minute walk across Burgos Drive, is Manila's old walled city, reminiscent of a tiny medieval enclave. Built in the 16th century by the Spaniards (aided by some 3,000 Filipino slaves), the fort was badly damaged during World War II.

Though it's partly in ruins, you can inspect crumbling walls, cobblestone streets, the ancient church of San Agustin (dating from 1599—the oldest stone church in the Philippines), Manila Cathedral, and the former palace of the Spanish governors-general. The city's original seven gates have been partially restored. Immediately outside Intramuros is the Zonta Aquarium of tropical fish, containing live and petrified marine life

Fort Santiago, one of Spain's oldest garrisons, stands at the northwest corner of Intramuros, between Aduana Street and the Pasig River. Built nearly 400 years ago near the river's mouth, the restored fort is a national shrine. It was once the seat of Spanish colonial powers; its dungeons and inner chambers served as a prison during the Spanish regime and the Japanese occupation.

In one of the dungeons, Dr. Jose Rizal spent his last hours before his execution in 1896. Inside the fortress is the Rizal Museum, housing memorabilia of the man who, to the Filipinos, is a martyr and a revolutionary symbol.

The fort attracts visitors not only for its historical significance but also as a pleasant place for evening strolls. Like Rizal Park, the fort is well lit and patrolled at night. Seasonal open-air drama is presented in the Rajah Sulayman Theater inside the fort.

North of the river

Short trips by taxi, jeepney, or a guided coach tour take you north of the Pasig River to the older sections of Manila.

Escolta district, just north of the Jones Bridge, is the heart of the city's old commercial district. As you walk along Escolta Street, you'll see many of

Ship-filled Manila Bay *presents an ever-changing scene from Roxas Boulevard and nearby hotels. The parklike thoroughfare, lined by palm trees and walkways, borders the bay for several miles.*

Cultural Center *of the Philippines is a Manila landmark, built on a peninsula near Roxas Boulevard. Inside the modern complex, you can enjoy local music, theater, and art.*

the big banks, insurance companies, and import-export houses (though many have moved to Makati —see page 26). Another reminder of Manila's early days is the imposing baroque structure of Santa Cruz Church.

The name *escolta* (meaning "escort") comes from the days when the Spanish viceroy and his mounted escort would clatter down the cobblestone streets. Shopkeepers would dash out at the "escolta" sound, hoping to make a sale.

Nearby, the Plaza Cervantes (named after the creator of the fictional Don Quixote) still retains its old Spanish atmosphere.

Chinatown, a few blocks north of the Escolta district, is the home of many of the city's Philippine-born Chinese. Ongpin Street, the center of Chinatown, is lined with dozens of noodle shops and family-run Chinese restaurants. Narrow streets branching off Ongpin contain hundreds of shophouses, including Chinese medicine shops. The district's architecture is more Filipino than Chinese, and most of the signs are in English. Though many Chinese families practice their ancestral ways, their children have names like Carlos, Manuel, Rosann, and Maria.

Quiapo district, just north of the Quezon Bridge, is one of Manila's oldest areas. Plaza Miranda, at the head of Quezon Boulevard, is Manila's Hyde Park and the people's political forum. Beneath the plaza is a pedestrian underpass with several shops, a bank, and young people selling lottery tickets.

Facing the plaza is Quiapo Church, containing the Black Nazarene shrine. On Fridays great crowds come to the church to venerate the ebony-carved image. Twice a year, at fiesta time and on Good Friday, a milling crowd gathers to watch the male penitents carry the Black Nazarene through the district's streets. Women devotees dress in the garb of the Nazarene—purple or maroon long dresses, with crowns of green branches around their heads.

Under Quezon Bridge you'll find the Quiapo Market, resembling an underground department store. Hundreds of stalls sell fresh produce, fruits, fish, and meats brought in from the provinces at dawn. By mid-morning, late arriving housewives are haggling with shouting vendors over the price of picked-over vegetables and dried-up fish. Some stalls sell handicrafts—hats, handbags, place mats —at lower prices (if you bargain) than in the city.

Central Market, north on Quezon Boulevard, is one of the city's largest markets. You'll understand the Manilans better after watching them shop. Here under one large roof are all the items a family will need in its lifetime. You'll see electronic items from Japan and expensive brocades from Paris, as well as hand-embroidered jusi cloth from Iloilo and hand-loomed cottons of the Ilocos. In the food section, you'll discover that the Filipino gourmet has a multitude of choices, among them snails, frogs, beetles, and choice New Zealand steaks.

University of Santo Tomas, a few minutes' walk east of the Central Market, occupies a 60-acre site fronting on Espana Street. Santo Tomas is an old university; it was founded in 1611—25 years before Harvard—by Spanish Dominicans. For 300 years the university was located inside the old walled city; the present buildings were dedicated in 1927.

Santo Tomas is noted for its medical school, its museum, and the tower, a historical landmark. A colorful student quarter surrounds the university. During the Japanese occupation, some 3,000 American and Allied men, women, and children were confined here for more than three years.

Malacanang Palace, on the north bank of the Pasig River, is the imposing official residence of the president of the Philippines. Originally built as a country residence by a 19th century Spanish aristocrat, the palace has also housed the Spanish and American governors.

The main building is closed to visitors, but by prior arrangement you can stroll through the gardens and visit the Executive Building. Just inside the main gate stands a nipa hut, shaded by banyan and acacia trees; the structure is made entirely of hand rubbed bamboo, with furnishings of bamboo and rattan. In one corner of the grounds you'll find a Japanese cottage.

South of Rizal Park

Heading south from Rizal Park, the "tourist belt" extends some 12 miles along wide Roxas Boulevard and its tree-shaded promenade to Manila International Airport. Some of the attractions are within

---

The Philippine jeepney—mobile folk art

That colorful, chrome-plated jeepney found throughout the Philippines was once a jeep before it received a Filipino-style face lift and its elongated body became a roaring and mobile abstract painting.

The Filipinos' natural competitiveness and love of flamboyance have developed the jeepney into a riotous blend of colors—crimson red on canary yellow, peacock blue on electric pink, or kelly green on adobe white. The long bodies, capable of carrying 10 to 12 passengers, are further adorned with gargoyles and hand painted with Filipino designs. Standard accessories might include white sidewall tires, chrome bumpers, shiny hubcaps, eye-catching hood ornament, tassels dangling from the windshield, and fringe draped from the roof along the open sides.

A short, fast, bumpy jeepney ride costs 20 centavos and follows a regular route in the cities and barrios. The jeepney picks up and lets off passengers anywhere along its route. They enter and exit through the rear and sit hunched together on side bench seats; during the rush hour, some people hang onto the rear door rails and balance precariously on the rear step.

Wherever you travel in the Philippines, you'll find the jeepneys. In many rural villages, they are often the only form of motorized transport. In Manila your seat companion may be a lovely Filipino girl going to work, but in the barrios you might sit beside a farmer who is balancing a cage of chickens on his lap.

Colorful history. The jeepney has an interesting history. After World War II, the Philippines had a taxi shortage and some form of transport was vitally needed. A group of enterprising Filipinos secured some surplus U.S. Army and Navy jeeps. By cannibalizing several of the jeeps, they managed to get a few running. These were outfitted with temporary tops against the sun and weather, fitted with extra seats, and used to haul passengers. The fancy decorations came later.

Visiting a jeepney factory. Not far from Manila, you can visit the Davao or Francisco jeepney factories where this process continues today. Both are located some 10 miles south of Manila on the Laguna Highway.

In the paint shop, jeepney bodies are primed gray, sprayed with rainbow colors, and decorated by freehand artists with fantastic, fanciful, and sometimes meaningful designs.

In the assembly yard, you can follow the entire reconstruction process of the surplus jeeps. Amidst tumultuous hammering on sheet metal and sparking welder's torches, new and longer bodies are added to the jeep chassis. The engines (gasoline or diesel) are all reconditioned—good for another 10 to 12 years.

If you'd like your own jeepney, you can buy one for about $2,700 from the factory. It takes about a week for local delivery.

Jeepney *receives a fanciful, brightly colored decoration by this freehand artist.*

walking distance of bayfront hotels, or you may prefer to hail a passing jeepney or taxi.

Many of the city's leading hotels, shops, art galleries, restaurants, and night clubs line the thoroughfare and streets running parallel to it. Before the war, Roxas Boulevard (formerly Dewey Boulevard) was considered Manila's "millionaires' row," and several stone-walled mansions still remain. On the bayside, the U. S. Embassy occupies spacious grounds. Further down the avenue is the headquarters of the Philippine Navy and the Manila Yacht Club; you board hydrofoils at the navy docks for the trip to Corregidor Island.

The Cultural Center of the Philippines, set on a 67-acre site beside Manila Bay, is the place where you can sample the music, theater, and art of Manila. A stop on city tours, the complex has architecture that combines modern sculptured forms with native Philippine materials.

A theater building contains two auditoriums and a restaurant; four museum pavilions house collections of antique art objects, colonial artifacts, Muslim and other folk art, and works by contemporary artists. Just behind the Cultural Center is the new, 10,000-seat Folk Arts Theatre.

Rizal Memorial Coliseum, on Vito Cruz Street east of the Cultural Center, is the country's largest sports stadium.

Vito Cruz Street is sometimes called Embassy Row, since many of its elegant mansions now house foreign missions. The Manila Zoo also occupies some 100 acres on the north side of the street.

Nayong Pilipino (Filipino village) stands within earshot of jets warming up at Manila International Airport. This Philippines-in-miniature complex of regional villages covers some 90 acres, giving you a good sample of the variety of architecture, crafts, and culture of the country's far-flung regions.

Focal point is the administration center, patterned after a typical town plaza during the Spanish era, with a *residencia* (town hall), chapel, and small shops. Eight miniature villages, a Filipino restaurant, and the Museum of Traditional Philippine Cultures surround a manmade lagoon.

Filipino guides and a fleet of jeepneys take you from village to village. Each of the settlements was carefully planned to depict a region of the Philippines — Mindanao, with a Muslim mosque, stilt houses in the lake, and some vintas anchored offshore; a Spanish-style, old Vigan house, representing northern Luzon; an authentic Igorot village, depicting the Mountain Province; the Bicol village, with a replica of the Mayon Volcano; women weaving *hablon* cloth in Iloilo; a Tagalog village, representing central Luzon; the re-created Chocolate Hills of the Bohol district; and a replica of the historic cross of Magellan at Cebu City.

Nayong Pilipino is open week days from 9 A.M. to 8 P.M. (Friday through Sunday until 9 P.M.), with varied activities scheduled throughout the year. Transit passengers at Manila's airport can see the complex as part of a local mini-tour.

Makati and Forbes Park

Some of Manila's sights overlap into the suburbs. Many tours include the spacious campus of the University of the Philippines near Quezon City, the nearby suburbs of Makati and Forbes Park, and the stirring Manila American Cemetery and Memorial.

Makati, some six miles southeast of the downtown district, is a planned community. Its stores, supermarkets, homes, and office buildings combine to make it one of the most modern suburbs in Asia. Trees shade the broad main street, Ayala Avenue — Manila's Wall Street. Modern glass buildings facing the boulevard house the stock exchange, banks, apartments and condominiums, the offices of some of the country's largest companies, and the Philippine branches of many foreign firms.

At the far end of Ayala Avenue is the Makati Commercial Center, a complex of stores, boutiques, restaurants, and dozens of small shops. Several hotels are within walking distance. Spreading out from the commercial area are some of the finest residential areas near Manila, including low-cost housing for Manila's growing middle class.

Ten to 15 years ago, Makati was rural grassland. Today its remaining open land is gradually being filled in with new hotels, apartments, and office buildings.

Forbes Park, just east of the Makati Commercial Center, is Manila's wealthiest residential area; its contemporary mansions are protected by an encircling wall with guarded gates and patrolled streets.

Fort Bonifacio, just a few minutes beyond Forbes Park, is the site of the impressive, 152-acre Manila American Cemetery and Memorial. Some 17,000 white crosses encircle the marble memorial, marking graves of American and Filipino World War II dead. On several walls of the memorial, mosaic

Colorful jeepneys *provide free transport around Nayong Philipino, where cultural features of the Philippines are exhibited.*

Tourists *roam remains of Battery Crocket; during battle for Corregidor, it sheltered a 360° disappearing gun.*

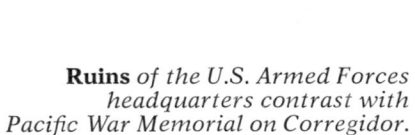

Ruins *of the U.S. Armed Forces headquarters contrast with Pacific War Memorial on Corregidor.*

maps record major battles and theaters of operation in the Pacific campaign.

Museums and art galleries

Throughout the city you'll find dozens of art galleries, some private and others public. Check with the local tourist officials or call ahead to find out if a particular gallery is open to the public. Here are a few you should include in your museum tour:

The National Museum of the Philippines is located in the Old Congress building on Padre Burgos Street. It houses interesting exhibits including a rich collection of ancient Chinese porcelains, many dating from the 14th and 15th centuries. The museum's west wing is dedicated to Philippine art and history and contains a display of the material culture of the Ifugao tribes of northern Luzon. The Ethnology Hall houses cultural artifacts of Mindanao's Muslims. Museum hours are 8 A.M. to 5 P.M. Monday through Saturday.

University of Santo Tomas, Espana Street, has a good zoological collection in its museum

Lopez Memorial Museum, 10 Lancaster Street, Pasay City, specializes in early Philippine prints.

The Museum of Traditional Philippine Cultures, Nayong Pilipino, has an interesting exhibit on the country's lesser-known minorities, including the Tasaday cave people.

Philippine Art Gallery, Arquiza Street, is open to the public; it contains modern Philippine paintings and sculptures.

Ayala Museum, in the Makati area, dramatically portrays the Philippines' past in 60 historical dioramas.

Excursions out of Manila

Popular excursions from Manila include a half-day trip by hydrofoil to Corregidor Island and its impressive wartime remains, and a half-day visit to the Tagaytay-Taal Volcano and Lake. The latter excursion provides glimpses of rural life en route.

Historic Corregidor

The island's fame as a World War II battleground does not prepare you for such a green and pleasant spot, tranquil and even a bit cooler than the city. Shaped like a giant tadpole, its head facing westward toward the South China Sea, the three-square-mile rock guards the entrance to Manila Bay, some 28 miles west of Manila.

Waterless Corregidor served as a pirate hideout during pre-Spanish times. By the early 18th century, it had become the site of a Spanish dockyard and navy hospital. In 1902 the island became a U.S. military reservation and six years later an Army post—Fort Mills. Its strategic site made it an important World War II stronghold; after the Japanese invasion of the Philippines in December 1941, the island became headquarters for Allied resistance under generals Douglas MacArthur and Jonathan Wainwright.

Now a national shrine, Corregidor's war memorial of white concrete and marble tablets is located at Topside, on the west side of the island. A sculptured steel "Eternal Flame" juts skyward and a museum contains war relics, photographs, and military papers.

Passengers are transported from Manila to Corregidor by hovercraft. Two hovercraft leave the Philippine Navy headquarters pier off Roxas

Blue green waters *of Taal Lake partially fill the large volcanic crater south of Manila. Often spewing steam from an island in the lake, Taal Volcano attracts the continuing study of volcanologists.*

Boulevard at 8:30 A.M. daily except for Monday, returning about 12:30 P.M. You can book the trip to Corregidor through any Manila travel agent. Each hovercraft accommodates 65 people.

After skimming across Manila Bay past a host of anchored freighters and small outrigger fishing boats, you transfer to a bus for a 1½-hour historic journey. You'll see the 900-foot-long Malinta tunnel (which sheltered the military command post) and its numerous side tunnels, the mile-long barracks where 8,000 soldiers once lived, skeletons of various military structures, giant rusting guns, and pockmarked walls amid the jungle growth. Nearly devoid of vegetation following World War II bombing, the rocky island is once again covered with dense jungle, mostly *ipil ipil* trees. At various spots on the island, you'll see wooden crosses inscribed in Japanese, erected by widows and family and still visited today.

Besides its historic significance, Corregidor has become a favorite weekend retreat for Manilans. The island has numerous secluded coves and beaches. Surrounding waters are extremely clear, and offshore coral reefs invite snorkelers. Those people wishing overnight accommodations can stay at the Corregidor Inn, situated on a small hill in the center of the island.

Tagaytay—Taal Lake and Volcano

You see a condensed version of rural Philippine life during an hour-long drive to Tagaytay, a hillside resort area 45 miles south of Manila. The half-day excursion provides an interesting contrast with the busy city. The road winds through fishing villages and farming barrios, past rice fields, neat *nipa* huts (stilt houses of bamboo), coconut plantations, orchards, and a succession of *sarisari* stores, the Philippines' version of the variety store.

As the road ascends, you have an exhilarating view of the lush, green countryside. From Tagaytay Ridge, 2,250 feet above sea level, you see Taal Lake and Taal Volcano, spewing steam from an islet in the middle of the lake. The volcano erupted in 1971 without much damage, but earlier eruptions in 1965 and 1911 killed hundreds of people in the fishing villages on the island over which it rises. (Volcano-watchers scrutinize the volcano year round.) Taal Lake itself is in the crater of a once mighty volcano.

Standing on the edge of the cool and quiet Tagaytay Ridge, you view a far-reaching mix of blues and greens—lake and convoluted shoreline and even the South China Sea beyond. Weather can be unpredictable, with fog sometimes sweeping in to hide the volcano in a matter of minutes.

At the rustic Taal Vista Lodge, perched on the edge of the ridge across from the volcano, you can enjoy the scenery from outdoor tables during a snack or lunch.

For a closer view of the volcano, you can arrange a trip to the crater through Sierra Grande Resort in Tagaytay. Your excursion includes the ride down to the lake, a motor launch cruise out to the volcano-island, the climb up to the crater, a swim in the lake, and return transportation to Tagaytay.

About a half hour outside Manila (on your return trip from the volcano) is the Las Pinas Church, renowned for its bamboo organ. Constructed by a Catholic priest in 1794, the organ (containing 950 bamboo tubes) is still in working order.

Southern Luzon

Some 250 miles southeast of Manila, on the east side of southern Luzon, are Legazpi City—named for the famous Spanish conquistador—and the Mayon Volcano, the Mount Fuji of the Philippines. From Manila you can reach Legazpi in an hour by air. By road, the trip takes 15 hours on the South Road — part of the Philippine-Japan Friendship Highway stretching the length of the island. In the port city of Legazpi, you can stay at the Al-Bay Hotel, Mayon Imperial, or Hotel La Trinidad.

A perfect cone rising 7,947 feet, often encircled by puffy white clouds, Mayon Volcano dominates the countryside some 16 miles northwest of Legazpi. Most visitors allow one day for sightseeing in the Legazpi area, including a trip to the government rest house 2,500 feet up the slope of the volcano. A single twisting road, lined with abaca plantations, leads to the rest house. You can stop at an abaca factory, where hemp rugs, slippers, belts, and other twine products are made.

Some 10 miles south lie the ruins of Cagsawa, a town buried in 1814 when the volcano erupted. Twenty feet of lava and the subsequent mudflow from torrential rains covered the village. You can still see rooftops and the church steeple rising out of the ground, now covered with green grass. Farmers cultivate the rich soil on the slopes and at the base of the sleeping giant. After the volcano's first recorded eruption in 1616, a major eruption has occurred approximately every ten years. Though Mayon's cone frequently belches smoke, the volcano was most recently active in 1968.

You can also stop at the thermal resort of Tiwi Hot Springs, noted for its boiling sulphurous va-

Shooting the rapids at Pagsanjan Falls

One of the more spectacular day trips out of Manila is the dugout canoe ride on the Pagsanjan River to roaring Pagsanjan Falls. The two-hour drive southeast from Manila to the river goes through rural towns and villages of palm-thatched stilt houses, rich green coconut plantations, and fields of rice and sugar cane. Often you'll see small boys riding a *carabao* (water buffalo), roadside fruit stands, or bright laundry spread on bushes to dry.

At the town of Pagsanjan, you stop at the Pagsanjan Rapids Hotel on the riverbank to change into a bathing suit or waterproof attire. The boat ride is neither dangerous nor strenuous, but you'd better plan on getting wet.

Two or three passengers and the oarsmen sit or kneel in the brightly-painted *bancas* (canoes) for the upriver ride to the main waterfall. Using short, snubnosed paddles, the boatmen push, pull, and shove the craft over 14 rapids. When the water is low or when the boatmen come to a tight squeeze between rocks and boulders, they jump out and actually lift the small boat over the rapids.

You pass between 300-foot-high gorge walls, hung with curtains of orchids and begonias. Dozens of small waterfalls cascade down the cliffs. Cries of monkeys and tropical birds break the stillness; palms and dense vines crowd the river's edge.

You disembark near the thundering, 300-foot main waterfall, taking in the vista of falling water crashing into the lagoon below. A small, makeshift refreshment stand sells cold drinks and snacks (prices are high, since supplies must be hauled upriver).

If you feel adventurous, ride a bamboo raft across the lagoon and go behind the falls (a drenching experience) to explore a cave. Or you can swim in the deep pool at the base of the waterfall.

Your return trip downstream is fast, through turbulent white water. You'll find yourself hanging onto the sides of the small but sturdy craft as the oarsmen maneuver around the rocks.

Bamboo raft *takes tourist behind Pagsanjan Falls after river trip over 14 rapids.*

Baguio children *eye visitor at City Market. Bananas are less than two U.S. cents each.*

Baguio Country Club, *in a rustic setting, offers members and guests a variety of sports, including golf.*

pors, and at Kalayukaii, a black sand beach resort. Most trips include a fishermen's village, where houses are built on stilts over the water and boats parked underneath, and the busy harbor of Legazpi, where hundreds of workers load copra onto waiting ships.

North to Baguio

The countryside north of Manila is a checkerboard of flooded rice fields and small farms, seamed by winding canals and dotted with hundreds of small villages. The road north to Baguio crosses the plains of central Luzon and then climbs into the Cordillera Mountains. You drive north from Manila on the MacArthur Highway, picking up the narrow, zigzag, mountain-climbing Kennon Road.

Along this route you pass rice fields, nipa huts, sugar and coconut plantations, Clark Air Force Base at Angeles, native markets in Tarlac, and the rice granaries of the central plains. Once into the mountains and away from lowland mugginess, you reach the most untropical and atypical countryside in the Philippines—pine-covered mountains, refreshed by cool breezes and brightened by beds of temperate-climate flowers.

You can reach Baguio by air (1 hour), by road (5 hours), and by train/car (6 hours). Philippine Airlines has two morning flights daily from Manila. Baguio's Loakan Airport, located on a plateau and surrounded by mountains, is usually swathed in fog or heavy mist by early afternoon. If you want to drive, hire a car and driver in Manila.

Baguio is within a day's drive of the famed Banaue rice terraces, the west coast beach resort of Bauang, and further south, the Hundred Islands National Park.

Pine-scented mountain air

Noted for its balmy, pine-scented air, Baguio is the summer retreat of the Philippines. Wedged between two mountain ridges, the city nestles on a mile-high plateau in the Cordillera Mountains.

An American architect, Daniel Hudson Burnham, laid out this pleasant city of pines and parks in the early 1900s. Its streets spill over the hills. Broad swatches of green brighten the landscape. Shaded by pine and oak trees, Baguio's hillside homes usually have terraced gardens. On the slopes outside the city, small wooden cottages and log cabins are sheltered by lofty pines. Clear streams tumble down the steep hillsides, and the aroma of moist evergreens drifts over the slopes.

Baguio has a gentler atmosphere than Manila— its parklike setting and cool temperatures lend a certain calmness to its townspeople (even the local jeepneys have a subdued decor). The city is also an important center of Igorot (Philippine Aborigine) arts and crafts. You can take trips from Baguio to Igorot wood carving villages.

Mild temperatures. Baguio's wintertime population of about 100,000 nearly triples each summer as lowlanders take up temporary residence to escape the hot, muggy weather below. A number of wealthy Manila residents own large, landscaped estates here.

Mild, year-round temperatures in Baguio range from an average high of 73° F. to an average low of 58° F. Since evenings are pleasantly cool, you'll want a sweater or light jacket. The rainy season lasts from May to September; January is the driest month. Humidity averages 86 percent.

Summer capital. In past years the entire government of the Philippines moved from Manila to Baguio in summer. Today, the summer residences of the cabinet members and justices of the Supreme Court are located in the area. Mansion House, the presidential summer home, is situated north of Camp John Hay, a rest and recreation center for American servicemen.

Where to stay, dine, and play

Baguio has also seen a rash of hotel construction with several new hotels recently completed. They will nearly double the number of rooms available at this popular mountain resort. Most of Baguio's hotels are located near the business center, though some are outside town in the mountains. Even with the new hotels, you need confirmed reservations, especially in summer.

Among favorite tourist hotels are the Crismar Mansion Hotel, Hotel Milton International, Pines Hotel, Ruff Inn, Terraces Hotel, and the Villa la Maja. Most of the hotels and inns have dining rooms and bars. Both the Pines and Terraces hotels have sports facilities.

Visitors who wish to enjoy the private golf courses and other sports facilities of the rustic Baguio Country Club or the U.S.-owned John Hay Air Base Club must be the guest of a club member or obtain a pass from the base commander.

Varied cuisines. Baguio's hotels and restaurants offer a pleasing variety of Filipino, Spanish, American, and Chinese dishes.

Restaurants specializing in Filipino food are the Jade, on Santo Tomas Road; Manila Cafe, on Abanao Street (near City Hall); Morlou's, on Carantes Street, and Bahay Kubo, on Session Road.

For Spanish dishes you might try the Hilltop, on Santo Tomas Road (across from the Baguio General Hospital); Sky View, 116 Session Road; Vallejo Hotel, also on Session Road; and Forest House, on Outlook Drive.

You'll find Chinese food at City Lunch, on Abanao Street; Dainty, on Session Road; and Mido Cafe, on Malcolm Square.

Night life. Most of Baguio's hotels offer dining and dancing; some feature floor shows. Among the city's numerous cocktail lounges and bars, favorites are the Sadiwan at the Pines Hotel, John Hay's Halfway House and Main Club, and the Woodhouse at the Baguio Country Club.

Continuous combo music, with dining and dancing, can be found at such cozy spots as the Vista Club House, Tip Top Key Club, Crystal Cave Nightclub, and the Down Under at the Crismar Mansion Hotel.

Sightseeing in Baguio

A leisurely day of touring allows you plenty of time to take in the sights in Baguio and its environs.

Baguio Cathedral, on Cathedral Loop, Session Road, dominates the heart of the town. The twin-spired structure rises above a gently sloping street.

City Market, Magsaysay Road, is a busy, well organized market with marked prices. Strolling through its long covered aisles, shoppers can select from an array of exotic fruits, poultry, household goods, handwoven mats, handkerchiefs, scarves, fabrics, woodcarvings, bamboo wares (trays, mats, and small gifts), abaca products, and silver filigree jewelry.

Burnham Park, resembling a displaced American town green, is a rectangular park just down the hill from the commercial center. Northwest of the park, the multistory City Hall overlooks a tree-shaded expanse of playing fields, athletic bowl, parade grounds, skating rink, children's playground, and a manmade lagoon (you can rent rowboats and vinta-styled sailboats by the hour).

From the city center, Leonard Wood Road takes you east to the following destinations:

Imelda Park, south of Leonard Wood Road, contains the "Ile Ti Igorot," a scale model of an Igorot village. You'll also find a Zoological and Botanical Garden, a children's playground, and a picnic pit.

Camp John Hay, a U.S. military rest and recreation base located southeast of Baguio, is the site of Bell Amphitheater, containing terraced lawn seating and a profusion of flowers and plants.

To reach the base's north gate from Leonard Wood Road, turn right at Park Circle onto Park Road, which becomes Country Club Road. Just outside the camp's north gate, you pass the Baguio

Session Road, *one of Baguio's main streets, leads uphill through the city's business district. Twin spires of cathedral rise in the distance.*

Cockfighting—a Filipino passion

Two glaring roosters, held by their owners, shake their feathered heads and scratch the hard packed earth. From around the amphitheater, tension-riddled Filipinos place bets with the *kristo* (bookie) by shouting or signaling with their fingers. At the sound of a bell, the cocks attack with a flying leap. The 2 to 6-inch razor-sharp blade attached to the cock's left foot flashes as each bird tries for the fatal mark.

With every deadly thrust, the screaming crowd goes into a frenzy. Feathers fly. Suddenly, one cock goes down for the count. The cock that remains standing wins; the decision of the *sentenciador* (judge) is final.

For centuries, cockfighting has thrilled and excited Filipinos, and visitors with strong stomachs usually enjoy the festival atmosphere and frenzied betting. On Saturdays, Sundays, and holidays (when betting is legal), almost every city and barrio stages a cockfight. Weekend village fairs are often held near the cockpits.

From midmorning to sundown, cockfights are held in quick succession. The fowls, specially fed and trained, are matched by their owners according to size and weight. When the owners agree to a match, steel fighting blades are attached to the cock's left foot, and the betting and fighting gets underway.

White rooster *arches his ruffled feathers after defeating the downed loser.*

Country Club and golf course. The base includes the U.S. Ambassador's summer residence, an 18-hole golf course, and the colorfully landscaped Italian Gardens.

William Wright Park, just past the traffic circle on the north side of Leonard Wood Road, features a reflecting pool canopied with trees. Children and adults go horseback riding here.

Mansion House, originally built for the American governor-general, now serves as the official summer home of the president of the Philippines. Surrounded by green lawns and flower gardens, the sprawling white mansion sits atop a gentle rise, opposite the reflecting pool in William Wright Park.

Mines View Park, located on Outlook Drive just north of Leonard Wood Road, perches on a cliff overlooking the Benguet gold mining district. From the sheltered lookout, you gaze across tree-denuded hillsides. Underground, miles of tunnels lead to gold-bearing rock.

Other nearby destinations

South of the city limits, 7,500-foot Mount Santo Tomas offers a splendid viewpoint on a clear day. From the rest house near the mountaintop, you have a broad panorama stretching from Luzon's central plains west to the South China Sea. An altar atop the mountain commemorates the establishment of Christianity in the Philippines.

Young Filipino men are trained for the Army's officer corps at the Philippine Military Academy, located at Fort Del Pilar. The academy—and even the cadet uniform—was modeled after the U.S. Army's West Point. During the last week of March, cadet graduation is marked by open house, intramural sports, and a dress parade and review. Philippine war memorabilia has been assembled in the school's museum.

Outside Baguio you can drive through the Trinidad Valley, only 10 minutes north of the city, where local farmers grow a multitude of fresh vegetables and strawberries. Roads lead southwest to Asin Hot Springs, an Igorot wood carving village, Lourdes Grotto, and Dominican and Mirador hills.

Mountain handicrafts

You'll find handicrafts of the mountain people in most of Baguio's stores and shops, especially those along Session Road (the main commercial center) and the nearby city market (see page 31). Prices for handicrafts and gift items are generally lower in Baguio than in Manila.

If you are interested in textile items, visit the Easter School of Weaving northwest of the city,

Mines View Park *lookout offers an impressive panorama of Baguio's pine-covered mountain country. Roadside shops display Igorot wood carvings for sale.*

Igorot tribeswomen *at the Easter School of Weaving deftly weave vivid strips of color on their upright and back looms. Many items are offered for sale on the premises.*

where Igorot tribeswomen weave vivid strips of color on upright and back looms. You can buy fringed belts, place mats, tobacco pouches, and bolts of material.

Another workshop open to visitors is the St. Louis Silver Shop, where young men make and sell silver filigree work.

Journey to the rice terraces

Sometime between 20 and 30 centuries ago, the Ifugao tribespeople drifted into the mountainous interior of northern Luzon and began the task of carving the precipitous land from valley floor to ridge top into neatly terraced rice fields. They toiled so diligently—with bare hands, wooden and stone tools, and empirical engineering skill—that today the terraces, if laid end-to-end, would extend halfway around the world.

Once known as fierce headhunters, many of the tribes of northern Luzon are still remote enough to be self-sufficient, raising their own food, weaving their baskets, and making their weapons.

The terraces are classed among the world's manmade marvels—though they are certainly among the least accessible. The long, tiring drive by car over mountain roads to reach the terraces is a memorable discovery trip in itself.

Banaue, base for exploring

Center of the rice terrace country is the village of Banaue, in the homeland of the Ifugao tribespeople. From Manila, you have a choice of two routes to Banaue. One is through Baguio; the alternate approach is from the east through Bagabag. You can use both routes to make a loop trip—in via Baguio to Banaue, returning to Manila via Bagabag (or vice versa). Philippine Airlines flies into both Baguio and Bagabag.

From Baguio, it's another eight hours by road to Banaue; from Bagabag, it's a three-hour ride. (The shorter route from Bagabag is far less interesting and serves only to create a loop trip.) Many of the best rice terraces are located between Banaue and Bontoc.

A memorable journey

Driving northward from Baguio, you follow the Mountain Province highway through the towns of Mount Data and Bontoc to Banaue. Scenically exciting, this road is no superhighway but a road engineering and maintenance feat. Just outside Baguio a road sign warns, "Drive with Care, Courtesy, & Discipline"—and you soon see why. The eight-hour ride is a jogging, erratic mountainside journey. Drivers frequently use their vehicle's horn to announce their approach to oncoming obstacles—jeeps, cars, trucks, open-sided buses, and out-of-sight road gangs repairing highway damage caused by erosion and landslides.

But you have exciting compensations for the rugged road trip: glimpses into tribal life styles and unforgettable scenery, sunflowers lining the road, bright green, terraced vegetable fields, pine forests, orchids growing wild, even a stretch of rain forest. The road winds upward to 7,500 feet, the highest point in the Philippine highway system.

As you careen along a straight stretch of the road, dusty buses—which started from the north before dawn—bounce past, piled high with baskets of chickens and sacks of rice. Trucks loaded with bamboo baskets of cabbages roll past. If you arrive at any town on market day, you'll see the mountain people trading for rice, dried fish, pots and pans, and clothing. All of these items are spread out on the ground.

Tribal dress

Travel deeper into rice terrace country and you'll notice that the style of dress becomes less westernized and more functional. Women with tattooed arms appear, dressed in wrap-around *tapis* (skirts with distinctive stripes) topped with faded shirts, heads encircled by snake spines, and balancing straw mats or baskets on their heads. Older women, wrinkled and bronzed by the sun, smoke long, skinny-stemmed pipes, sometimes with a cigarette sticking out of the bowl.

In some regions the men still wear G-strings or loincloths; some sport eye-catching back tattoos. They stuff their long hair up under straw pillbox beanies, each topped with a big button or wisp of feather, worn perched on the back of the head. Since a loincloth lacks pockets, money and betel-nut-chewing paraphernalia are also cached under the beanie.

Little children wear whatever is handy and are usually the most friendly toward visitors.

The rice terraces

For years Filipinos have urged visitors to see the rice terraces—and even those who have viewed this monument to man's ingenuity and fortitude find it difficult to comprehend what they see.

Imagine yourself looking across a river canyon at a sharply sloping mountain. Visualize that entire mountainside, from river bed to ridgetop—reaching as high as 5,000 feet—cut into hundreds of curving steps, each stone staircase a product of laborious hand cutting and digging. Picture these terraces with rice plants forming patterns of green—from delicate rice seedlings to strips of dark green mature rice—and with water falling gently from one level to the next.

The builders tapped springs and constructed channels (often stone-lined) to transfer the water along the breadth of the slopes and down from plot to plot so that it moistens (rather than washes away) topsoil and terraced banks. Rims along each terrace form little dams and also serve as walkways. These are the rice terraces—built before the time of Christ—by a tribe of people who reshaped the earth by hand.

Winding deeper into the terraced country, the road often cuts across planted slopes, becoming another lateral terrace itself, with rice fields stepping sharply above and below. Some steps cover several acres, others just three square feet. You'll see villages clustered along the riverside flats and other tiny settlements perched at isolated spots on the terraces. This vista continues intermittently all the way from Mount Data through Bontoc to Banaue—more than three hours of driving.

Mountain hotels

On your trip to the rice terraces, you can stay overnight at Mount Data, Bontoc, or Banaue. Mount Data Lodge, located on the Baguio-Bontoc route, is halfway to the terraces. Bontoc has the Cawed Hotel and the Pines Kitchenette & Inn. The newer Banaue Hotel offers a superb view from atop a Banaue ridge, just a gully or two from the center of the terraces.

West coast excursions

Luzon's west coast, stretching from the ancient city of Vigan south along Bauang's resort beaches to the Hundred Islands National Park on Lingayen Gulf, offers approximately 150 miles of historic sights, sandy beaches with calm surf, and deserted islands.

If you use Bauang as a base, you can include these destinations in a three to six-day Manila-Baguio-Bauang-Manila loop trip. From Baguio, it's an hour's drive (30 miles) to the beach resort area of Bauang along the Naguilian Mountain Road. Or you can fly from Manila to San Fernando, a port city eight miles north of Bauang.

Vigan, early Spanish center

Founded in 1574, historic Vigan became a seat of Spanish culture and power second only to Manila. Located some 75 road miles north of Bauang, the ancient city was built in the same style as Manila, with narrow streets, Spanish architecture, and ornate churches. Many Filipinos say that old Vigan resembles the walled city of Intramuros in Manila.

Bauang, a restful beach resort

Washed by the calm blue waters of the Lingayen Gulf, Bauang is considered one of the best beach resorts in the Philippines. Shaded by coconut palms, its long, beautiful, white sandy beaches offer swimming, fishing, skin-diving, water-skiing, and boating. Pleasant beach front cottages and hotel rooms are available in four hotels: the Cresta

Ancient calesa *(horse-drawn buggy) plods along a quiet Vigan street. The 300-year-old town resembles Manila's walled Intramuros.*

Thatch-roofed *huts cling to the lush hillside amid the famed rice terraces on the route through the Baguio-Banaue district.*

Nalinac Beach Resort, *one of several palm-shaded resorts in Bauang, caters to skin divers and other water sport devotees.*

Roadside market *in Abatan enlivens the journey to Banaue. Fresh fruit and vegetables are colorfully arrayed under white awnings.*

PHILIPPINES

Willowy palm trees, *grazing water buffaloes, nipa huts, and beached fishing boats mark this pastoral countryside near Iloilo on Panay Island. Nearby villages are weaving and craft centers.*

Rice threshing *to separate grain from the stalk requires hardened feet and a strong back. Bamboo structures such as these have dotted the Philippine countryside for many generations.*

Ola Beach Resort, Long Beach Resort Hotel, Nalinac Beach Resort, and Sun Valley Beach Hotel.

Hundred Islands National Park

Recognized as the second largest marine park in the world, the Hundred Islands are 150 road miles (a 6-hour drive) north of Manila and some 60 road miles (3 hours by car) west of Baguio. Jumping-off place for the scattered islets is Barrio Lucap in Alaminos town.

Quezon Island is the most popular destination among the 400 rocky islets. Its white sand beach edges shallow waters ideal for swimming. Scattered around the island's shore are several fishing nooks and coves, perfect for snorkeling. You can hire a native launch for a picnic excursion among the islets, cave exploring, and viewing undersea coral gardens.

The southern islands

The southern islands of the Philippines—the Visayas, Mindanao, and the Sulu Archipelago—are a world removed from the big, fast-paced city of Manila. Key tourist destinations are Iloilo on Panay Island, Cebu in the Visayas, and Zamboanga and Davao on Mindanao. The Sulu Archipelago and its port city of Jolo are the home of the Muslim Tausugs; continual outbreaks of warfare curtail this region's desirability as a tourist destination.

On these southern islands you find one of the least westernized of the Filipino peoples—the Badjao nomads of the sea, known as sea gypsies; the primitive Yakan people, with long hair and knee breeches; turbaned Filipino Muslims, known as Moros; and the southern Filipinos, who retain the gracious manners and language of Old Spain.

Philippine Airlines operates daily flights south from Manila. Flying time is an hour to Iloilo and Cebu and another 50 minutes to Zamboanga and Davao. Zamboanga will one day become an official international entry-exit point for the Philippines, making it possible for visitors to enter the Philippines at Manila and leave through Zamboanga (or vice versa) en route to other countries in Southeast Asia.

Travelers with more time can travel by ship. From January to May several steamship companies operate cruises from Manila through the Visayas (Iloilo and Cebu) to Mindanao (Zamboanga and Davao); for more information, see page 11. You can even take a 4-day, sea-land-air trip out of Manila to the islands.

Iloilo and Panay Island

Located about midway down the island chain on the southeast coast of Panay Island, Iloilo combines a feeling of Spanish antiquity with black sand beaches and rural tranquillity. Backed against the island's hills and valleys, this busy port—a city of about 200,000 people—is also something of an educational center. Outrigger fishing boats grace the city's waterfront. Iloilo's easygoing charm is typified by women weaving delicate fabrics from fibers of native plants on century-old Spanish looms.

You can stay in the city center or near the beach in any of several good hotels: Kahirup, del Rio, Royal Palms, Madia-as, and the Anhawan Resort.

The waterfront, with its brightly painted fishing fleet, tops the city's attractions. You can break the afternoon's sightseeing with a bowl of *batchoy* (a noodle soup with pork, liver, and chicken). In the evening, you'll find music and dancing at the Hotel del Rio, River Queen Hotel, and Park Hotel.

Iloilo handicrafts. Several villages outside Iloilo are your best shopping bets for woven goods, flowers, and shellcraft. The village of Arevalo, four miles from Iloilo City, is the weaving center. Also known as a flower village, Arevalo can supply you with leis, corsages, bouquets, and potted plants. You can purchase shellcraft articles at the village of Oton. The round, paper-thin seashells found locally are called *kapis;* they are made into attractive boxes, trays, chimes, and even chandeliers.

History display. The island's history and art are showcased at the Museo Iloilo. Exhibits include prehistoric tools, grave artifacts (among them ancient gold eye and nose masks), pottery, and jewelry. War relics date back to the early revolutions against Spain and the United States and to World War II. Other collections feature antique porcelain, colonial religious sculpture, and old weapons. The museum is open daily.

Iloilo's environs. The Spanish influence is most evident in the countryside surrounding Iloilo, where a succession of sturdy, old Spanish-Filipino churches and watchtowers are strung out along the coast.

The coast road provides a charming, easygoing route through bougainvillea-splashed villages—past nipa-thatched huts, bright green fields, and palm and banana-framed beaches. Probably you'll see people working in the fields, perhaps threshing rice on a bamboo platform, stamping their feet so that the grain cascades into a golden pile beneath the frame. In areas where experimental farming methods are being practiced, rice is harvested as many as three times a year.

Spanish churches. Perhaps the best known church is on the coastal road west of Iloilo in the town of Miagao. It combines European and Filipino influences in relief sculpture, depicting coconut and papaya trees surrounding the figure of St. Christopher. Two massive sandstone towers give the church a fortresslike appearance; when constructed in 1787, it was planned both as a religious edifice and a fort against Muslim pirates. Today you see fish merchants strolling past the church, baskets of fish balanced on a pole over their shoulders, and townspeople buying rice and other necessities at a row of shops across the street. Roaring three-wheeled tricycles add a noisy, modern touch to the street scene.

Another favorite church for sightseers is San Joaquin, a white coral church built in 1369, located 10 minutes west of Miagao on the paved coast road. A military scene decorates its unique facade, built a decade after the invading Spanish troops conquered the Moroccans at Tetuan.

Preservation and restoration of old churches and watchtowers are a continuing project in Iloilo Province. In recent decades, well-meaning priests attempted to repair many ancient structures by plastering over interior and exterior walls. Restoration work has included the removal of these layers to reveal structural brick and coral stones.

Crumbling watchtowers. Also being preserved are some old watchtowers, built during the era when Muslim pirates terrorized coastal villages. Guards manning the towers used smoke signals to warn

Molo Church *in Iloilo shows Spanish and Filipino influences with its tall, spired belfry, moss-covered stone work, and sturdy columns.*

townspeople, who then fled into the mountains. You can see one of the cone-shaped sandstone watchtowers at Guimbal; though covered with moss and other vegetation, it retains the aura of those unsettled days.

Black sand beaches. Lining the calm blue waters of the Panay Gulf are exotic black sand beaches, marked by resorts of bamboo cottages. At Anhawan Beach Resort at the town of Oton, about 7 miles west of Iloilo, you can enjoy the beach scene and feast on Filipino seafood specialties. You can laze away the afternoon under a thatched pavilion, free to enjoy a cool drink along with the peaceful setting; a solicitous attendant stays close at hand to flick away flies with a tassel of streamers.

Cebu, Philippines' oldest city

Discovered by Ferdinand Magellan in 1521, Cebu was officially established by Legazpi in 1565, making it the oldest city in the Philippines. Using Cebu as a base, the Spanish moved up the island chain, Christianizing Filipinos along the way. They eventually occupied Manila in 1571. Today Cebu is recognized as an important historical center of old Spanish culture. The island is the most densely populated in the Visayas, with some 350,000 inhabitants. Cebu city has good tourist accommodations in half a dozen hotels, the most popular of which are Hotel Magellan, Skyvue Hotel, Cebu Plaza, and the Montebello Hotel.

City sights. Sheltered by a tile roof near the city's waterfront, the Cross of Magellan honors the navigator who planted the cross here in 1521, claiming the land for the Spanish crown. Nearby stands the Basilica of San Agustin, renowned for its famed Santo Nino image encrusted with precious jewels. Fort San Pedro, more than 300 years old, is one of Cebu's most interesting historic sights. Its crumbling stone steps and silent guard towers are mute testimony to the period when the fort was the settlement's main defense against Muslim piracy.

A popular excursion is a trip by the causeway to Mactan Island, off Cebu's east coast. In the town of Opon, a monument marks the spot where Magellan lost his life in 1521 at the hands of the native chief

---

Morion Festival—a Holy Week tradition

A centuries-old tradition is celebrated during Holy Week on Marinduque, an island off southern Luzon where, some 200 years ago, Spanish shipbuilders constructed galleons. The unique and colorful events climax on Easter Sunday with the Morion Festival, a Lenten play based on the miraculous cure of the blind eye of Longinus, the Roman centurion who speared Christ's side on the cross. According to the story, a drop of blood hit the Roman's blind left eye, restoring his sight. Longinus proclaimed this a miracle and professed his belief in the divinity of Christ.

First presented about a hundred years ago in Mogpog, one of the province's villages, the drama spread to nearby towns. Today's festival center is Boac, the island's capital city, where events begin on Holy Thursday. Enthusiasm for the religious events, including reenactments of the Last Supper and the Crucifixion, have developed into a provincewide celebration and masquerade.

Participants in the Morion Festival (called *moriones*) purchase licenses for a few *centavos*, entitling them to wear huge papier-mâché masks and Roman costumes. These licensed moriones join the masqueraders as a form of penance; for four days they roam about the towns—Boac, Gasan, and Mogpog.

The main event takes place at noon on Easter Sunday along the dried river bed outside Boac (shelters shield visitors from the sun). Milling about dressed as Roman centurions, moriones attend the reenactment of Longinus's miracle and his "pugutan".

When Longinus bursts forth from the crowd, yelling that he can see, the authorities arrest him. A protracted chase follows, he is captured, and the drama climaxes with his symbolic beheading. The one-eyed mask of Longinus appears above the crowd at the end of a sword, raising cries of sorrow from the moriones. Longinus' body is carried on a shield to the town's churchyard to conclude the drama.

Marinduque is a 45-minute flight from Manila. During Holy Week, special flights are added to the scheduled air service. Packaged tours combine transportation, accommodations, and meals.

Pugutan *(beheading) climaxes the Morion Festival; participants wear Romanlike masks.*

Sausage seller *and his youthful helpers operate a family business in the central market in Cebu.*

A single vinta *(Muslim sailboat) with its sail unfurled glides across a palm-fringed Cebu lagoon.*

Lapu Lapu. Nearby, a monument has been erected honoring the warrior chief, regarded as the first Filipino hero against outside aggressors. You can also see these monuments on your way to or from Cebu Airport, which is located on Mactan Island. Horse-drawn carts, called *tartanillas*, provide most of the local transportation on Mactan.

Mountainous Mindanao

At the southern end of the Philippine archipelago lies the mountainous island of Mindanao (second largest island in the Philippines). Here the Muslim influence is strong, especially in western Mindanao, where you'll see turreted mosques more often than Christian church steeples.

The Cotabato coastal range encloses much of Mindanao's southern coast. In recent years it has attracted world-wide attention, for it was here in the early 1970s that the Tasaday tribe was discovered. Existing in a primitive manner, they live off the land, collecting food rather than cultivating plants; stone axes are their main implements. The government created a 50,000-acre tribal reserve to protect the Tasadays' ancient way of life.

Zamboanga, an intriguing seaport

Situated at the tip of the Zamboanga Peninsula, the ancient seaport of Zamboanga blends an intriguing variety of cultures with cloak-and-dagger history. Approximately 540 miles south of Manila, Zamboanga is actually closer to Indonesia.

A wide choice of accommodations are available to visitors. Hotels in the Zamboanga area include the Astoria, Embassy, Hotel Zamboanga, Lantaka, Pasonanca, Zamboanga Plaza, Sultana, and Zambayan.

Though a city of 200,000, Zamboanga has a small town atmosphere—sparked by horse drawn *calesas*, a fish market, outdoor food stands, Moro fishing villages on stilts, domed mosques, and many roaring, three-wheeled tricycles. Palm trees shade the lovely gardens of Pershing Plaza; betel nut trees line Mayor N. S. Valderosa Street. Flowers brighten the city's parks, home gardens, and window boxes. Offshore waters are alive with the colorful *vintas* (narrow, hollowed-out logs with bamboo outriggers and huge sails) of the sea gypsies *(Badjaos)*.

The city officially dates from 1635, when the Spaniards laid the cornerstone of the future Fort Pilar, and Zamboanga became a seat of Spanish culture. Three centuries of Spanish rule left a strong impression, including a language—Chabacano—that is 70 percent Spanish.

Waterfront markets. Downtown Zamboanga centers on the waterfront public market—a clamor of bargaining voices and a maze of covered stalls offering everything from freshly caught seafood to brightly colored Indonesian batiks, from Muslim brassware to pieces of coral. You'll see fishermen unloading catches at the docks in the early light, a gutted shark being wheeled along at midmorning, and young boys selling *matangbaca* (fish with cow's eyes) in plastic bags until late in the evening.

Beside the public market, behind a chain link fence, is the Barter Trade Market. Under the

Sheltered *by coconut palms, nipa huts are scattered along the coast north of Zamboanga. Family's water buffalo is tethered to a tree.*

Coiled hemp rope *in bright colors is displayed at Zamboanga's public market. Outriggers and coastal steamers sail from the port.*

Boatman poles *a cargo-laden dugout past a cluster of stilt houses, part of Zamboanga's Muslim village of Taluksangay.*

Spreading tree *at Fort Pilar shades an improvised, open-air barber shop. Fort guards the southern approach to the port of Zamboanga.*

awning-covered stalls, you'll see imported goods from around the world—Japanese lighters and ornate umbrellas, French perfumes, Russian caviar, and bolts of cloth of every fabric, color, and design.

Across the street at Pershing Plaza, you can stroll among the greenery or sit and watch the jeepney traffic.

Fort Pilar. Not far away, on the town's southern edge, is historic Fort Pilar. Built by the Spanish for protection against Muslim pirates, it was recently used by Philippine Army troops engaged in continuing battles with the Moros. The fort contains the Shrine of Our Lady of Pilar, honored every October 12 in a fiesta. Eventually the fort will have a museum, an aquarium, a small hotel, restaurants, open-air auditorium, and landscaped gardens. From the south walls of the fort, you can see the Muslim village of Rio Hondo and its gleaming-white, minareted mosque.

Pasonanca Park. Zamboanga is known as a city of flowers. One of its most colorful areas is Pasonanca Park, a 125-acre, orchid-adorned stretch of green on hills overlooking the city. Zamboangans cool off in a large, spring-fed swimming pool here, and both the Boy Scouts and Girl Scouts have camps in the park.

At the park's south end is the Zamboanga Tree House, a one-room cabin about 30 feet above the ground in a huge tree, available free to honeymooners. The house is equipped with a bathroom, running water, and electricity.

Shopping for seashells. One of Zamboanga's natural resources is seashells, which come in a dazzling variety of shapes, colors, and patterns. Sea gypsies sell the shells along the waterfront, or you can visit the Rocan Shell Shop outside town. Its factory-showroom has dozens of varieties of shells prepared for export, from giant clam shells to delicate black coral jewelry (rings, necklaces, bracelets) set in sterling silver.

Santa Cruz Island. Travelers who enjoy collecting their own seashells or who want to sunbathe on a deserted stretch of beach can take a half-day excursion to Santa Cruz Island. Just a 10-minute ride by motorized *banca* (from the waterfront at the Lantaka Hotel), the low-lying island offers a beach tinged pink by crushed coral. Clear waters offshore attract swimmers and snorkelers. (Diving gear may be rented at the Lantaka.) Near the shore the ocean bottom is rocky, so bring along some old sneakers. For lunch, you can buy fresh shrimp and fish at the public market and have your boatman prepare a meal over an open fire.

If you feel adventurous, spend some time exploring along the island's shoreline. About a hundred yards down the beach, east of the landing site, look for an ancient Muslim cemetery with wooden figures as headstones. About three-fourths of a mile beyond, separated by an inlet, is a cluster of thatched huts—a Samal Muslim fishing village. The Muslims collect shells from the sea and then process them for sale in Zamboanga.

After divers gather the shells, they place them at the bottom of a lagoon for a full day, haul the shells onto the beach the second day, and boil them in a huge cauldron for five minutes. The process not only cleans the shells, but also it bleaches them white. With a little haggling, you can buy your shells here at a lower price than in Zamboanga.

The Moros. Filipino Muslims were given the name Moros by the Spanish, after the Moors of Africa. The first Arab teacher-missionary arrived toward the end of the 14th century. During the 17th and 18th centuries, Muslim pirates made raids as far north as Manila, and later, they battled fiercely against the Spanish and Americans. Today, fighting still continues between some Moros and Philippine government troops in parts of Mindanao and the Sulu Archipelago.

The Muslims' life style hasn't changed in centuries. Expert fishermen and pearl divers, the Moros live off the water—harvesting the fish-rich Sulu Sea.

They have their own legal system based on the Koran, and the young learn Arabic script in classrooms in the shadows of turreted mosques. Nipa huts built on stilts over the bay are connected by narrow foot bridges. Occasionally a Moro ceremonial dance can be seen by special arrangement at one of the local Muslim villages.

Zamboanga's major Moro settlements—Taluk-

Taluksangay/youngsters *frolic in the water on a warm afternoon. In the southern islands, you'll see numerous mosques, a reminder of the strong Muslim influence.*

Pearl culture *attracts visitors to Aguinaldo Pearl Farm on Samal Island, offshore from Davao.*

Bocaue River Festival *features large barge carrying a Holy Cross. Villagers surround float in decorated boats.*

sangay, Rio Hondo, and Recodo—are usually included as part of a city tour.

Davao . . . pearls and a luxury resort

Mindanao's largest city and shopping center is Davao, on the island's southwestern coast. One of Davao's oldest landmarks is Osmena Park, now transformed into a zoological and botanical garden.

The city on the Davao Gulf attracts visitors seeking a relaxing tropical resort. You'll find here three hotels—two in the city and one along the beach. Most tourists prefer the Davao Insular Hotel in its suburban setting, a beach resort with sailboats and outrigger canoes for day excursions. You can make arrangements to visit an abaca plantation, go deep sea fishing, play golf, or just relax beneath tropical trees along the tranquil beaches.

Just offshore from Davao is Samal Island, famous for the Aguinaldo Pearl Farm. For centuries the pearls of the Sulu Archipelago have attracted buyers from the Orient. Holding his breath, each Muslim diver makes dozens of dives each day from a small boat in search of the pearl-bearing oysters. The shells are sold for their mother-of-pearl, which is fashioned into necklaces and curio items.

Southwest of Davao, 9,690-foot Mount Apo dominates the countryside. Mount Apo National Park covers approximately 7,000 acres around the mountain's base, providing a scenic preserve rich in orchids, waterfalls, lakes, and hot springs.

Hidden within the overgrown jungle on Mindanao's southern side is the forest reserve of the Tasaday Tribe, natives who were recently discovered still living in Stone Age style.

Festivals and events

In the Philippines you'll discover the magic of the fiesta deeply rooted in Filipino history, tradition, and culture. Festivals—real, non-manufactured celebrations—fill the Philippine calendar.

Each village has its saint's day, harvest time, and *carabao* (water buffalo) festivals. There are fiestas celebrating birth and marriage, feasts honoring the dead, fertility rites, and numerous other festivals reflecting traditional customs and religious practices—not only of the Christian and Muslim Filipinos but also of some 50 other ethnic groups. Most fiestas feature music, dancing, and feasting. Some include colorful dramas, competitive sports, and cockfights.

Listed below are a few of the events occurring about the same time each year:

Feast of the Three Kings. On the first Sunday in January, Manila social organizations recreate the royal visit to the Christ child.

Feast of the Black Nazarene. Manila's largest religious event occurs from New Year's Day to January 9. At the climax of the celebration, devotees walk through the city's streets, pulling a carriage bearing a 200-year-old image of the saint.

Ap-pey. Each January, rites and offerings are made in Bontoc (Mountain Province) to insure a successful rice crop (see page 12).

Ati-Atihan Festival. Kalibo residents and guests dress in bizarre costumes during a three-day January festival honoring the child Jesus.

Hari Raya Haji. This Muslim holiday in March is observed by those who have been to Mecca (see (see page 13).

Practical information for visitors to the Philippines

Here are some important practical details to help you plan your trip:

Entry requirements. No visa is required to visit the Philippines for up to 21 days, but you need a passport and proof of onward passage. For stays longer than 21 days, apply for a visa at the nearest Philippine consulate. The visa is free to U.S. citizens and good for 59 days. You pay an airport tax of about $3 on departure.

You will need an international health certificate showing inoculation for smallpox. Cholera and yellow fever inoculations are required for visitors arriving from an infected area. The U.S. Public Health Service suggests you have cholera, typhoid, paratyphoid, tetanus, and gamma globulin shots.

Philippine consulates are located in San Francisco, Los Angeles, Seattle, Honolulu, Chicago, New Orleans, and New York. The embassy is in Washington, D.C.

Customs. Tourists are not required to fill out a customs declaration, and baggage is usually not examined. You can bring in duty-free 300 cigarettes, 50 cigars, one kilo of pipe tobacco, two kilos of packaged tea, one quart of liquor, and one camera with a reasonable amount of film.

Currency. The rate of exchange of the Philippine peso is about P7.35 to U.S. $1. There is no limit on the amount of foreign currency brought in, but it should be exchanged only with authorized agents of the Central Bank located in most hotels.

Health conditions. Medical facilities are very good in Manila but limited in the rural areas. You can buy everyday medicines and toiletries.

Tipping. Light tipping is the rule in Manila, where most hotels and restaurants add a 10 per cent service charge. In rural sections, tipping can be misconstrued as an affront to hospitality.

At air, rail, and ship terminals, a tip of P1 per piece of luggage is sufficient. In first-class restaurants with no service charge, a 10 percent tip is customary. Taxi drivers are usually not tipped but will accept 10 percent. At beauty and barber shops with no service charge, tipping is at the customer's discretion—usually P1.

Climate. Weather in the Philippines is tropical, with cool, dry, and wet seasons. In Manila, the best time of the year is November to February, when daytime temperatures average 78°F. Warm, summer weather comes from March to June, with average daytime temperatures of 82°F. During most of the year, ocean breezes cool Manila and low areas at night. The rainy season (also the typhoon season) lasts from July to October with frequent heavy rains. All of the islands receive an average of 80 inches of rain per year. Serious flooding occurs in many low areas on Luzon Island. The southern islands of the Visayas and Mindanao (cooled by steady breezes) are best from January to May.

For more information. Contact the Philippine Ministry of Tourism, 556 Fifth Avenue, New York 10036; or 447 Sutter Street, San Francisco 94108; or 3325 Wilshire Boulevard, Los Angeles 90010; or 30 N. Michigan Avenue, Chicago 60602; or their headquarters at Agrifina Circle, Rizal Park, Manila.

Holy Week. A week-long celebration, culminating on Easter Sunday, combines centuries-old traditions, Catholic liturgy, and native practices.

Morion Festival. From Holy Thursday to Easter, Marinduque Island participants masquerade in colorful masks and the costumes of Roman soldiers to reenact the story of the Roman centurion Longinus. Climaxing the festival is the "beheading," or *pugutan*, on Easter Sunday (see page 38). Hundreds of visitors travel from Manila for this event.

Turrumba Festival. Residents of Pakil (Laguna Province) celebrate on the second Tuesday after Holy Week. They sing and dance in the streets in honor of the town's patroness, Our Lady of Sorrows. *Turrumba* means to jump with joy.

Maolod en Nabi. On April 26, Muslims celebrate the birth of Prophet Mohammed (see page 13).

Santa Cruzan. Month-long festivities in May with street extravaganzas commemorate the finding of the "True Cross of Christ"; the cast of characters is drawn from the Bible, history, mythology, and pure fantasy.

Harvest Festival. On May 15, farmers in Sariaya and Lucban (Quezon Province) honor the patron saint of good harvests (see page 12).

Independence Day. On June 12 a national celebration commemorates Philippines' independence.

Bocaue River Festival. On July 2, the Holy Cross is borne by barge down the river near Manila.

Bayombong Fiesta. Held on the first Sunday in August in Nueva Vizcaya Province, the fiesta honors San Domingo de Guzman, the town's patron saint. Highlight is the *sumbali* dance, performed by the Aeta Tribe.

Penafrancia Fiesta. Held during the third week of September in Bicolandia Province, the statue of the town's patron saint—the Virgin Mary—is taken down the Naga river on a flower-bedecked barge.

Pagsanjan Fiesta. On December 12, gaily decorated arches are carried in procession, and parties are held in this town known for its waterfalls.

Christmas Day. A 22-day celebration is highlighted with midnight Mass on Christmas Eve, and church bells are rung throughout the country.

Terraced rice fields (top), *built centuries ago, are found throughout Indonesia. Bicycles and becaks* **(right)** *roll along Yogyakarta's streets. Bali fisherman* **(far right)** *casts his net in the island's offshore waters.*

Indonesia

The world's largest tropical archipelago

A fabled collection of more than 13,000 tropical islands strung out along the equator, Indonesia is the world's largest archipelago. The countryside is lush and fertile, its face scarred by rivers descending from towering volcanic mountains.

A land of contrasts, Indonesia has modern cities that belie rural districts where gentle people exist on rice terraces still farmed as they were thousands of years ago. Ancient temples, monumental in size, contrast with tiny field temples on nearly every farmer's plot, built to appease the rice gods.

The hospitable Indonesians still follow time-honored rituals, including colorful festivals set against dramatic backgrounds. This intriguing country has also become known for its traditional crafts, costumed dance performances, and puppet plays presented by wandering minstrels.

Jakarta, Medan, and Denpasar are the gateways to Indonesia. The prime attraction is Bali. For the adventurous traveler, the country's far-flung island groups offer some of the least visited discovery areas in today's travel world.

Indonesia—then and now

Indonesia's 13,677 islands stretch more than 3,000 miles from east to west, sharing portions of the Pacific and Indian oceans and the South China Sea. From an orbiting satellite, the islands must resemble giant stepping stones linking Australia and Southeast Asia. The mountainous island backbone of Sumatra, Java, and Bali is punctuated with the cones of more than 400 volcanoes.

A necklace of islands

The principal islands of Indonesia are Java, Sumatra, Kalimantan (Borneo), and Sulawesi (Celebes); these are known as the Greater Sunda

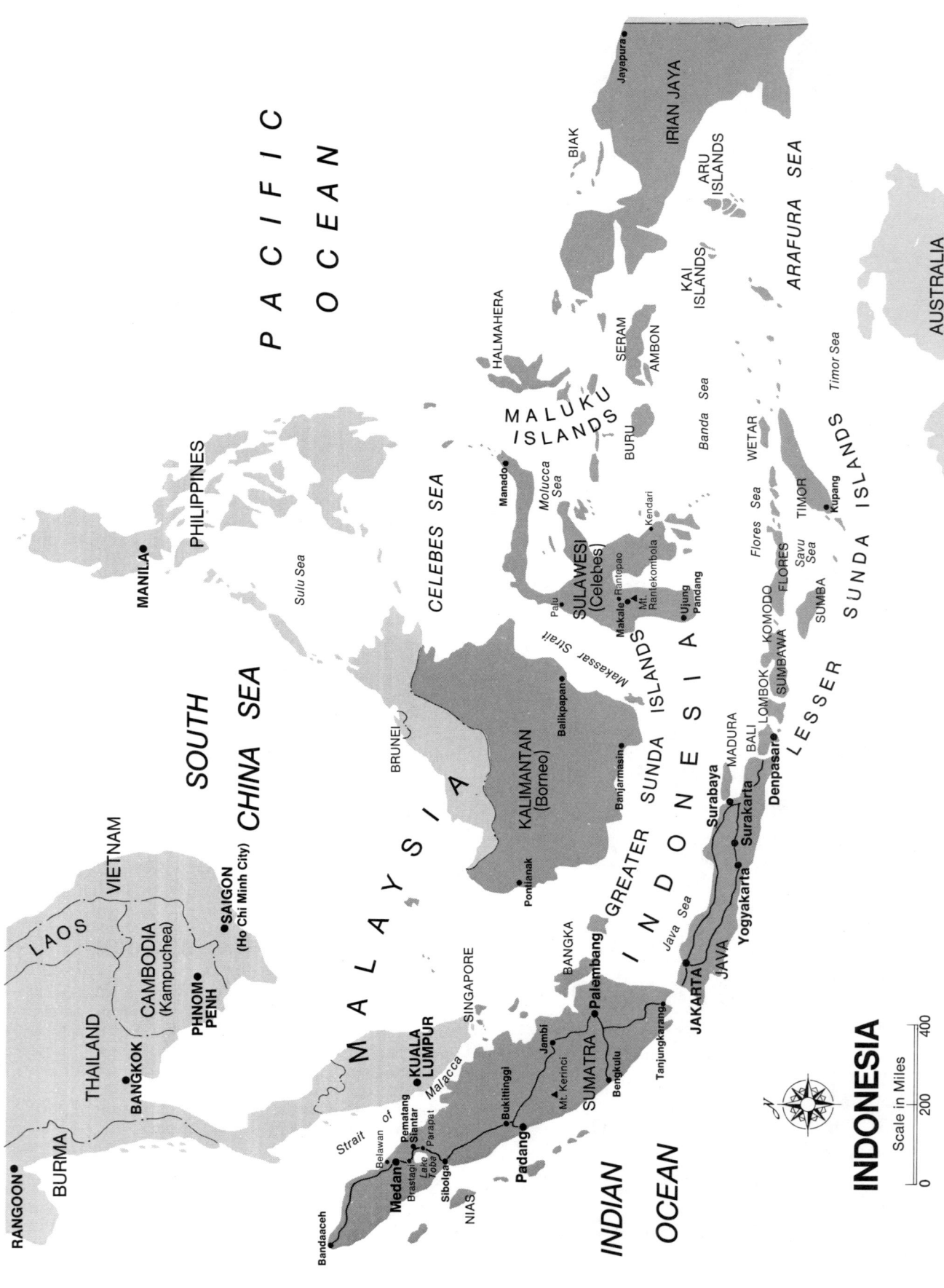

Islands. East of Java are the Lesser Sunda Islands—the principal ones being Bali, Lombok, Sumbawa, Sumba, Flores, and Timor. Strung out along eastern Indonesia are also the Maluku Islands, the Kai Islands, the Aru Islands, Irian Jaya (the western half of New Guinea), and smaller island groups.

Only about half of the country's islands have permanent settlements, and two-thirds of Indonesia's 135 million inhabitants live on Java.

Plants and animals

The Indonesian islands are known as a "transitional" region—one containing plants and animals typical of both Asia and Australia. More than a fifth of the land is carpeted with jungle vegetation, yielding valuable woods. The coastal plains are abundant with coconut palms, bamboo, *trengguli* (pudding pipe tree), shrubs, and flowers. Orchids and water lilies grow in a great profusion.

Animal life includes many kinds of reptiles and mammals, among them elephants, rhinoceroses (including the nearly extinct one-horned rhinoceros), tigers, small grey monkeys, apes, and tapirs. On Borneo, Sumatra, and parts of Java are found orang-utans, gibbons, and lemurs. Included among the reptiles found here are many snakes, some venomous. Crocodiles inhabit the jungle rivers and swamps; nine-foot lizards are found on the island of Komodo. Domesticated animals include the water buffalo, Balinese cattle (which resemble overgrown deer), and pigs descended from wild hogs.

An ancient history

Most of today's Indonesians are descended from waves of people who entered the area from the Asiatic mainland between 3,000 and 500 B.C. However, these islands were inhabited half a million years ago by some of the earliest known examples of mankind (the Java man, whose bones were discovered in 1891).

Hindus and Arabs. As early as the 5th century B.C., Indonesia was introduced to Indian culture and religion through the influence of Indian traders, settlers, and Buddhist and Hindu monks. By the 16th century the native empires, with their strong Buddhist and Hindu influences, were replaced by the Islamic religion. Hindu followers who resisted Islam fled eastward to Bali, where much of the population still embraces Hinduism.

First Europeans. Marco Polo landed at Sumatra in 1292, the first Westerner to visit Indonesia. Portuguese, Spanish, English, and Dutch traders followed, and in 1596 the Dutch defeated their rivals and took over the government of Indonesia under the name of the Netherlands Indies—a rule that was to last more than 300 years.

Growth of nationalism. The Indonesian movement for independence began in the early 20th century and lasted through the World War II occupation of the country by the Japanese forces (1942-1945). Two days after the unconditional surrender of Japan, Indonesian nationalists proclaimed the Republic of Indonesia on August 17, 1945, in Jakarta. The Dutch did not recognize the legality of the Indonesian Republic, and "police actions" continued until August 1949, when the U.N. effected a cease-fire. A Dutch-Indonesian conference, held at The Hague in 1949, transferred sovereignty from the Dutch to Indonesia with Sukarno as president.

On September 30, 1965, the Indonesian Communist party attempted to turn the country into a Communist state, a move crushed by the Indonesian Armed Forces under General Suharto. Though Sukarno remained the country's symbolic leader for a brief period, the Communist uprising was his downfall. In 1967 General Suharto was elected president, with the task of rebuilding the economy and leading the country back to independence.

Indonesia is still emerging from centuries of foreign domination. A fascinating part of your visit is to see first hand how this development is taking place—to talk with the people, see the changes and the growth, and feel the fervor of a new nation.

The people of Indonesia

Original "Indonesians" were a Mongoloid type of primitive man similar to those still found in the Dyaks of Borneo, the Bataks of Sumatra, and the Torajas of Sulawesi.

Though predominantly of Malayan and Polynesian stock, present-day Indonesians reflect a complicated mixture of peoples, representing some 130 ethnic groups and more than 200 dialects. With a population exceeding 135 million, Indonesia ranks fifth among the nations of the world.

Outside the main cities and towns, the Indonesian life style is still governed by the family, the community, and the dictates of religion. Life is communal—families cooperate with one another in growing rice or building a house. Patience and *musyawarah* (the habit of discussing things) serve to make the Indonesians a peaceful people.

Moderation in all things is the Indonesian ideal, whether it be in speech and behavior, eating and drinking, or the possession of worldly things. Extremes in emotion are avoided; the loud voice, hearty laughter, or cries of anguish are regarded with disapproval and considered unbecoming.

The Indonesian language

Of the 200 languages spoken in Indonesia, only one is the national language—Bahasa Indonesia. Adapted in 1928 from the traditional Malay, it has evolved into a national language. Within the country, the people of each region also have their own language: Sundanese in West Java, Javanese in Central Java, Madurese in East Java, and Balinese in Bali.

The Indonesian language is written in the same Roman letters used for English. Letters are pronounced as they would be in English with a few exceptions: C is like Ch in "Chip"; Sy is like Sh in "Shop"; and Kh is like "ich" in the German language.

Words that were formerly spelled with a Dj have been changed to J—thus Djakarta has become Jakarta; the letter J in old spellings has been changed to Y—Surabaja has become Surabaya; the Tj combination of consonants has been changed to C—*betjak* has become *becak*. You will find many similar changes.

To ease communication problems, all hotels, transportation facilities, and tour offices have multilingual employees. You will find, though, that once you get off the beaten track, very few people speak English.

Religious beliefs

Most Indonesians live by the Muslim behavioral code—the Koran is law—yet only a small percentage are Muslims in the traditional Middle Eastern sense. In East Java this is particularly true; people are Muslim by affiliation but continue to cling to ancient animistic rituals and customs. In West Java and Sumatra, Islamic instruction is required in parochial schools; classes are also available on a voluntary basis after school and on Friday, the Muslim holy day.

Although Buddhism waned on Java and Sumatra after the introduction of Islam, you can still find Indonesian Buddhists along the coasts and in Central Java.

On Bali religious practices are dominated by the Balinese-Hindu faith. Bali's brand of Hinduism has been highly modified by ancient Balinese beliefs, including animism (attributing a spirit to inanimate objects and natural phenomena) and ancestral worship, as well as doctrines adapted from Buddhism, Sivaism, and Christianity.

Christian converts are scattered throughout the country, chiefly among the Toraja and Minahasa peoples on Sulawesi and the Batak tribesmen on Sumatra. Frequently, Christian worship is tempered with animist practices.

Planning your visit

Indonesia lies some 8,000 air miles west of the United States—a trip taking about 17½ hours from California. The time difference between the west coast of the U.S. and Indonesia is 15 hours. When it's noon Monday in Jakarta, it's 9 P.M. Sunday in San Francisco.

Many international airlines—including Garuda Indonesian Airways—serve the country, and regional airlines fly into Indonesian airports from many cities of Southeast Asia and the Orient. Both passengers, freighters and cruise ships include Indonesian ports of call on itineraries.

From planes to pedicabs

Although the fastest and most reliable way to travel between Indonesian cities is by air, you can also see parts of Java, Sumatra, and Bali by rail and bus. Traveling through the countryside provides interesting personal impressions of both the people and the land.

Daily ferry service links Ketapang on Java with Gilimanuk on Bali. Ferry services also operate between several other island groups.

In the major tourist centers, the best way to sightsee is by taxi. Most taxis have meters or per-mile tariffs. In addition, it is possible to hire taxis by the hour or day. Make arrangements through your hotel for a car with an English-speaking driver and have the price negotiated in advance. Metered taxis operate between the two airports and the international hotels.

Chauffeur-driven cars are available for long trips (you are expected to pay for the driver's accommodations and meals). Car rentals are not readily available nor recommended because of road congestion and right-hand controls.

For short journeys around town, try the *becak* (three-wheeled pedicabs), which are cheap, convenient, and usually available. In Jakarta they are banned from crowded downtown streets until after dark.

New hotels available

In recent years, many new hotels have been built on Java and Bali under the management of large

High priest *in ceremonial dress blesses the site chosen for a new hotel. This Indonesian custom is part of a Hindu religious ceremony.*

international hotel chains. Most of them provide restaurants, nightclubs, sightseeing services, guided tours, shops, pavilions for theater and native dance programs, and swimming pools. Around-the-clock service is provided by friendly and willing room boys. Hotels charge a 11 per cent room tax and many also add a service charge of 10 per cent to the bill.

If you are traveling on a very tight budget, you can try some of the inexpensive "national-standard hotels." Outside Jakarta or Denpasar, though, some of these still do not meet western standards, either in facilities or cleanliness.

A good way to get acquainted with a middle class Indonesian family is to share their home. A government-sanctioned organization finds homes for paying guests in Yogyakarta, Jakarta, Bandung, Malang, and Surabaya. The homes are regularly inspected, so they are clean. Air conditioning is rare, but most are fan cooled. For details, write Biro Pariwisata and Perusahaan Diy, c/o Kepatihan Danurejan, Yogyakarta, Indonesia.

Your choice of cuisines

Indonesian food offers great diversity in ingredients, styles of preparation, and manners of serving. Aromatic eastern spices, famed for centuries, are used lavishly to give variety to Indonesian dishes. Thousands of restaurants serve local specialties—varying from region to region, and island to island—as well as Chinese, Japanese, and western cuisines. Travelers preferring familiar western-style foods will find continental menus at most international hotels.

The basic Indonesian staple is rice, eaten with a mixture of dishes—meat, eggs, fish, and vegetables—often served as *rijsttafel*, a Dutch-Indonesian sampling of many local dishes. Two of the best known menus are Javanese and Sumatran. Javanese food is spicy and sweet, but not hot. Sumatran food is very spicy and full of chili peppers.

Tea and the good local beers are favorite drinks, but wines and liquors are also available. *Sirsak* is the local fruit-flavored soft drink. Most coffee is exported, but you can request it in restaurants. Except in international hotels, you should drink only boiled water or bottled drinks.

Entertainment

Indonesia's cultural tradition of music and dance dominates the entertainment scene; you'll enjoy ceremonial dances, music programs, puppet shows, and shadow plays. Western-style entertainment and floor shows are limited to the large hotels and a few nightclubs in Jakarta, Bandung, and Surabaya.

Most larger Indonesian cities have a People's Park, which can be an inexpensive (usually about 100 Rps to enter) and delightful way to spend an evening the way the local folks do. Entertainment possibilities include carnival rides, cock fights, movie theaters, snack bars, concerts, and traditional Indonesian theaters, such as shadow plays

Hostess in Tretes *awaits her guests, her table laden with Indonesian food. Fingers, forks, and spoons—no knives—are used in eating.*

(wayang kulit), dance operas *(wayang orang)*, or puppet plays *(wayang golek)*. The plays may last for hours; but it's acceptable to wander in and out of the theater, eat a snack, or even take a nap during the production.

Shopping for handicrafts

For centuries Indonesians have blended themes from Arabia, India, China, and the West with their native styles and techniques to create art works of exceptional beauty. They excel in painting and sculpture, woven and decorated textiles, woodcarving, metalwork, and floral creations.

Among attractive items you'll find are antiques, jewelry, basketwork, handwoven fabrics, pewter tea and coffee sets, woodcarvings, leather work, paintings of ancient and modern subjects, and batik cloth or clothing made from batik. Look for batik *kemben* (strapless dresses); *kebaya* (shirt or jacket) of silk and velvet or of homespun material, such as those worn by the peasants of Central Java; sarongs of all types; and *slendangs* (long colorful scarves).

Jakarta, busy island capital

A hustling, noisy city of five million people, Jakarta is the political and economic capital of Indonesia and the main entry-exit city on the island of Java. International airlines arrive daily at the city's handsome new Halim Airport, 10 miles southwest of the downtown area. Tanjung Priok, the city's congested and busy port, lies five miles north of the city on Jakarta Bay.

The city sprawls over 240 square miles of former marshland. From your hotel room window, your view encompasses a sea of red tiled roofs stretching almost to the horizon, broken occasionally by trees, mosque domes, and the soaring outlines of modern skyscrapers.

Midday traffic jams are commonplace, the noisy congestion created by a mixture of cars, trucks, buses, bicycles, handcarts, and (at night) *becaks*, the three-wheeled pedicabs. The most unique vehicles are the *helicak*, a motorized becak with driver in back and passengers sitting in an enclosed, helicopter-type bubble in front, and the *bemo*, a little three-wheeled truck, usually loaded with locals carrying an assortment of purchases and belongings.

Ruled by many nations

Through the years, Jakarta has seen many rulers. In its earliest days it was the site of a Hindu kingdom, then a Portuguese fort; later it became a Muslim city named Djayakarta. Next came the Dutch, who razed the city and built a new town, Batavia.

During World War II, the Japanese occupied the city, changing its name to Djakarta. Following the war and the country's struggle for independence, it was proclaimed the capital of the new Republic of Indonesia.

As you might expect after more than 300 years of Dutch occupation, the Dutch influence remains strong. Old Dutch buildings still stand in older parts of Jakarta. The canals, often flanking wide thoroughfares, are also a remnant of the city's colonial days.

Batik, Indonesia's national cloth

Wherever you go in Indonesia, you'll see women dressed in batik sarongs and blouses. In this free and individual art form, cloth is decorated with bold designs and bright colors using a wax and dye process to obtain successive colors. The original technique of hand decorating cloth in this manner was developed by Persians and Egyptians, brought to Indonesia by the early traders, and amplified and improved by the Javanese.

To make fine, hand-decorated batik, the cloth first has its original starch removed; it is re-starched, then softened by beating with wooden mallets. Artists create the design on paper, then trace it onto the cloth. Liquid wax is applied to some areas using a copper funnel, called the *canting*. Dyes are applied, then the material is washed in hot water to dissolve the wax. The wax-covered parts remain uncolored, while the dyed parts carry the design. This process is repeated with each color until the design is completed.

Less expensive batiks are made by stamping a design in various colors onto the material or by printing a batik design on the fabric by mass-production methods.

While it is sometimes difficult to distinguish a handmade batik from a mass produced one, the handmade batik usually shows more irregularity of design and is considerably more expensive.

Hand drawn batik takes time; dyeing of material for a sarong sometimes requires two or three months. Proper batik technique is as difficult as etching or painting. It is practically impossible to correct a mistake in the design or the color.

Though Java is the center for batik, every district in Indonesia has its own peculiar colors and designs and each pattern its own name. The best-known come from Yogyakarta, Surakarta, and Pekalongan in Central Java.

One of the best places to watch batik being made is the Batik Research Centre, a few miles from downtown Yogyakarta. Here you can watch demonstrations of batik making, and view displays of batik from almost every district of Java. Old pattern stamps, too worn for batik making, are often for sale at the center and make unusual souvenirs. In Jakarta, the best place to shop for batiks is the showroom of G.K.B.I., the Batik Federation, situated near the Senayan Sports Complex in the Kebayoran Baru area.

Delicate handiwork *results in intricate batik patterns. Small pot holds liquid wax.*

High-rise office buildings *and hotels line busy Jalan Thamrin, Jakarta's busy main boulevard. In the distance, the impressive Senayan Sports Complex rises above the flat countryside.*

A hotel building boom

In recent years a boom in hotel building has greatly improved the level of accommodations available in Jakarta. More than 30 major hotels provide rooms in the city and its suburbs.

Among these hotels are the Hyatt Aryaduta, Borobudur Inter-Continental, City, Hilton, Horison, Indonesia, Kartika Plaza, President, and Sari Pacific. Smaller hotels, many of which have opened recently, are the Airport International, Gadjah Mada International, Garden, Inter House, Kartika Chandra, Marcopolo, and Sabang Metropolitan.

All of these hotels are air-conditioned, and some of the larger ones have swimming pools. The new Hilton is part of a 32-acre complex that includes sports facilities, an open-air Balinese theater, and an Indonesian bazaar.

Dining adventures

Most of Jakarta's better restaurants are located in the city's hotels, though you'll also find European, Japanese, and Chinese restaurants elsewhere offering variety in both menu and surroundings. Here are a few of the best:
- George and Dragon, Jalan Thamrin (near Hotel Indonesia), has a British "pub" atmosphere. It offers such Anglo-Saxon favorites as steak, mushroom and kidney pie, ploughman's cold lunch, lobster bisque, and Irish coffee.
- Istana Anggrek, Taman Ria Remaja Senayan, serves Indonesian specialties.
- Istana Naga, Case Building, Jalan Gatot Subroto, tempts the palate with tasty Chinese dishes. Its specialty is roast pork.
- Oasis, Jalan Raden Saleh, occupies an old Dutch colonial-style mansion decorated with antique furniture. Rijsttafel leads off the menu, but you can also order Western food, especially French and Italian dishes.
- The Cellar Bar, Jalan Gondangdia Kecil, caters to the pizza, hamburger, ravioli, spaghetti, and apple pie crowd.
- Sky Room, Jalan Blora, attracts a mixed crowd with its international bar, restaurant, and delicious Chinese food.
- Yoshiko, Jalan Museum, offers Kobe beef and authentic Japanese dishes prepared by a chef from Tokyo.
- Vic's Viking, Jalan Thamrin (near Kartika Plaza Hotel), is highly rated by both residents and visitors. The restaurant features European and Oriental dishes.
- Mataram Restaurant, Hotel Borobudur Inter-Continental, features authentic Indonesian decor and food, especially rijsttafel, and performances of the Ramayana Dance by costumed dancers.
- Ramayana Restaurant, Hotel Indonesia, offers Indonesian and Continental cuisine.
- Tiara, on the rooftop of Hotel Kartika Plaza, tantalizes diners with a fantastic view of the city. It offers an international menu.

Entertainment and night life

In Jakarta you can enjoy presentations of Indonesian music and dance at several cultural centers.

Near Halim International Airport, the Indonesia in Miniature complex features performers from various parts of the far-flung nation in a program of music and dance. Traditional homes and craft workshops are displayed on the grounds.

Cultural and artistic programs are presented at the Taman Ismail Marzuki Cultural Center on Jalan Cikini Raya. Programs are listed in a monthly guide published by the center and available at your hotel or from local travel agencies.

You can see performances of the famed Ramayana, Mahabharata, and other epics of ancient cultures at Panca Murti Theater on Jalan Senen Raya.

Sundanese gamelan music, *wayang topeng* dancing, and *wayang golek* puppetry are performed at

Awning-covered stalls *create a flea market on Jalan Surabaya, a short ride from Jakarta hotels. Buyers and sellers bargain over secondhand furniture, brass urns, lamps, and antiques.*

Jakarta museum visitors *examine a Bhairawa, a 14th century figure of Buddhist origin. Other exhibits display pre-Hindu arts and crafts. A museum guide book in English describes the collection.*

the Bakti Budaya School on Jalan Bunga.

The most ambitious amusement center in Southeast Asia is the Jaya Ancol Dreamland complex, on the north edge of the city. This 343-acre amusement and sporting center features an oceanarium, nightclubs, restaurants, a casino, and facilities for horseback riding, golf, swimming, and bowling. You can also attend jai alai matches and automobile races.

After dark. In recent years Jakarta's night life has become more lively as new clubs and casinos have opened. La Casa Cosyndo, in the Kosgoro Pavilion at the center of Merdeka Park, has a good band, floor shows, and hostesses. Popular, too, are the Blue Ocean on Jalan Hayam Wuruk, the Latin Quarter on Jalan Majapahit, the Nirwana Supper Club in the Hotel Indonesia, and the Flaming Night Club in Jaya Ancol Dreamland.

Jakarta's four licensed casinos are new attractions; garishly appointed and crowded with locals, visiting Asians, and a few Caucasian tourists, they offer gamblers a chance to try their luck at blackjack, fan-tan, *dai-sai* (a dice game), roulette, slot machines, and baccarat.

Shopping in Jakarta

Jakarta is a shopper's delight. You can buy from streetside stalls or shop in neighborhood markets or modern department stores. The Sarinah department store, on Jalan Thamrin near the Hotel Indonesia, is Indonesia's largest—15 floors, all air-conditioned and stocked with every imaginable type of merchandise.

On Jalan Haji Agus Salim, the street running behind the big department store, you'll find boutiques with French and Italian designs, excellent leather shops, and numerous handicraft and batik stores. The major hotels have shopping arcades, and the hotel front desk personnel can suggest where you can look for special items. Many interesting new shops are opening in the restored Old Batavia district.

A fascinating flea market, on Jalan Surabaya in Menteng—about ten minutes from the major hotels—is certainly worth a visit. Lining one side of the street for about three blocks, its stalls display everything from old furniture to Ming China, from new shoes and Chinese porcelain to old coins and brasswork. Though some of the "antiques" were obviously manufactured yesterday, you can often find some excellent authentic pieces. Be prepared to bargain with a vengeance.

Sightseeing in the capital

Though Jakarta has little natural beauty because of its flatness, it does have some unusual sightseeing attractions, including its many monuments.

Mostly built during the regime of President Sukarno, these massive structures dot the city's squares and circles. Among these city landmarks are the Peasants Monument on Jalan Menteng

Prapatan, the Welcome Monument at the Hotel Indonesia Circle, and the Irian Jaya Liberation Monument—a striking representation of a slave bursting his chains—found near the Borobudur Inter-Continental Hotel.

Merdeka Square

Jakarta's most impressive landmark is located at Merdeka Square, core of the city; the National Monument is a 350-foot white tower topped by a flaming torch. Containing 70 pounds of gold leaf, the torch commemorates Indonesia's nationhood and is called the "flame of freedom." Inside the monument are dioramas, depicting the country's history from prehistoric times to independence. An elevator ascends to the top for a panoramic view.

Around the square are the Merdeka Fountain, Freedom Park, the hundred-year-old Presidential Palace, City Hall, Gambir railway station, and numerous Greek-styled government buildings. Within camera range to the east is the striking Istiqlal Mosque, as yet unfinished but destined to be the country's finest. Its huge white dome and minarets tower high above their surroundings.

Jalan Thamrin, the capital's spacious main boulevard, runs from Merdeka Square to the Hotel Kartika Plaza; high-rise hotels, apartments, and office buildings line the wide street.

National Museum. Recognized as one of the finest of its kind in Southeast Asia, the National Museum is located on Merdeka Barat bordering Merdeka Square. Its halls include excellent collections of the arts and crafts of various Indonesian peoples and sculptures from pre-Hindu times through the 14th century. One of the museum's most prized possessions is a skull of a prehistoric Java man. Other exhibits display old Chinese porcelain (excavated from various parts of Indonesia), native folk art, and jewels of past kingly rulers.

Old Batavia

Work will be continuing for several more years on a restoration project destined to recall the sights and atmosphere of early Jakarta. Called Old Batavia, the development encompasses a three-block-wide, two-mile-long stretch of the old city and includes three areas: Fatahillah Square, site of the Stadhuis (city hall) built in 1710; Pasar Ikan, the old port and today's fishermen's wharf; and Glodok, the historically important Chinese quarter.

Fatahillah Square. Historically unimportant old buildings have been removed and the square has been handsomely landscaped with plantings and brick and cobblestone paving. Shops surrounding the square are being redone to simulate the architecture of earlier days. You can shop here for a range of antiques, paintings, porcelains, spices, and batiks. Restaurants and street signs will also carry out the historic motif.

The Kota Museum, housed on the site of a 1640 Dutch church near the square, contains old etchings, paintings, coins and other currency, weapons, beautifully carved furniture, and other relics of the days of the Dutch East India Company.

Near the railway station is the oldest Christian church in Jakarta; known as the Portuguese church, it was built around 1695. Its baroque architecture provides a well-preserved glimpse of early colonial settlement, and its old graveyard marks the final resting places of various governors and their families.

Pasar Ikan. If you visit Pasar Ikan, the old harbor area, you can see much of the current work underway. Two thick-walled spice warehouses built in 1652 have been restored—one as the Spice Trade Museum, and the other as a display area for past and present ships. You'll see the Burgis schooners and other boats of the fishing fleet anchored here in the old 17th century Dutch canal.

Best time to visit the fish market is at dawn—when the day's catch is being sold and the market is bustling with activity. If you poke around, you'll find some of the fishermen have turtle shells, coral, and a fine assortment of seashells for sale.

Chinatown. The Chinese quarter comes to life each evening when hundreds of small shops and stalls are set up along the narrow streets. The local inhabitants jam the streets, moving from stall to stall, squabbling with the sellers for a better bargain. Stalls and shops carry all types of food, clothing, household goods, and gifts. Handcarts and pedicabs add to the congestion.

Other city attractions

Jakarta offers several opportunities to browse through colorful markets where strange produce

Fatahillah Square, *in the heart of Old Batavia, recalls the past with 18th century Stadhuis, remodeled shops, and landscaped environs.*

and handmade wares are sold. The Cikini Market features fresh fish, fruit, poultry, and vegetables. South of the city center is Pasar Minggu, the main fruit market. Satay men, fanning tiny braziers on street corners, offer charcoal-broiled skewers of beef, chicken, and shrimp. At night, when sea breezes moderate Jakarta's hot and humid atmosphere, streets fill with portable stalls, lit by bare electric bulbs, where proprietors sell a variety of merchandise.

The Jakarta zoo at Ragunan Pasar Minggu, a favorite with weekend picnickers, is about 30 minutes from the main downtown hotels. The zoo is attractively laid out in a parklike setting, its broad walkways edged with trees and shrubs. Its animal collection includes a superb cross section of Indonesia's animal world—including the Komodo dragon, tigers, rhinos, crocodiles, a marvelous bird collection, and a snake house that alone is worth the visit.

Several other city attractions will be found in the vicinity of Kebayoran Baru, the new residential area just south of the Hotel Indonesia. Here are the Senayan Sports Complex, site of the Fourth Asian Games in 1962 and now used for badminton, swimming and tennis meets; the Batik Federation near the Sports Complex, with probably the country's best display of the national fabric (batiks may be purchased); the Parliament Building; and the new Constitutional Assembly Hall, just north of Kebayoran.

Elsewhere are art galleries, batik factories, orchid gardens, flower markets, and theaters where you can see Javanese opera, Balinese dance, and puppet shows.

Sportsmen will find a variety of opportunities: motor car racing, ice skating at a new and surprisingly popular rink, beach sports, golf (at one of three courses), tennis, horse and greyhound racing.

Day trip to Thousand Islands

For an easy day trip out of Jakarta—a day devoted to golden sun, white sand beaches, and swimming or diving—you should try Pulau Seribu (Thousand Islands), about 40 miles northwest across Jakarta Bay and easily reached on a 20-minute flight (or three-hour boat trip). Although the bay is dotted with more than 600 islands, only a few of them have been developed for tourists. A bird sanctuary, found on Pulau Rambut, can be reached by boat; Pulau Genting is the most popular for snorkeling and diving; and Pulau Opak Besar has some rather basic accommodations (bring food and bedding).

The most developed island, Pulau Putri, has an airstrip and a 100-room resort with fan-cooled bungalows and *pondoks* (Indonesian-style cottages). These have kitchens and outdoor barbecue pits, and the resort also offers a restaurant and bar. Sports available include water-skiing, sailing, fishing, snorkeling, and skin diving (scuba gear is available).

Seeing the Java countryside by rail

Trainside vendors, *balancing boxes on their heads, hawk food and souvenirs to passengers.*

Unquestionably the best rail trip in Indonesia is the run between Jakarta and Surabaya on the island of Java. Three trains make the journey—the Bima Express, an overnight air-conditioned sleeper, and two all-coach daylight trains that have some air-conditioned cars.

The Bima leaves Jakarta daily at 4 P.M., arriving in Yogyakarta at 1:54 A.M. and at Surabaya at 7:39 A.M. A similar run goes westward from Surabaya. The train contains sleeping compartments, a dining car serving both European and Indonesian food, and hostesses who ply passengers with hot chocolate, fruit, tea and cakes, and liquor.

On the daylight trip you travel through Java's green rice fields and past red-roofed bamboo villages squatting under clusters of banana trees. You see farmers at work in the fields with their water buffaloes. In the stations, children mingle with peddlers selling fruits and other foods.

Another excellent rail trip is the 3½-hour run through West Java's most dramatic countryside to Bandung. You traverse jungle-covered canyons, and gorges terraced with rice, tapioca, and cassavas. There are three departures leaving Jakarta daily beginning at 6:15 A.M. Food and drinks are served on board.

Youthful helpers *outside Bandung assist farmers in loading cabbages destined for the local market.*

Presidential Palace *at Bogor, south of Jakarta, is surrounded by lawns where deer roam and graze.*

West Java, a splendid tapestry

West Java, with Jakarta and Bandung as its principal cities, is probably the easiest part of Indonesia to explore. Good road and railway systems radiate from Jakarta, providing access to several interesting regions.

Home of the friendly and happy Sundanese, West Java is a rich tapestry of rice paddies and terraces, tea plantations, dense jungles, towering mountains, and beautiful beaches.

Bogor and a Presidential Palace

An easy and rewarding day excursion goes 35 miles south from Jakarta to Bogor, famous for its Botanical Garden and the Presidential Summer Palace. Full-day and half-day trips to the area are offered by several Jakarta tour operators.

Your drive to Bogor takes about 1½ hours, first on a busy, traffic-clogged highway, then through the green countryside, where you see women working in the rice fields, and farmers guiding their water buffalo.

Begun in 1817, the Botanical Garden covers 275 acres and has an impressive tropical plant collection exceeding 10,000 species of trees, 15,000 species of plants, and 5,000 orchid hybrids. Scientists from many parts of the world have studied this exceptional collection.

Adjoining the gardens is the Summer Palace, surrounded by parklands where deer roam freely. The present colonial mansion was built in the early 1800s and became the official residence for the Dutch Governor General in 1870. President Sukarno made it his summer palace, and it remains so with President Suharto. You'll need special permission to enter the palace grounds; your hotel or a local travel agent can help you obtain the necessary permission.

Just south of Bogor is the Puncak Mountain region, a popular holiday resort for Jakarta residents. The district has a number of small hotels, several featuring swimming pools, gardens, and golf courses.

On to Bandung

A winding road leads from Puncak to Bandung, the capital of the province of West Java, third largest city on Java and one of the island's educational and cultural centers. Situated atop a plateau at 2,500 feet elevation and ringed by higher mountains, Bandung's mild, springlike climate produces a rainbow of temperate zone flowers. The surrounding hill country is intensively farmed with rice fields, cinchona trees (source of quinine), and tea plantations.

About 100 miles southeast of Jakarta, Bandung may be reached in about four hours by road or rail or in 20 minutes by air. The Puncak Pass Hotel at Puncak makes a pleasant stop on the route from Bogor to Bandung.

The colorful folk dances and melodic music of the Sundanese have been particularly well preserved in Bandung by performances at the Sundanese Department of the Indonesian Conservatory. Here you can hear the *angklung*, a unique local musical instrument made of bamboo, a string instrument called the *kecapi*, and various metal percussion instruments making up a gamelan orchestra. Live dramas, dances, and puppet shows are performed frequently in the town and surrounding area. Check with your hotel as to when and where performances will be presented.

If you feel adventurous, you can make short trips to the rims of extinct volcanic craters on Mount Tangkuban Prahu (meaning overturned boat) and Kawah Ratu (Queen's Crater). Looking over the rim, you see and smell the pungent, steaming sulphur beds in the craters.

Samudra excursion

You can visit Samudra Beach, on the southern coast of Java, on an overnight trip. Lodging is at the Samudra Beach Hotel, at the edge of a palm-fringed beach. A swimming pool is adjacent to the open-air dining terrace, where Javanese dances and music are performed on Saturday nights.

The drive to Samudra—through forest and rice fields and villages—is superb; or you can fly (and the hotel will pay half the air fare). An enjoyable side destination is the nearby village of Pelabuhan Ratu, with its armada of black-hulled, outrigger fishing boats. Air service to the village is available several times a week.

Central Java, rich in tradition

For more than a thousand years, Central Java has been the cultural center of the Javanese people. Here, clustered in and around Yogyakarta and Surakarta (Solo), you'll discover some of Indonesia's greatest treasures—antique artifacts and works of art, traditional dance forms, the age-old art of batik, palaces dating back many centuries, and massive architectural relics capturing some of Java's mysticism.

Captivating Yogyakarta

Many visitors to Indonesia consider Yogyakarta the country's most fascinating city. It is a showcase of Javanese arts, crafts, culture, and history. Nearby are masterpieces of early Buddhist and Hindu architecture, Borobudur and Prambanan. The area is famous for an array of attractions: spectacular performances of the Ramayana ballet, the puppetry artists who perform the wayang kulit plays, many museums, gamelan music, the Sultan's palace, fine theater and dance performances, and the Batik Research Centre (see page 50).

Only 310 miles east of Jakarta, Yogyakarta can be reached by air, rail, or bus. Among the city's eight hotels and guest houses, the large Ambarrukmo Sheraton Hotel is the most popular with tourists.

A center of artists. If you are interested in Indonesian arts, you can visit galleries including that of the renowned painter Affandi. At the silverwork center of Kota Gede, silversmiths are at work, dressed in the traditional *lurik* (striped cotton garment) and batik headgear. Some of the finest modern batik artists live in Yogyakarta, including the internationally recognized Amri Yahya and Saptohoedojo.

Batik shops, art shops, restaurants, and offices line the city's main street, Jalan Malioboro (pronounced "Marlborough"). You can also visit Pasar Beringharjo, where Yogyanese women sell batiks, and Pasar Ngasem, the bird market.

Shadow plays. An intrinsic part of the Javanese way of life is the *wayang kulit*, a shadow play using leather puppets. The play is based on one of the popular episodes from the Mahabharata legend. A single puppeteer—the *ki dalang*— is the narrator for all the roles and also conductor for the gamelan orchestra.

Traditionally such a play goes on all night, from 9 P.M. to 5 A.M., with children falling asleep on their mothers' laps (and some adults also dropping off to sleep). A shorter, two-hour evening performance is presented by the Ambarrukmo Sheraton on Mondays and alternate Thursdays. On other nights, the hotel features Javanese dances and the Ramayana ballet.

Sightseeing in Yogya

Sightseeing opportunities are varied in and around Yogyakarta. You can visit the Sultan's Palace, view Javanese art, and journey to the royal tombs.

Sultan's Palace. Originally built in the mid-1700s, the palace (called the *kraton*) is more than a half mile long; it remains essentially unchanged except for some of its decorations. The first president of Indonesia was sworn in here. You are shown through the palace and its courtyards by some of the Sultan's retainers, who add to the quiet mystique of the palace and its grounds.

Just west of the palace is Taman Sari, a 16th century water palace built by the Sultan as a bathing place for his princesses.

Sono Budoyo Museum. One of the country's finest collections of Javanese art is housed in Sono Budoyo Museum, also near the palace. Exhibits include a variety of brass and bronze pieces, old gamelan instruments, ancient puppet figures, and early Buddha figures.

Royal tombs. About 10 miles south of the city at Imogiri are the tombs of the Mataram kings, where royal families have been buried since 1645. To reach the tombs you must climb 345 steps up a shaded stairway. If you wish to enter the courtyards (possible on Mondays and Fridays), you are asked to wear formal Javanese court dress (available at the site). The view from the hilltop graveyard is superb.

Buddhist sanctuary at Borobudur

Lying about 24 miles north of Yogyakarta is Borobudur, the largest Buddhist sanctuary in the world. Probably built in the late 8th century, the massive monument is over 150 feet high and consists of

Bamboo laden carts, *pulled by yoked animal teams, roll through the Java countryside on the way to nearby markets.*

Gamelan players *in rural Yogyakarta provide instrumental accompaniment to performances of dance drama or* wayang kulit.

Backstage *at* wayang kulit *(shadow puppet plays) a* ki daleng *works behind the screen, blending characters' voices to gamelan music.*

Wedding party *in Yogyakarta wears traditional Javanese dress for Muslim ceremony. Each island has its own marriage ceremony.*

INDONESIA 57

six square lower terraces and three circular upper terraces.

About 200 years after its completion, the center of the Buddhist culture shifted, and Borobudur was abandoned for nearly a thousand years. It was discovered again in the 19th century, nearly covered with layers of earth and lava dust. Excavations early in this century uncovered the huge monument, which is now undergoing extensive preservation and restoration work.

Reliefs depicting the life of Buddha decorate the lower galleries, which you approach by walking to the left after entering the east gate. Above each gallery are niches containing meditative Buddha statues—432 in all. The three upper terraces contain 72 latticed *stupas* (dome-shaped shrines), each with a seated, transcendental Buddha. On top is a large, hollow stupa.

Along the main road approaching Borobudur, you see stone carvers at work making small replicas of the head of Buddha, along with statues of legendary figures and garden lampposts. Huge, ornately carved gates are also made to order.

Prambanan, the Hindu complex

The Hindu temple complex of Prambanan is a 10-mile trip east from Yogya on the road leading to Solo. This 9th century grouping, built by the first Hindu king of Central Java, includes a main temple (some 160 feet high) dedicated to Shiva, God of Destruction. Other temples in the group are dedicated to Vishnu and Brahma. Elaborate carvings decorate the temple walls, and small sanctuaries hold images of Hindu deities. In one courtyard are the ruins of 224 minor shrines or temples.

An open-air theater in front of the Prambanan is used for staging the colorful Ramayana Ballet Festival, held on four successive nights during periods of the full moon from June to October. Nearby are several Buddhist structures, among them Candi Sambisari; it is currently undergoing excavation, a process that is fascinating to watch.

Surakarta side trip

Another worthwhile excursion from Yogyakarta is the 40-mile trip to Surakarta (also known as Solo), another superb repository of Javanese art and culture. You'll see the Kraton Kasunanan, a palace built in 1745 when the sultan moved his capital to the Solo River and named it Surakarta Hadiningrat. Most of the superb decorations in the palace —gilded columns, marble statues, crystal chandeliers—were chosen by Sultan Pakubuwono X, who reigned in the early part of this century.

Next to the palace is the Royal Museum, containing exhibits of Solo's social, cultural, and poli-

Market place *in Surabaya offers a wide range of products to buy—including baskets, conical hats, woven mats, and vases. Curious and friendly faces return your smile.*

Ancient steps *lead visitors to main temple of Prambanan complex, site of the Ramayana Festival dances from June to October. Stone carvings decorate the walls of the 9th century Hindu temple.*

tical history. Established in 1963, it is one of Java's best. Of special interest are the royal coaches and figureheads from some of the royal barges.

At city handicraft centers you can watch craftsmen making gamelan musical instruments and the leather puppets and costumes for the *wayang kulit*. The *wayang orang* (Javanese opera) is performed nightly at the Sriwedari Recreation Grounds by the finest group in Java.

Solo also has an ample antique market, Pasar Trewindu, with lots of brass, copper, and glass household goods left from centuries of Dutch occupation. If you bargain, you can get some good buys. Other interesting markets in Solo are the Toy Market, where you can buy imaginative (if fragile) toys made on the spot; Pasar Besar, the big general market; and Pasar Klewer, where hundreds of stalls offer thousands of varieties of batik and a few other local fabrics.

Mountainous east Java

On your way to or from Bali, you can explore East Java, a countryside of smoking volcanoes, pleasant mountain resorts, and ancient temples. Jammed with 26 million people, it is Indonesia's most densely populated area. Strongly Indonesian, the women wear brightly colored sarongs usually topped with lacy, long-sleeved overblouses; most of the men also wear sarongs.

Southeast of Surabaya, the provincial capital, is Mount Bromo, an active volcano you can examine at close range. Off the north coast lies Madura Island, famous for its bull races.

Industrial Surabaya

Second only to Jakarta in size and economic importance, the commercial and industrial city of Surabaya is located on the Kali Mas River at the western end of Madura Strait. Its harbor, Tanjung Perak, is the eastern terminus for ocean-going ships sailing between Europe, Asia, and Indonesia. Nearby Ujung is Indonesia's famous naval base. With a population exceeding 2,200,000 and with hundreds of factories, Surabaya is one of the country's principal industrial cities.

By air Surabaya is an hour from Jakarta, a half hour from Bali; you can also reach it by rail or road. If you fly in at night, you will undoubtedly see the fiery red glow of Mount Semeru—one of several active volcanoes in the region—far southeast of the city.

Hotels. The Surabaya hotel picture includes the Majapahit, Mirama, Natour's Simpang, and Jane's House. All are fully or partially air-conditioned, and the Mirama has swimming pools. Jane's House is furnished in restored Javanese and Chinese antiques.

Javanese dances. Surabaya's entertainment offerings feature classical and folk dances. You can see *wayang orang*, composed of episodes from the Ramayana and Mahabharata, performed nightly at the People's Park.

Another favorite is the *reog Ponorogo*, in which a man supports a huge, befeathered tiger's head (weighing from 55 to 110 pounds) with only his neck muscles and teeth. The reog is performed by a number of troupes; your hotel can tell you where to see it and a companion dance, the *kuda kepang*. In the latter, an entranced performer behaves like a horse, whipping himself and eating grass.

The Ramayana classic and local dances are also performed during a six month period in an open-air amphitheatre at Pandaan near Tretes (see page 60).

Sightseeing. Surabaya's architecture mixes old and modern structures, with numerous Dutch colonial buildings adding pleasant accents. Because the people are predominantly Muslim, minaret-topped mosques and men wearing black fezlike hats are common sights. Dominating many street corners and public squares are boldly executed, heroic

Whip dancers *flay each other during a performance at amphitheater near Pandaan.*

Diminutive ponies *carry visitors along narrow dirt roads near mist-shrouded Mount Bromo.*

military memorials, commemorating Indonesia's 1945 war of independence.

The usual city tour of Surabaya takes in Chinatown, the Arab quarters, the harbor, and the city zoo. The latter, largest in Southeast Asia, is home to the fierce-looking Komodo dragons, sloe-eyed sambars, playful orang-utans, and black apes. Stops are also made at the Governor's mansion, city hall, local fruit and vegetable markets, Joko Dolog (Surabaya's oldest Hindu statue), and the city's museum. Evening tours visit the People's Park, an amusement and shopping complex popular with the local people.

You can also visit some of Surabaya's numerous antique shops, where you can discover interesting examples of Javanese and Chinese furniture and woodcarvings. Tunjungan shopping center is a good stop for bargain hunters—sometimes you can purchase watches, cameras, and electronic equipment at prices lower than you would pay in Hong Kong or Singapore.

Rugged trip up Mount Bromo

From Surabaya you can arrange for a day trip to 7,176-foot Mount Bromo, an active volcano about 80 miles southeast of the city. The steaming crater, which last erupted in 1842, is part of the massive Tengger Mountains, a chain of volcanic peaks ranging across this part of East Java. On your trip you can also see a Ramayana performance and other local dances at Pandaan, stop at the mountain resort of Tretes, and visit the villages of the Tenggerese people, a small group of animists who mix their worship of the mountains with Hindu beliefs.

Many people make the trip up to Mount Bromo in the middle of the night so they can watch the sun rise over the dramatic, rugged landscape. You leave the hotel in Surabaya about 11 P.M., drive by way of Probolinggo, and arrive at the small mountain village of Ngadisari about 2 A.M., where you transfer to ponies. Wind soughs through the tall pine trees, and stars seem incredibly close in these clear southern skies as the sure-footed pack animals carry you up the slopes of Bromo's neighbor, Mount Batok, and down into the desolate Sea of Sands.

After two hours on ponyback, you dismount and climb steep stairs to Bromo's crater rim in time to see the sunrise. From the rim you gaze down on steaming sulphur beds, the cone veiled by smoke and encrusted with striking lava formations. Nearby Batok looms above you, and other volcanic peaks rise on the horizon — including 11,034-foot Mount Semeru, Java's highest mountain and one revered in local legend.

You can be back in Surabaya by midday. The trip can also be made during daylight hours, but you miss much of the mountain's mystique. Night or day, it's cold on the mountain—so come prepared with a heavy sweater, jacket, and gloves.

Pandaan. If you are in the area from May to October, you should arrange to see the classical dances of East Java performed in Candra Wilwatikta amphitheater near Pandaan. Presented on two successive nights during the period of the full moon, dances feature a version of the Ramayana based on carvings on an East Java temple.

Tretes. Situated on the slopes of Mount Melirang about 35 miles south of Surabaya, the town of Tretes is a delightful, refreshing mountain resort.

It is a better base than Surabaya from which to make the Mount Bromo trip and explore the surrounding countryside. Horses are available, and guides can lead you to waterfalls and temples.

Tenggerese villages. More than 300,000 Tenggerese tribesmen live in the mountains south of Mount Bromo in a series of villages surrounded by forestland and extensive vegetable gardens.

A frugal, rugged people, the Tenggerese have learned to respect Bromo. They make an annual pilgrimage to the crater, carrying offerings to the God of Fire whom they believe lives in the crater. Known as *Kesada*, the ceremony is a midnight event held on the 14th of the Kesada month; it precedes *Kara*, a fortnight of lively village celebrations.

Majapahit ruins

One hour south of Surabaya (via Mojokerto) lie the ruined temples and archaeological treasures of the Majapahit empire. Your route cuts through rice, sugar, and tobacco fields and follows along canal-lined roads toward a volcano-dominated horizon.

Dating from the 13th century, the empire was an advanced and powerful Hindu civilization that controlled many parts of East Java. Today you can visit the remains of Gajang Ratu and Brahu temples, Wringin Lawang (a huge brick gateway marking an entrance to the empire), and the Trowulan museum containing many artifacts.

Madura Island festivities

Across a narrow strait from Surabaya is the island of Madura, best known for its championship Brahmin bull races held on the first Sunday of every month (except January). You reach the island on a 35-minute ferry ride.

Each year in September, at the close of the harvest season, the championships are held on the outskirts of Bangkalan in combination with a harvest fair. From each district of the island, the two best bulls are brought to Bangkalan. The night before the race, the bull owners, gamelan musicians, family, and friends congregate for a festive evening.

The morning of the race, owners decorate the carefully groomed bulls and parade them through town to the race course. Huge crowds, accompanied by musicians, add to the festivity.

The bulls are yoked in pairs, with a narrow wooden sled harnessed between them, the end of the sled trailing on the ground. A jockey balances on the sled to guide the team. Normally plodding and slow when you see them in the fields, the racing Brahmin bull team really moves at a fast clip—10 seconds is considered a good time to run the 121-yard-long course.

Magical, charming Bali

For centuries—from the days of the early traders to the cruise ship and jet travelers of today—Bali

Racing bulls, *with jockey on dragging sled, competes during the Madura Island festival. This annual event attracts hundreds of visitors.*

has been the enchanted island. Much of its charm lies with the people—the graceful, beautiful Balinese who live in mystical harmony with their natural surroundings. Thousands of temples—set in villages, amid fields, on beaches, under banyan trees, in caves, on hilltops—are the settings for colorful religious festivals and holy days that help to maintain that harmony.

Another part of the enchantment is the island itself: a richly foliaged countryside, edged by palm-fringed beaches, dotted with villages, and sliced down the middle by a chain of sacred volcanic mountains whose slopes are seamed by muddy rivers and terraced with padis.

Separated from the eastern tip of Java by a narrow two-mile channel, Bali is a rather small island, shaped like an elongated diamond, stretching about 90 miles eastward; it is 50 miles at its widest point. Though predominantly mountainous, it is one of the richest agricultural islands in the world.

Rice and religion

Two major elements in Balinese life are readily apparent to the visitor: rice and religion. Rice, the mainstay of the economy, is cultivated in an ingenious complex of terraced *sawahs* (rice fields) which climb the hills and carpet the slopes and plains. The lands are cultivated communally by families that cluster together in villages, each surrounded by walls enclosing temples, the village meeting house, and a series of ancestral family compounds.

Dominating the life of the Balinese is their religion, continually manifested in temple festivals, processions to the sea, purification rites, and cremations—all of which the visitor may watch.

The chain of volcanic mountains traversing the island from east to west is considered the home of the gods and the holy source of water. Of the conelike peaks, 10,308-foot Mount Agung is the highest and most sacred.

Rice and religion play an important role in many of the Balinese dances and festivals, and certainly no visitor should leave Bali without seeing some of these events.

Distinctive arts and crafts

When the early Javanese Hindus moved to Bali in the 13th century to escape Islam, they took with them their Javanese classics and poetry, arts and crafts, music, dance, sculpture, and theater. On Bali, they continued to cultivate these arts with little influence from outside sources. As a result, you'll find distinctive arts and crafts unique to this island and differing from village to village. Things to look for: paintings of Balinese village life or Balinese legends; carvings of wood, ivory, and stone figures; the traditional *kris* (sword); ceremonial or comic dance masks; and hand woven fabrics.

Hotels and cottages with charm

In recent years, several international class resort hotels have been built on Bali's Sanur Beach—the Hotel Bali Beach Inter-Continental and Seaside Bungalows, and the Hotel Sanur Beach. All these resorts are built to capture the spirit of Bali.

Some travelers prefer the smaller, Balinese-style bungalow or cottage hotels in the Sanur Beach area. Many of these are one-story cottages or duplexes nestled amid jungle growth and gardens; others are two-story "tree-house" structures with walls of woven bamboo splits and thatch roofs. Some have pools, others offer only the clear blue ocean.

Elsewhere on the island there are small hotels: on Kuta Beach, at the Pertamina Cottages, in Ubud, at Nusadua Beach, and in Denpasar itself, where you'll find the classic old Bali Hotel and the Denpasar.

Traveling around the island

Rental cars are available on Bali, but you can hire a car and driver for about U.S. $5 a day more. Taxis are expensive, costing several dollars to go just a few blocks. You can also get around on mini-buses that make tours to points of interest on the island. Motor scooters and bicycles are also available.

Denpasar, the island capital

Bali's largest city (75,000 people) and provincial capital is Denpasar, site of the island's international airport. Bustling, traffic-congested, and perhaps over-commercialized, Denpasar is a place to

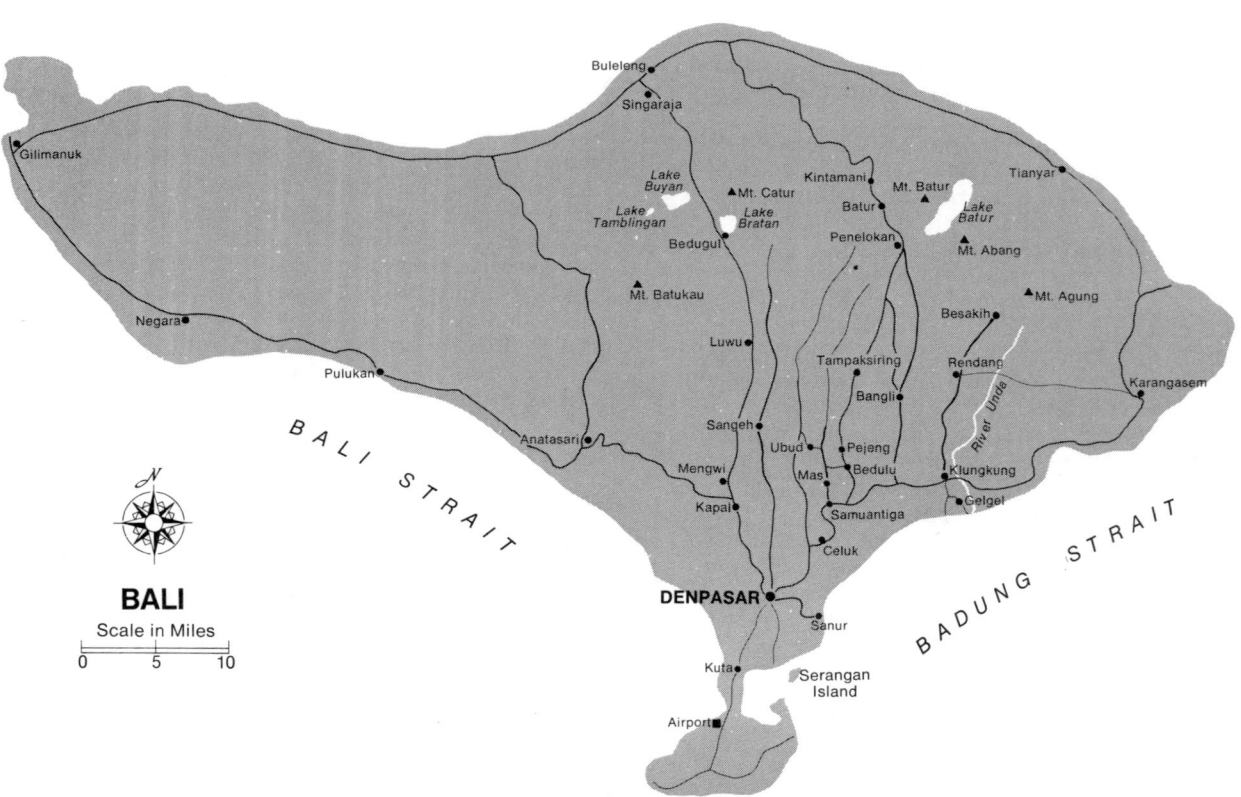

Sanur Beach *is Bali's main resort area; resort accommodations range from thatched-roof bungalow complexes to luxury hotels.*

Balinese fisherman *unfolds his meager catch on the beach. Rich offshore fishing grounds are reached by outrigger boats.*

Dawn at Ubud *silhouettes Balinese women walking to market. Loads up to 60 pounds are carried on top of the head.*

Cremation tower, *led by procession of mourners, carries deceased through the streets to the cemetery where fire liberates the soul.*

INDONESIA

Walking pigs to market *is a morning scene on Bali. Women feed and fatten these tame descendants of wild hogs and then sell them at village markets.*

browse in curio shops, visit the Denpasar Museum, and wander through the big city market. One sour note: this may be your first stop in Indonesia where you'll be besieged by vendors, touts, and children wanting money if you take their picture.

Exploring Bali

Bali's popular sightseeing paths are well worn, most of them emanating from the Denpasar-Sanur Beach area and limited to a few popular villages, dance and craft centers, and temples. With time and a car and driver, though, you can go beyond these well-trodden routes. The island has a good road network. With rough going here and there (and in some areas, little of interest to see), you can circle the island by car; but most of the roads run on a north-south axis into the mountains or cross-island.

Here are some of the highlights:

Excursion to Ubud. The main road north from Denpasar takes you to Ubud, an exquisite village that is home for several hundred artists, superb dance groups, and gamelan orchestras. On the way to Ubud, you pass through Celuk, famous as a silversmith center; Mas, known for its woodcarvers; and Batuan, a village of weavers.

Samuantiga cultural center. The village of Samuantiga includes an interesting cultural center. It is located a few miles northeast of Denpasar. You can watch programs of music and dancing, as well as demonstrations of local arts and handicrafts.

To Mount Batur. On a full day tour, you can visit Ubud and still have time to drive into the mountains to Tampaksiring and the upper slopes of Mount Batur. Tampaksiring, set in a vale near one of Sukarno's palaces, is the site of holy springs used by people to "cleanse" themselves—no photographs are allowed.

The road continues north to Penelokan, on the rim of the Mount Batur crater, then runs along the edge of a mammoth caldera—7 miles across—in the center of which is the steaming cone of Mount Batur. To the east, Lake Batur shimmers in the sunlight. Looming above the edge of the caldera to the east is 7,058-foot Mount Abang, and to the southeast, the towering sacred peak of 10,308-foot Mount Agung.

Bedulu-Pejeng-Bangli. The approaches to Mount Batur are worth considerably more time than a one-day excursion. North from Denpasar, roads take you into districts where you can see dozens of ancient temples, including some of the oldest architectural relics on Bali.

You can visit Bedulu and its Elephant Cave Monastery; Pejeng, a village of 40 temples housing grotesque demon statues; and Bangli, capital of an early kingdom and site of about ten ancient temple complexes.

Mother Temple of Besakih. The oldest and most sacred temple complex on Bali is located northeast of Denpasar at Besakih, on the slopes of Mount Agung. This "mother temple," probably built in the 2nd century, is the largest temple on Bali and is considered to be the royal ancestral sanctuary.

On the trip to Besakih, stops are usually made at Klungkung, a handicraft center where highly ornamental gold and silver jewelry is made, and Karangasem, site of the "water palace" of Ujung. You can also see the devastation wrought by the eruption of Mount Agung in 1963; the lava flows are particularly visible near Klungkung, Gelgel, and in the valley of the River Unda.

Through Mengwi. The road northwest from Denpasar through Mengwi (the main south to north highway) goes by superb temple compounds at Kapal, Mengwi, and Taman Ayun. Kapal is noted for its excellent examples of temple sculpture. The lakeside water temple at Taman Ayun is considered one of the island's most beautiful temple complexes.

Farther north and east of the main road lies the sacred forest of Sangeh, home of hundreds of monkeys. Protected as sacred, the monkeys will flock around you for peanuts (these you can purchase on the site from an eager group of children).

Other diversions. The beautiful beaches of Sanur and Kuta offer swimming, sunbathing, fishing, and boating. Balinese boatmen, using small outrigger sailboats, will take you out to the edge of the reef;

or you can travel by boat to Serangan Island a few miles offshore to see a turtle farm.

Jungle-clad Sumatra

Sumatra, second largest of the Indonesian islands (and fifth largest island in the world), is bursting with tourism potential but it remains short on accommodations and other tourist facilities.

Part of its attraction, of course—for the traveler willing to forego some of the amenities—is its noncommercial, undeveloped atmosphere. For here are tribes of people living in much the same way as their ancestors did centuries ago, villages with unique architecture based on designs handed down for generations, and roaming wildlife that includes gibbons, panthers, tigers, elephants, and rhinoceroses.

The island is canted on an angle, running 1,110 miles from northwest to southeast, with the equator slicing through its middle. A rugged range of mountains parallels its western coast, in places crowding to the edge of the Indonesia Ocean. More than 90 volcanoes are strung along this thousand-mile chain — and thus its name, Bukit Barisan (Parade of Mountains).

The peaks range in elevation from 5,000 to more than 12,000 feet, the highest being Mount Kerinci at 12,484 feet. East of the range lies a wide coastal plain, crossed by broad rivers, edged on the eastern coast by mangrove swamps. Much of the inland area is impenetrable, a land of dense rain forests.

The northwestern half of the island parallels the Malaysian peninsula, so close in places that on a clear day portions of Malaysia are visible across the Strait of Malacca.

The Sumatran people and their life style provide strong cultural contrasts with Java and Bali. Here the Muslim influences are stronger, as evidenced by the number of mosques (except in the predominately Christian Batak country in North Sumatra). The wedding costumes and the festival of *Lebaran*, marking the end of Muslim fasting, are as colorful as anything you'll see in Indonesia.

Getting there

You can fly from Jakarta to Medan (North Sumatra's capital) by Garuda Indonesian Airways or Merpati Nusantara Airlines.

International flights link Medan with Singapore, Tokyo, and the Malaysian tourist centers of Kuala Lumpur and Penang Island. A twice-weekly ferry service also links Belawan with Penang.

Intra-island service is available between Padang on Sumatra's west coast, Palembang on the southeastern coast, and Medan in the north.

Medan, tropical trading center

Sumatra's capital and largest city, Medan, is a cosmopolitan trading, processing, and manufactur-

---

Dramatic dances relate Balinese epics

Each Balinese village has its own dance team and gamelan orchestra which perform a great variety of dances at religious festivals, marriages, and other ceremonies. Most of the dances are based on religious or mythical origin. Many are stories derived from the Ramayana or Mahabharata—the great Hindu epics; their plots are simple contests between good and evil. Some of the dances are vigorous; others reflect stylized patterns of movement.

Among the most important Balinese dances are the *legong*, the *kecak*, and the *barong*. In the legong, a storyteller relates the epic while costumed girls enact the story with facial expressions and graceful movements.

The *kecak* or monkey dance tells a story from the Ramayana in which King Rama searches for his abducted wife. More than a hundred dancers, sitting in concentric circles, accompany the dance by swaying and flinging their arms while chattering and hissing in a monkeylike manner.

In the *barong* dance, a mystical lion helps the people in their fight against evil. The lion's followers, in a trance, "stab" themselves with ceremonial daggers.

In barong dance, *lion clashes with an evil witch while dancers "stab" themselves.*

Domed turrets *and inlaid tile facing mark the Medan mosque, one of Indonesia's finest. Fronting the mosque are stone grave markers.*

ing center. Trees shade many of its wide streets, and the city's rather dilapidated downtown buildings reflect Western architectural influences. But the traffic streaming around the buildings is Asian: pedicabs, small cars, umbrella-shaded vehicles, oxcarts, bicycles, motorcycles, and brightly colored carts drawn by red-capped horses.

The oldest part of Medan is near Kesawan Road, which once circled the city. Today it is the capital's busiest shopping street. Fourteen miles east of the city is Belawan, Medan's port, a regular stop for freighters and coastal steamers and an occasional stopping point for cruise ships.

Sumatra's ethnological variety is displayed on the streets and in the markets of Medan: Malays, Bataks, Acehnese, Europeans, Americans, Javanese, Indian Sikhs and Tamils, and many Chinese. The economy is based upon the rich Deli agricultural district, reaching from the mountains around Lake Toba to the Strait of Malacca. Medan exports the Deli tobacco (used for cigars and claimed by the locals to be the best in the world), rubber, petroleum, palm oil, tea, cocoa, and sisal.

Comfortable hotels. Medan has about a half dozen hotels, the newest being the completely air-conditioned Danau Toba International Hotel. Other tourist quality hotels are the Pardede International and Wisma Deli Hotel. Amenities at all three include restaurants serving Indonesian, Chinese, and European cuisine, swimming pools, and a full range of shops and services.

Mosques and markets. Sightseeing opportunities in Medan are limited, but you should certainly visit the big central market, destroyed by fire in 1971 but once again in full swing and offering a fascinating panorama of Medan's polyglot population. Also worth a visit are the palace of the Sultan of Deli, built in 1888, and the great mosque, Mesjid Raya, built in 1906 and one of Indonesia's finest.

Lake Toba and the Bataks

Lake Toba, a crater lake in North Sumatra about 110 miles southwest of Medan, is Sumatra's only developed tourist area. Lying 3,000 feet above sea level, the 50-mile-long lake is surrounded by high mountains and jungle-covered plateaus; Samosir Island fills more than half the lake basin.

Besides enjoying the attractions of the lake itself, you can visit villages and see the life style of the Batak tribesmen, about 300,000 of whom live in hundreds of villages scattered over the mountains between Medan and Sibolga. The Bataks are thought to be descendants of Malay tribes driven from their homeland by invading Mongols.

Two main roads lead to Lake Toba: one through the mountain resort of Brastagi, and the other—called the "plantation road"—which passes through mile after mile of rubber, palm oil, and cocoa tree plantations. The Brastagi route is longer but more scenic and less traveled. You can combine the two for an enjoyable loop trip; if possible, allow two days and spend the night at the lake.

Batak villages. On the Toba excursion, the traditional houses of the Batak tribesmen are the prime attraction. Though they retain many aspects of ancestor worship, most of the Bataks are Christians; you'll find the countryside fairly bristling with church steeples.

Near Brastagi you can make several side trips to villages where native architecture remains almost intact—communal dwellings built on stilts and topped by elaborate, high-peaked roofs. Each village has a well-preserved longhouse, used for generations as the residence of the kingly family.

In Brastagi you can stop for lunch or tea at the Massa Rest House, a small hotel sitting atop a hill overlooking its own small golf course. On either route, you go through Pematang Siantar, a city located in tea plantation country. You can lunch on rijsttafel at the quaint, old Siantar Hotel.

Lake Toba. Tourist accommodations at Lake Toba are located in the small town of Parapat, set back in a deep bay with a sweeping view of the lake and its surrounding mountains. The two most popular hotels are the Hotel Parapat, a vintage establishment with bungalow rooms set on garden-clad slopes above the bay, and the Danau Toba Hotel, a relatively new hotel.

You can mix sightseeing around the lake by boat with walks along pine-shaded roads, fishing, swimming, water-skiing, and strolling around Parapat

Lake Toba *fills a vast mountain crater in northern Sumatra. Tourist accommodations are available overlooking the lake, and you can take a boat to Samosir Island to visit Batak villages.*

Christian church, *topped with a corrugated metal roof, graces a hilltop on Samosir Island. On the road below, village women take a break from their field chores.*

and poking into its shops (some offering authentic antiques for sale).

Samosir Island. Lake Toba sightseeing concentrates on the Batak villages of Samosir Island. Considered sacred by early Bataks, the mountainous island almost overpowers the lake with its mass. Launches take visitors from Parapat to the island.

In Samosir's villages, houses are built with sway-backed roofs that peak sharply at both ends, and house facades are elaborately carved and painted. In the village of Ambarita, you can see stone chairs and tables used by early-day rulers; old Batak tombs, each shaded by a tree planted at the time of burial; and sacrificial stones used to behead the captured "enemies" from tribal wars. (Cannibalism was practiced here as late as 1914.)

Performances of local music and dance are usually arranged for tour groups. Local handicrafts include Batak calendars carved into bamboo or pieces of bone, brass containers for betel nut, snuff boxes, and handsome, hand woven fabrics.

South to Sibolga. Some of the most interesting Batak villages are found on the road leading south from Lake Toba to Sibolga on the Indian Ocean. Crumbling stone and dirt walls, topped by dense stands of timber bamboo, still partially ring many of these villages. In earlier days when tribal warfare was common, the villages were tightly surrounded by these impenetrable stands of bamboo, a living wall that had only two tightly guarded entrances.

The road down to Sibolga offers a fascinating sample of tropical agriculture, rain forests, and the botanical abundance of an equatorial climate —including such plants and trees as philodendron, cinnamon, rubber, kapok, clove, tapioca, manioc, nutmeg, banana, papaya, and mahogany. At Gurgur you can look back over the sweeping panorama of Lake Toba and its surrounding mountains and deep valleys.

West Sumatra, home of the Minangkabau

The two main towns of West Sumatra, Bukittinggi and Padang, are not tourist attractions in themselves, but they provide access to the Minangkabau hill tribes. The Minangkabau live in villages in the Padang highlands in houses with roofs curving skyward to a sharp point (see page 63). Raised well above the ground on beautifully carved pillars, the houses are covered by the black fibers of palm trees. The tribesmen are skilled farmers, excellent woodcarvers, metalworkers, and weavers. A matriarchal society, the people are noted for their resplendent costumes and headdresses.

Padang is the area's main seaport and a departure point for trips to the island of Nias (see page 68). Bukittinggi, 57 miles north, is the capital of Western Sumatra and its main commercial center. Bukittinggi's attraction is its museum; set in the zoological garden, it is housed in a century-old building designed in the traditional sway-backed style. A short drive from town takes you to Ngarai

Sianok, the Buffalo Hole, a deep chasm with precipitous walls carved by heavy rains and edged by a densely forested plateau.

Back country loop trip. An excellent way to see the Minangkabau country is to hire a car and driver and make a loop from Padang to Bukittinggi and back, past huge Lake Singkarak and through magnificent mountain country. In this lush countryside, turreted mosques supplant the church steeples found in the Batak country in North Sumatra. The journey from the lake back to Padang is on an up-and-down twister of a road, but the villages and scenery make the long day a rewarding experience.

Padang has air connections with other Sumatran cities and with Jakarta. Comfortable overnight accommodations are available in several small hotels in Padang and Bukittinggi.

Nias, a mysterious past

The island of Nias, lying off the upper west coast of Sumatra, is inhabited by more than 300,000 people still living in a Stone Age culture. On the island you'll see ancient pyramids and stone terraces (believed to have been the center of sacrificial ceremonies), and ritual dances and festivals. You can reach Nias by boat from Sibolga or Padang or by plane from Medan.

If you arrive by cruise ship, it anchors offshore from the village of Teluk Dalam. From dockside you ride about five miles up the hillside to the foot of a stone stairway leading up to the village of Bawomataluo, home of some 3,000 people.

The village is a stunning surprise: a series of tall, thatched-roof houses raised off the ground on piles and joined together. The village chieftain's house towers above the surrounding buildings. In the main square are stone chairs, used by village leaders during their meetings and while presiding over important ceremonies.

Groups visiting the village are entertained by men attired in full battle regalia—headdresses, face masks, shields, and spears. Women participating in the ceremonies wear beautifully embroidered dresses and gold headdresses. Carrying on a tradition performed by Nias warriors for centuries, some of the younger men exhibit their jumping skills; barefooted, they leap over a seven-foot-high stone wall set up in the main square.

Eastern foothills and Palembang

Lying between the mountains and the swampy coastal region on Sumatra's east coast is Palembang, an ancient seaport situated on the Musi River, about a hundred miles from the sea. In the city, land-people live on one side of the river and water-people on the other.

Minangkabau villages celebrate an ancient legend

Throughout the Padang highlands of midwestern Sumatra, the houses have roofs shaped like buffalo horns, the distinctive architecture of the Minangkabau tribes. The word Minangkabau is actually two words, *minang* and *kabau*, meaning "triumphant water buffalo." It refers to an ancient West Sumatran legend, telling of the victorious baby buffalo fitted with iron horns that saved West Sumatra from a foreign prince by killing the prince's powerful buffalo in a "fight-to-the-death." The appreciative tribesmen named the country Minangkabau and decreed that the roofs of all houses should take the shape of buffalo horns.

In all of the area's villages the roofs have a scooped design with high spirelike tips—the buffalo horns. The "horns" are the sharpened ends of long poles elevating the house about six feet above the ground and extending through the roof. Structures housing large families have many spires, as each pole represents a division of the living quarters for each group living in the house.

The Minangkabau tribes were long ago converted to Islam, but the ancient tribal custom of the woman dominating the family still exists. A daughter who marries stays with her family, and the husband has a choice: He can stay with his family and visit his wife as a guest, or he can establish himself permanently with his wife's family.

Each Minangkabau village has its own *mesjid* (mosque), *balai adat* (council house), and *lumbung adat* (communal storehouse for rice). Beautiful terraced mountain slopes reveal farming skills of the Minangkabau tribes.

Minangkabau council house *has saddle-shaped roof; pointed ends resemble buffalo horns.*

Morning mist *shrouds a rural village near Bukittinggi. This fertile mountain region is known for its jungle-clad valleys, scenic waterfalls, and Minangkabau tribal villages.*

Barefoot Nias Island warrior *high jumps a 7-foot stone wall, displaying a talent passed down from his forefathers. Cruise ships and planes provide access to the island.*

On the land side of the city are Chinese stores, freight yards, and warehouses for the rubber, tobacco, coffee, ebony, spices, and other products waiting to be shipped. The huge public market attracts housewives and other buyers dressed in the colorful costumes of their region and cult. The town's only important buildings are a small mosque and the university.

Across the river live the water-people—a floating population inhabiting small houseboats built atop huge bamboo rafts anchored to heavy log foundations. Some of the river houses have gardens and fences, and all have most of the amenities enjoyed by their neighbors on shore. Each houseboat has its own long fishing pole with a circular net, used to provide the family with a perpetual supply of fresh fish. Services are furnished by floating vendors, tradesmen, and professional people from houseboat offices and shops.

The best way to see the water-people is to rent a sampan with an outboard motor. You not only get a close-up view of the city's floating population, but you also see the freighters, barges, and deep-water *prahus* with their cargoes of coconuts, livestock, and lumber.

The mystical outer islands

Indonesia has thousands of other islands, some unexplored and uninhabited, but many that can be visited by an adventurous traveler. The largest of the outer islands are Kalimantan (on Borneo), Sulawesi (Celebes), Maluku, and Irian Jaya (the western portion of New Guinea). On these and on some of the numerous smaller groups, you'll find age-old cultures as yet uninfluenced by technological changes. Accommodations and transportation are negligible, but the experience of visiting them and seeing primitive life styles can be rewarding.

How to explore the islands

Some of the outer islands are accessible only by boat, but many of them can be reached by one of the Indonesian domestic air services. Airports are located at several places on Kalimantan, Sulawesi, and Irian Jaya; on Ambon in the Malukus and on Timor, Sumba, Flores, Sumbawa, and Lombok in the Lesser Sundas.

Kalimantan, forested nature world

Three quarters of the island of Borneo (third largest island in the world) is called Kalimantan and belongs to Indonesia; the northeastern portions of the island are part of Malaysia and the independent Sultanate of Brunei.

The mountainous land is covered with dense equatorial forests. Flowering plants abound—including many varieties of orchids and rhododendrons. Wildlife ranges from crocodiles to orangutans, proboscis monkeys, gibbons, panthers, and rhinoceroses.

Three of Kalimantan's major coastal cities have long been trading centers and timber shipping ports: Banjarmasin, capital of the province of South Kalimantan; Balikpapan, in East Kalimantan; and Pontianak, capital of West Kalimantan. The original people of the island were Dyaks, a wild inland people once notorious as headhunters; many Dyak tribes still remain. The island is a paradise for hunters and nature photographers, but only minimal accommodations exist. Transportation is limited almost entirely to boats that can navigate the rivers. Air taxis are available.

Spider-shaped Sulawesi

Straddling the equator east of Borneo is the spider-shaped island of Sulawesi (formerly known as Celebes). This mountainous, irregularly shaped island is developing as another of Indonesia's tourist centers, though it still lacks adequate accommodations and transportation facilities.

The four peninsulas comprising the island rise abruptly from the sea into mountains that are creased by rivers and dotted with lakes. Volcanoes are located near the tip of the northeast peninsula near Minahasa, and in the southwest near Ujung Pandang. The island's tallest peak, Mount Rantekombola, rises 11,314 feet and is one of the highest mountains in Indonesia.

Ujung Pandang. Formerly called Makasar, Ujung Pandang is the chief port on Sulawesi.

Despite its early Malay influences and 20th century touches, this city of a half million people still resembles a 16th century town. Overlooking the water is the centuries-old Dutch fort, Benteng Ujung Pandang (also known as Fort Rotterdam), dating back to the days when the Dutch East India Company waged war against the Makasar warrior king, Sultan Hasanuddin.

The harbor is crowded with *prahus*, the unique hand-hewn sailing ships built of teak logs and manned by the seafaring Buginese, who still travel the trading routes of their ancestors. Often you will see water-skiers pursuing their favorite sport and fishermen spreading nets to dry, mending sails, and paddling dinghies across the harbor.

Between the port and business district, you pass through a rural area of rice fields and coconut palms. Open parks and broad tree-lined streets grace the center of town; you can go sightseeing in a *becak* or *tigaroda*, both bicycle-operated pedicabs. The town's most important structures are the mosque and the cathedral. Two hotels provide accommodations.

The Toraja tribes. About 190 miles north of Ujung Pandang lies the scenic countryside inhabited by an ancient race called the Torajas. Known by its people as the "Land of the Heavenly Kings," the Tana Toraja district is inhabited by villagers who believe they are the direct descendants of the king of gods and are members of one huge family. Tours by jeep or mini-bus leave from Ujung Pandang.

The present day Torajas, in their cultural capital of Rantepao and their political capital of Makale, live in imposing boat-shaped houses richly ornamented with geometrical designs and life-size wood carvings of a buffalo at each door.

Nominally Christians or Muslims but animists by nature, the handsome, stocky Torajas eagerly welcome visitors into their villages. They serve as guides to the markets, show you woodcarvers at work, and perhaps will escort you to a festival—including their most intimate ceremony, the Toraja Feast of the Dead. Even if you miss one of these elaborate, month-long funerals, you will undoubtedly have an opportunity to help celebrate a circumcision, the dedication of a new house, or a good rice harvest—almost every day is a festival day.

Primitive Irian Jaya

Irian Jaya, the easternmost territory of Indonesia, occupies the western half of New Guinea. From its sweltering, swampy lowlands to snowcapped mountains, this is probably Indonesia's most primitive and undeveloped area.

Marsupials and thorny anteaters are among the fascinating animals while the bird of paradise is probably the most outstanding of the island's varied tropical birds.

The jungle island is inhabited by Papuans, Negritos, and Melanesians, though Indonesians began settling some of the interior lands after Irian Jaya was established as part of Indonesia in 1962.

Air service is available between Jakarta and several towns in Irian Jaya, including Jayapura, the capital (formerly called Sukarnapura). Accommodations are meager. A special permit, obtainable through local Indonesian travel agents, is needed to visit Irian Jaya.

Coastal villages. Occasionally a cruise ship will stop at one or more of Irian Jaya's ports, and passengers can go ashore to visit villages rarely seen by tourists. On a recent voyage, the *M. S. Lindblad Explorer* stopped at two coastal villages in the Asmat area, Agats and Biwar, both on the southeast coast. (Author-anthropologist Michael Rockefeller disappeared in the Asmat area in the early 1960s.)

The ship anchored about 15 miles off the mouth of the Betsj River—an anchorage necessitated by heavy silting at the river mouth. Traveling by rubber raft, passengers went about 2 miles upriver—through swampy lowlands and sago palm forests—to the Biwar village. The sago palm is not only the diet staple of the local tribes, but its wood is used for household implements, dugouts, bows and arrows, spears, and building materials. The area has no stones, and tribesmen must trade for them.

Many villages are built on low, swampy ground, with wooden walkways between the houses and between adjoining villages. Many rivers lace the Asmat area, and villagers do most of their traveling in dugout canoes.

An estimated 12,000 tribesmen live along the coast in the Agats-Biwar area, another 10,000 inland along the numerous rivers of the Asmat area. These people of Papuan stock have a highly developed,

Costumed *medicine man leads an Irian Jaya ceremonial dance.*

Asmat warriors *of Irian Jaya create a fearsome sight as they paddle decorated canoes out to greet cruise ship passengers.*

Body paint, *feathered headdresses, and nose shell decorations are everyday dress for these warriors of the Agats-Biwar area.*

Bare-shouldered women, *holding gourds for rice wine offerings, participate in lavish village welcoming ceremony on Flores Island.*

Village dancer *performs for visitors near Ambon in the fabled spice islands of Maluku. Metal helmet is from the Dutch colonial era.*

though primitive, culture and a developed artistic sense. They live today much as their ancestors did centuries ago.

Visiting cruise ships are a big event, and all the villagers turn out for a big welcome. They make no special effort to dress up: the men normally paint their faces and bodies, wear shell nose pieces and ragged shorts, and carry spears and other warmaking implements. In long war canoes they glide out to greet visitors.

These isolated areas offer a great opportunity to buy fine examples of the unusual Irian Jaya masks, carvings, basketry, and other art forms. However, purchases are restricted by the government, because most of the carvings are part of the tribe's religious life — pieces not made for the tourist trade, but for tribal rituals.

Maluku, the spice islands

The fabled spice islands of Maluku (formerly called the Moluccas) lie between Irian Jaya and Sulawesi. Ambon, the provincial capital, is the main port of this island group and a key center for air travel in eastern Indonesia. In centuries past, early mariners carried reports of the rich spice islands home to their rulers in England and Europe.

Lesser Sunda Islands

The island chain lying east of Java—consisting of Bali, Lombok, Sumbawa, Sumba, Flores, Alor, Timor, and a few smaller islands—is known as the Lesser Sunda Islands. Several of these are of special interest to the tourist.

Lombok, Bali's eastern neighbor, has an aura of discovery. You reach it by air from Surabaya or Denpasar or by ferry from Padangbai on Bali. Tourists enjoy its thick albizzia forests, towering mountains, beaches, native art and handicrafts, colorful traditions and festivals. You'll find small hotels in Mataram, Ampenam, and Cakranegera.

Ferry service from Sumbawa takes travelers to Komodo Island, home of some 800 giant monitor lizards. Called the Komodo dragon, an adult reptile can weigh 300 pounds and reach 10 feet in length.

Kupang, the port city of Timor, is where Captain Bligh is reputed to have ended his voyage after the mutiny on the *Bounty* in 1789.

Festivals and events

Practically every event in an Indonesian's life calls for a colorful ceremony. Ethnic groups of each island have their own individual festivities connected with birth, marriage and death.

Celebrations are an integral part of the country's different religions, and festivals are held for the fishing and harvest seasons, and for historical, military, and national holidays. The following list covers some of the more intriguing events occurring at about the same time annually.

Waicak Day. Annual full moon festival held at Borobudur Temple near Yogyakarta in early May, commemorating the birth and death of Buddha (see page 13). Climax of the event comes at 4 A.M. when the worshippers, each carrying a lighted candle, walk up the stairs of the temple and circle clockwise toward the main stupa.

Ramayana Dance Festival. Annual dance drama held June through October at Prambanan Temple near Yogyakarta (see page 58).

Komodo dragons, *the world's largest lizards, roam freely on Komodo Island. You can also see them at Jakarta zoo.*

Welcoming committee *waits at the Muslim village of Yamtil. Houses are built on stilts over the water.*

Practical information for visitors to Indonesia

To help you in planning your trip, here are some important details you will want to know:

Entry requirements. To visit Indonesia you must have a valid passport and a visa issued by an Indonesian embassy or consulate. To apply, you will need two copies of the visa application, two photos, and proof of onward transportation. A tourist visa, costing $3.00, is valid for 30 days from day of entry; but it may be extended not more than 15 days by payment of an additional fee of $16.50. You pay an airport tax amounting to about $1.50 on your departure from the country.

If arriving from an infected area, you will need an international health certificate showing inoculation against smallpox, cholera, and yellow fever. In addition, the U.S. Public Health Service recommends that you have typhoid, paratyphoid, tetanus, and gamma globulin shots. If you intend to go into remote areas, check with your doctor regarding anti-malarial treatment.

Indonesian consulates are located in San Francisco and New York; the embassy is in Washington, D.C.

Customs. You're allowed to bring in one bottle of liquor and 200 cigarettes. It is wise to register your camera, tape recorder, and similar equipment so you'll have no trouble when you leave the country.

Currency. The official rate of exchange for the Indonesian rupiah (Rp.) is approximately 617 Rp. per U.S. dollar. The rupiah cannot be purchased outside the country nor carried out on departure. You can bring in an unlimited amount of U.S. currency. Money may be converted at the Bank of Indonesia, or at any other authorized bank or money changer. You'll find that credit cards are seldom honored in the country's outlying areas.

Health conditions. Hospitals and medical services are good in the major cities, but quite limited when you get into the countryside. Medicines and toiletries are available in the major hotels and in drug stores in Jakarta and the other main cities. Bring mosquito repellant.

Tipping. Though some hotels ask that you not tip their staff, tipping is expected for most other services (some hotels add a 10 percent service charge). At air, ship, and train terminals, prices range from 100 Rp. to 150 Rp. per bag, depending on size. In restaurants the usual tip is 5 to 10 percent of the bill.

Taxi drivers expect an extra 100 Rp. to 200 Rp., depending on distance traveled. Guides and tour conductors are generally not tipped.

Climate. Indonesia straddles the equator, and its hot, tropical climate is influenced by monsoon winds. The best time to visit is from April through November during the "dry season."

The average year-round temperature at sea level is 79°F. The highlands are cooler, with temperatures dropping about 1° for each 300 foot rise in elevation. Humidity remains high throughout the year, but cooling breezes come in from the sea or down from the mountains, making evenings quite pleasant.

Annual rainfall in Jakarta is approximately 80 inches, though the mountains will usually get more than 240 inches during the wet season from December to March.

For more information. Your best sources of information on travel in Indonesia are the Directorate General of Tourism, 81, Jalan Kramat Raya, Jakarta; Jakarta Metropolitan City Tourism Development Board, 8-9 Merdeka Selatan, Jakarta, Indonesia; and the Indonesian Tourist Promotion Board, 323 Geary Street, San Francisco 94102.

Ram fighting. Grand finale of ram fighting takes place annually in Bandung on the first Sunday after August 17th. Highlight of the event is the singing and dancing of the *gendang pencak* (traditional fighting dance).

Below are some festivals and ceremonies occurring at different times during each calendar year. Exact dates may be obtained from the Directorate General of Tourism.

Galungan Day. A 10-day celebration of the Wuku calendar, which divides the year into 210 days. The Balinese spend the holidays in happy reunion with their ancestral spirits. Festivities include offerings and colorful ceremonies in villages across the island of Bali.

Idul Qurban. A Muslim holy day when meat from slaughtered goats, sheep, or cows is given to the people. It celebrates the occasion when the prophet Abraham was ordered to sacrifice his son Isaac.

Odalan. An all-day, all-night Balinese temple festival occurring in each of thousands of temples every 210 days on the anniversary of the consecration of the temple.

Grebeg Maulud. Muslims celebrate Mohammed's birthday (see page 13). In Yogyakarta, a procession travels from the Sultan's Palace to the mosque. Booths and stands turn the route into a marketplace, and a puppet show runs through the night.

Kesada. Held at the crater of Mount Bromo (see page 61), this is a midnight ceremony of offerings by the Tenggerese people to the fire god.

Idul Fitri. The end of the Muslim fasting month is celebrated with mass prayers in mosques and public squares.

Striped minarets *adorn the magnificent Ubudiah Mosque* **(top)** *in Kuala Kangsar, north of Kuala Lumpur. Dugout canoes* **(right)** *are the chief means of transport in many areas of Sabah and Sarawak. Jungle-edged beaches* **(far right**) *line the east coast of Peninsular Malaysia.*

Malaysia

Kampongs, turreted mosques, island resorts

Malaysia is a kaleidoscope of images: gilded mosque domes towering above the green fronds of palm trees; sparkling cities mixing Moorish and colonial architecture with modern high-rise structures; *kampongs* (Malay villages) of wooden houses nestled among coconut and banana trees; Anglican churches, their steeples reaching to the heavens; cool, rolling highlands covered with tea plants. The aromas of outdoor food stalls mingle with the scent of frangipani and steamy tropic odors.

Adding greatly to the Malaysian panorama are the people—a cultural and racial mix of Malays, Chinese, Indians, Dyaks, and Europeans—who enjoy a fascinating collection of religions, customs, languages, costumes, and festivals. Some are city dwellers; others live in highland villages, in stilt houses rooted in the swampy lowlands, and in huge longhouses stretching a few hundred yards through the rain forests.

European colonists have left their mark. A 400-year-old lighthouse built by the Portuguese still guards the Malacca headland; elsewhere, a Dutch-built church and fort lie in ruins. In most cities, government and commercial buildings recall the colonializing impact of Victorian England.

Tropical forests and lush cultivated lands sweep inland from the edge of the sea up into the refreshing highlands. Along the coast are hundreds of miles of quiet, unspoiled beaches. Offshore lie a handful of islands, idyllic resorts vying for the label of tropical paradise.

Malaysia is an inviting country to visit. Hotels range from comfortable to luxurious. Cities are clean and well run by an efficient civil service organization. Language is no problem: English is widely spoken—a legacy of the British colonial period—and is still taught in the schools. Malaysia has a fine transportation system and the best roads in Southeast Asia. Food comes well prepared and in surprising variety. A well-ordered society and a

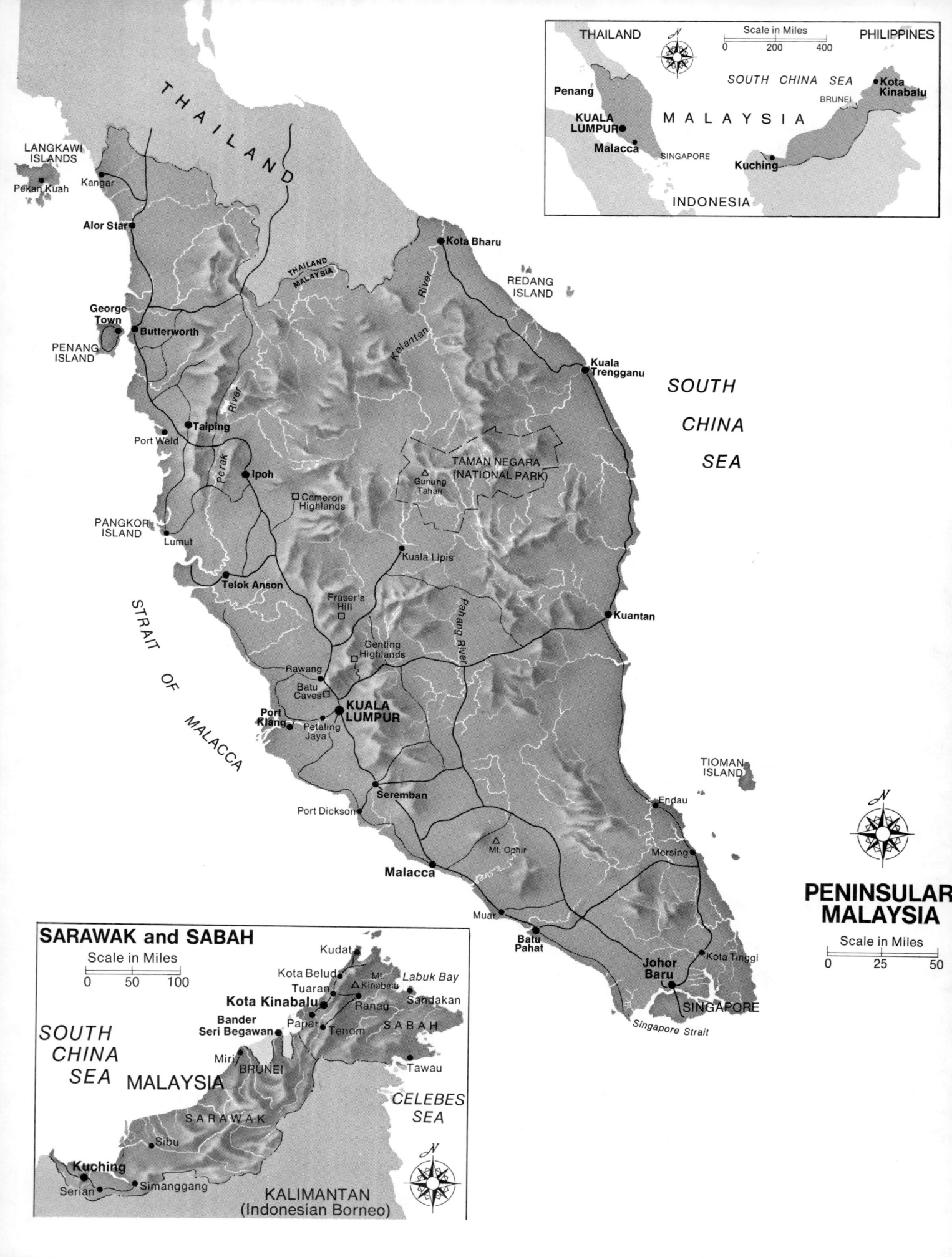

feeling of prosperity go with one of the highest standards of living in Southeast Asia.

You can glimpse Malaysia simply by driving the few miles from Singapore across the causeway into Johor, but there's much more: the capital of Kuala Lumpur, the resort island of Penang, historical Malacca, the hill stations, and the states of Sabah and Sarawak.

Malaysia—then and now

Malaysia consists of two separate regions—Peninsular Malaysia and the states of Sabah and Sarawak, lying about 600 miles east, across the South China Sea along the northern edge of Borneo.

This far-flung nation covers 129,000 square miles, a total area slightly larger than the state of New Mexico. It borders Thailand in the northwest and reaches toward the islands of the Philippines in the northeast. The peninsula's southern tip is joined to the island nation of Singapore by the Johor Causeway. On the island of Borneo, the states of Sabah (formerly British North Borneo) and Sarawak share borders with Indonesia's Kalimantan; both states also share a frontier with the sultanate of Brunei, a British protectorate.

Major towns and cities are located along the peninsula's densely settled and highly developed western coastal plain. Clean and prosperous Kuala Lumpur is Malaysia's federal capital and largest city. Main ports are George Town (on the island of Penang), Port Klang, and Malacca. Kuching, the capital of Sarawak, is a riverside town of 70,000. Modern Kota Kinabalu, capital of Sabah, has a population of about 50,000.

Lush, green countryside

Tropical rain forests cover about three quarters of the peninsula and most of Sabah and Sarawak. Most of the country is mountainous. Southeast Asia's highest peak is Mount Kinabalu in Sabah, towering 13,455 feet. On the peninsula, 7,184-foot Gunung Tahan is the highest peak.

The three largest rivers on the Malay Peninsula are the Perak, emptying on the west coast into the Strait of Malacca, and the Pahang and Kelantan, draining into the South China Sea on the east coast. The numerous rivers of Sabah and Sarawak are often the principal means of transportation and communication.

Important offshore islands include Penang, Pangkor Island, and the Langkawi group—all off the peninsula's west coast—and the islands of Tioman, Rawa, Redang, Perhentian, and Kapas off the east coast.

Jungle trees and wildlife

Located only a few degrees from the equator, Peninsular Malaysia is a land of dense tropical jungle, mangrove swamps, and mountainous terrain. Tall casuarinas and banyan trees, up to 100 feet tall, form a natural canopy. High-yield rubber trees, introduced from Brazil, and oil palm plantations produce more than half of the country's exports. Orchids of every size, shape, and color are found throughout the country.

Many kinds of mammals and reptiles inhabit the country — among them elephants, rhinoceroses, tigers, leopards (black and spotted), bears, tapirs, deer, wild oxen, crocodiles, wild goats, monkeys, and squirrels. Over 130 species of snakes inhabit the jungle and the sea. Sharing trees with some of the snakes are frogs and lizards—and the rare flying lemur. Most of the 600 species of birds hide amid the jungle growth. Those easily seen or heard include orioles, swallows, and magpie robins.

The historic route to independence

Archeological findings in Sarawak's Niah Caves—dating back to about 50,000 B.C.—identify Malaysia's first inhabitants as Negroid tribes with characteristics similar to those of the Aborigines of the Philippines, Indonesia, New Guinea, and Australia. Descendants of these primitive peoples still live in the Perak hills and other isolated areas, with little change in their Stone Age level of civilization.

Ancestors of present-day Malays, however, were Mongoloid people from southwest China who arrived from 2,000 to 250 B.C. Malaysian artifacts reveal that the earlier immigrants—called Proto-Malays—lived in wooden houses, cultivated crops, and domesticated their animals. The later arrivals, known as Deutero-Malays, contributed a knowledge of metal work. Eventually the two groups merged, and their descendants became the Malays who inhabit many countries of Southeast Asia.

The early traders. During the early Christian era, trading ships sailing between India and China brought the first outsiders to the Malay Peninsula. These traders explored the coastal area for tin, gold dust, and jungle products. Indian traders set up trading posts along the west coast. At first the Chinese made little attempt to settle, but in succeeding centuries, they gained a stronghold.

Following the traders were Buddhist and Hindu Indian missionaries and colonists, who set up small independent Malayan states and kingdoms that flourished until the 8th century.

Wars with invaders from Indonesia and Thailand indirectly resulted in the establishment of the Malacca Sultanate. Located on the Strait of Malacca (one of the world's great arteries of sea commerce), the Sultanate was a rich marketplace exporting gold, ivory, and spices and importing cotton, silk, and metals. The Malacca Sultanate lasted from 1400 to 1511, a period marking the golden age of the Malay court and tradition. During this period Malays began to convert to Islam, which became the national religion following independence.

Colonial rule. The capture of Malacca by the Portuguese in 1511 ended the Malay empire and ushered in colonial rule. In 1641 the Dutch besieged

Malacca, overcoming the Portuguese, and Dutch influence was to dominate the next 180 years. In 1786 Britain obtained permission for a naval base in Penang, establishing its first foothold in Malaya. In 1824 the Treaty of London defined Dutch and British "spheres of influence" in Southeast Asia, and Malacca was transferred to the British.

Two years later the British East India Company incorporated Penang, Malacca, and Singapore as the Straits Settlement, later making them a British Crown Colony.

Sarawak and Sabah (both in northern Borneo) became British protectorates in 1882. During the next three decades, British suzerainty was extended over the remaining states of the Malay Peninsula.

A series of treaties induced all the Malay states to accept British advisers.

Independent Malaysia. At the outbreak of World War II, Malaya's vital geographic position was recognized by the Japanese, who quickly invaded the country and occupied it from 1942 to 1945. After the war, the British attempted to replace pre-war arrangements with the states, dissolving the former colony and establishing a Malayan union. Resentment against the union plan resulted in the creation of the Federation of Malaya. Independence of the Federation of Malaya was granted on August 31, 1957. Singapore, Sabah, and Sarawak joined the Federation in 1963 to form the nation of Malaysia.

Malaysia's hill stations — cool retreats from lowland heat

Mountain retreats in Malaysia were usually patterned after their British counterparts in India. In the early days, the bare necessities for a "hill station" were a cool climate, spectacular views, and comfortable accommodations. From Kuala Lumpur you can reach three areas meeting these requirements and adding a few modern amenities. The elevation cools temperatures to about 70° F. during the day and about 60° at night.

Genting Highlands. Overlooking the jungle from atop 5,614-foot-high Mount Ulu Kali, the Genting Highlands hotel-casino complex is often shrouded in clouds and enveloped in mist. Situated 32 miles northeast of Kuala Lumpur, Malaysia's newest hill station offers five hotels, the country's only licensed casino, a cable car ride, and a manmade lake. You can reach the complex by car in about an hour or by helicopter in about 10 minutes from Kuala Lumpur.

Close at hand is thick jungle greenery, where sounds of birds break the stillness. On a clear day you can see the capital city and the distant Strait of Malacca. Inside the casino you'll find both western and oriental games of chance.

Included in the resort complex are an 18-hole golf course and a clubhouse. The golf course is linked to the main part of the complex by a 1½-mile cable car system.

Fraser's Hill. Once the hideout of adventurer Louis James Fraser, a dealer in opium and tin ore in the late 1800s, Fraser's Hill has been developed into a popular hill resort. Situated at 4,000 feet, the resort is popular with KL residents for its cool, fresh air and peaceful jungle surroundings. Well-kept gardens surround English-style bungalows and a small hotel. Located 64 miles northeast of Kuala Lumpur, the resort can be reached by rail/bus, taxi, or private car.

From the moment you enter the gate, you'll be surprised by the complete holiday atmosphere of Fraser's Hill. The main street is lined with stone buildings—reminiscent of an English township. Nestled in a hollow at the end of the street is the 9th and final hole of the golf course. Paved roads, narrowed by encroaching jungle, lead to the guest bungalows, a restaurant, tennis courts, and children's playground. Marked jungle walks lead to Jeriau Falls, with its swimming lagoon and picnic area.

Cameron Highlands. Further north, 140 miles from KL, is Cameron Highlands, discovered by government surveyor William Cameron in 1885. Mile-high mountains surround the plateau. Chinese tea planters first claimed the Highlands and built a road to take their product to market. Soon wealthy rubber planters discovered the route and built weekend houses in the area.

Today the Highlands has three townships with a half dozen hotels. The main village of Tanah Rata—known for its clean air, streams, lakes, and mountain views—offers Swiss-style chalets, Chinese hotels, small cottages, restaurants, and an excellent steak house. Year-round activities include golf, tennis, badminton, swimming, and jungle walks.

Tudor-style bungalows *at Fraser's Hill appear as an oasis in the green jungle.*

Two years later Singapore seceded from the Federation to become an independent republic.

A constitutional elective monarchy

Malaysia is a constitutional elective monarchy, composed of 13 states: Sabah, Sarawak, and 11 states of the former Federation of Malaya. Hereditary Malay sultans who rule nine of the states elect the Supreme Head of State, the Yang di-Pertuan Agung, from their royal group within the Conference of Rulers. The Conference also includes the non-royal governors of Penang, Malacca, Sarawak, and Sabah. On his election, the royal monarch relinquishes his functions as ruler of his own state but remains head of his state's Muslim religion.

The national executive power is vested in a Prime Minister and his cabinet. A 58-member Senate has 32 members appointed by the royal monarch and 26 elected members. The 154 members of the House of Representatives are elected by popular vote.

Malaysia's people

Malaysia is multiracial, a society composed of Malays, Chinese, Indians, and several other minorities. Their diverse cultural traditions are still evident in dress, festivals, foods, religions, crafts, drama, music, and architecture. In contrast to the country's modern cities, many tribal people in Sabah and Sarawak retain ancient customs seldom seen in the 20th century.

Nearly half of the country's 12 million population are Malays and other indigenous people, including Ibans (Sea Dyaks), Land Dyaks, and the Kadazans, Bajaus, Muruts, and Kedayans of Sabah. Malaysian Chinese number about 4 million, Indians and Pakistanis account for another million, and Eurasians and Europeans—mostly British—make up most of the balance.

Dress. Malaysia's varied cultures are reflected in the colorful clothing worn by her people. Malay women dress in the fitted *kebaya* and skirtlike *sarong*. Men often dress western-style, in shirtsleeves and trousers, though on festive days they may wear the Malay shirt, called a *baju*. Indian women drape themselves in flowing *saris;* Chinese women wear the tightly fitted *cheong-sam*, slit to the thigh, or a *sam foo*, a loose tunic and trousers.

Language and religion. Malaysia's cultural melange is also reflected in the variety of languages spoken and religions practiced.

Malays speak Bahasa Malaysia, the national language, and most of them are Muslims. The Chinese usually speak Mandarin or one of many Chinese dialects; most adhere to Buddhism, though many are Christians or Taoists. Most Malaysian Indians come from southern India; they are Tamil-speaking people who follow the Hindu faith. The people of Sabah and Sarawak are mainly animist, though many have embraced Islam and Christianity.

Both the national language and English are compulsory school subjects, though primary school in-

Chinese Market, *shaded by colorful umbrellas, offers shoppers fresh vegetables, fish, meat— and a chance to use their bartering skill.*

struction may also be in Mandarin or Tamil. About one out of three Malaysian children attends secondary schools. English is the common language of all races and is widely used in hotels, shops, restaurants, and offices.

Visiting Malaysia

Malaysia is situated some 8,000 air miles from the west coast of the United States—a trip requiring about 19 hours from California. The time difference between the U. S. west coast and Malaysia is 15½ hours. When it's 9:30 A.M. Saturday in Kuala Lumpur, it's 6 P.M. Friday in California.

Some 20 international airlines—including the Malaysian Airline System (MAS)—serve the country from cities around the world. A number of steamship companies include Malaysian ports on itineraries of passenger freighters and cruise ships.

Transport in Malaysia

Frequent daily air service is provided by MAS to all the major towns. The Malayan Railway's main line runs from Butterworth Station, opposite Penang Island, south to Singapore; the railroad also operates an east coast service. At the Butterworth Station you can board the International Express for Bangkok. In Sabah rail service is offered by the government-operated Sabah State Railways.

Vehicular ferries *ply the waters between Penang Island and the mainland on a frequent daily schedule. They connect with the train traveling from Bangkok via Kuala Lumpur to Singapore.*

Small roadside stand *on Penang Island offers passers-by a selection of fruit, snacks, and even imported beer. Owner's son, above, efficiently trims the husk off a coconut.*

Passenger ships of the Straits Steamship Company provide regular service between Singapore and the ports of Sarawak, Sabah, and Brunei.

The principal cities of Malaysia are linked by regularly scheduled bus service, and some bus companies have charter services and supply guides.

In addition to buses, all large towns have *teksi* (taxis) that you can hire on a per-mile tariff or by the hour. Taxis are required to have meters, and fares run about M $0.60 for the first mile or M $4 for the first hour. For short trips around town, the trishaw (bicycle-powered rickshaw) provides a leisurely way to view local sights.

Malaysia has a good and extensive road system, making it one of the best areas in Asia for travel by rented car. Although traffic moves on the left side of the road, you soon become accustomed to right-hand drive and the location of your car's controls. Most of the highway signs use international picture symbols.

Wide range of hotels

Malaysia offers excellent modern hotels in its larger cities, Malay village-type homes on stilts at Rawa Island resort, informal living in government rest houses, visitors' lodges, and thatch-roofed huts elsewhere in the country.

Most of the hotel accommodations are oriented to western visitors, providing private baths and air conditioning along with friendly attention and good service. Most hotels add a 10 percent service charge and a 5 percent tax.

Government rest houses provide more informal accommodations outside the main cities. If you are interested in camping or using a rest house, contact the Tourist Development Corporation (see page 101) for more information.

Dining out

Food in Malaysia is generally very good, and dining out literally adds spice to the evening. You'll find an interesting range of cuisines—Malay, Chinese, Indian, and Western-style.

In addition to restaurants and hotel dining rooms, numerous shops and small roadside stalls offer a peppery selection of favorite local treats for adventurous diners.

Satay, Malaysia's national dish, consists of slender skewers of meat—mutton, beef, or chicken—grilled over a charcoal fire and then dipped in spicy, sweet, pungent sauces. Distinctive Malay curries have their own flavor derived from such ingredients as coconut, chili, and lemon grass. Indian restaurants offer curries of mutton and vegetables served on banana leaves and eaten with the fingers. A Chinese specialty is the selection of piping hot Cantonese "tidbits" served from portable carts.

Beers and stouts are locally brewed—among them the favorite of the Far East, Tiger Beer, which tastes best ice cold. In a spirit of adventure try *samsu*, similar to vodka and distilled from rice mash; *tuak*, the popular native drink of Sarawak, made from fermented rice; and *today*, made of coconut juice and tasting like champagne.

Entertainment scene

Since Malaysia has such diverse cultures, you'll find many different types of entertainment. Luxury hotels and many restaurants have supper clubs with imported floor shows, where acts range from international stars to the latest Paris or Australian nightclub dancers.

Throughout the country you can enjoy folk dances depicting various cultures, become absorbed in the fanciful world of Chinese theater, or watch the intricate movements of the dancers in a Malay Joget.

On the east coast of the peninsula, look for skilled demonstrations of *bersilat*—the Malay art of self-defense—giant top spinning, and kite flying. Other popular diversions include the *wayang kulit* (shadow plays), the unusual Malay drama called *Menora*, theater club presentations of modern plays, and Chinese, Indian, and American films.

Shopping in Malaysia

In Malaysia you can shop in well-stocked stores and hotel shopping arcades or examine merchandise at roadside stalls. Fixed prices prevail in larger stores, but expect to bargain at smaller shops and markets. Shops on Penang Island offer good prices on some luxury items.

Malaysian handicrafts are your best buy. You can purchase lengths of colorful and washable batik fabric or buy ready-made clothing and accessories. Fine pewter articles range from beer mugs to tea sets; some are hand engraved with Malaysian scenes. Wooden carvings made by tribal people are available at handicraft centers.

Cosmopolitan Kuala Lumpur

Clean, green Kuala Lumpur is set against a backdrop of jungle-clad hills often hidden by billowing white cumulus clouds. Familiarly known as KL, this city of a million people is located about halfway down Peninsular Malaysia near the west coast. A horizontally open city of wide streets and well-tended parks, it operates at a leisurely pace.

The most vivid quality of this hundred-year-old city is its heterogeneous mixture of races, religions, and cultural influences. As you tour around KL, you'll see the sharp, sleek lines of the National Mosque next to the Moorish baroque domes and arches of the Railway Station. On the streets, amid people in western dress, Malay girls in *sarong-kebayas* pass Chinese girls in *cheong-sams* and Indian girls in *saris*. Food stalls serving satay and curry offer their wares not far from restaurants.

Now a federal territory similar to Washington, D.C., KL did not officially become a city until 1972. Actually, it has been the seat of the central government since 1957 when Malaysia gained its independence. The city has come a long way since 1857, when less than a hundred Chinese miners sailed up the Klang River and discovered rich tin deposits. Within weeks, all but 18 in the party died of fever. However, the first shacks had gone up at the junction of the Klang and Gombak rivers; soon the waterways were busy with boats hauling supplies and tin ore.

When KL became the capital of Selangor state in 1880, it was still a scrubby little town of thatched huts and narrow streets. In the following year a fire destroyed much of the city, and it was rebuilt with brick, street by street. By 1897 the elaborate Moorish-style Secretariat Building had been completed; one of the town's landmarks, it still sprawls along Jalan Raja.

Obtain a city map at your hotel or from the Tourist Development Corporation (see page 101).

Modern hotels galore

Kuala Lumpur now has more than 20 hotels, many located along Jalan Treacher and other streets south of the Selangor Turf Club. Larger hotels attracting many tourists are the Equatorial, Federal, Kuala Lumpur Hilton, Holiday Inn Kuala Lumpur, Merlin, and Kuala Lumpur Regent. The Travel Inn has been completed recently. Smaller hotels and motels include the Fortuna, Malaysia, Majestic,

Moorish-style *Secretariat Building on Jalan Raja recalls turn-of-the-century days in Kuala Lumpur. Modern hotels and office buildings are nearby.*

Shah's Village Motel, and the motel and cottages at Mimaland Tourist Complex.

All these hotels and motels are air-conditioned, with restaurants and a full range of services.

KL food fare

You'll find a wide variety of Asian and European foods in KL's major hotels, but most Malaysian dishes served have been tempered to suit foreign tastes. To sample the country's authentic foods, you'll have to try some of the smaller city restaurants and eating stalls.

• Shawal Restaurant, on Jalan Tuanku Abdul Rahman, is one of the city's good Malay restaurants. Dishes are described on the menu. The restaurant is noted for *soto ayam* (flavored chicken soup).

• Akbar, near the Loke Mansion, offers excellent Indian food. Mogul Court upstairs has tasteful decor and friendly waiters.

• Le Coq d' Or, 121 Ampang Road, offers European and French cuisine in a former Chinese mansion.

• Malacca Grill, in the KL Hilton Hotel, Jalan Treacher, serves Western and local cuisine in an elegant atmosphere.

• Imperial Room, Malaysia Hotel, is noted for its full course Chinese dinners.

• Sri Yazmin, at the Ampang Shopping Complex, offers a good selection of Malay dishes and has cultural shows in the evening.

• Cempaka, at the Holiday Inn, is known for its superb Malay cuisine.

For local food and atmosphere, make an evening visit to either the food stalls along Jalan Campbell or to the Old Market or Medan Selera in Petaling Jaya. You point and order from an array of foods served from carts and stalls. You can sample satay and other Malaysian favorites at modest cost.

Around town at night

Other than the evening markets, night life in KL is pretty much limited to hotel nightclubs. These provide music for dancing and, in some cases, floor shows and cabarets. The young at heart will find two good discotheques: Tomorrow at the Merlin Hotel, and the Tin Mine at KL's Hilton.

You'll find Malaysian-style entertainment at both the Federal and Merlin hotels. A nightly cultural show at the Yazmin in Ampang Park and at the KL Hilton offer classical and folk dances.

Several tour operators offer an evening entertainment package that takes in the illuminated city sights, visits several food stalls, and concludes with dinner at a restaurant serving Malay, Chinese, or European food.

Most Kuala Lumpur nightclubs and restaurants stop serving liquor at midnight on week nights, slightly later on weekends.

Shopping in KL

KL offers goods from around the world, but you'll have to move around a bit to do your shopping. Although KL has no specific shopping district, it does have some new shopping centers. Stores, shops, and hotel arcades are cropping up all over the city. The best bargains are in batik, silver, pewter, woodcarvings, and pottery.

Along KL's main streets, look for excellent locally made goods at the Malayan Handicraft Center on Jalan Mountbatten and the MARA Arts and Crafts Center and shopping arcade on Jalan Tuanku Abdul Rahman; browse through the shops on Jalan Petaling (Chinatown) for Chinese porcelain, jade figures, antiques, and jewelry.

For Selangor pewter, visit the Pewter Showroom and Demonstration Center, housed in a 1930s-style Malaysian bungalow at the junction of Hot Spring Road and Jalan Genting Klang. You can watch demonstrations of pewter production and shop for items ranging from beer mugs to coffee and tea sets. Most KL countryside tours visit the center.

KL's Tourist Development Corporation has recently opened a handicraft center at the Bukit Nanas Complex in the city center. Goods for sale in the seven center shops include pandan and mengkuang leaf products, tooled copper, silver and brasswork, woodcarvings, and ceramics.

Among KL's other shopping areas are the UDA-Ampang Shopping Complex, the Pertama Complex, and the Wisma Central. The Wisma offers a good choice of handicrafts—especially batik and aboriginal wood carvings—at reasonable prices.

A visit to one of the local markets gives you a glimpse of what KL citizens buy and how they go about it. The Sunday Market (held on Saturday nights) in Kampung Bharu, a Malay section of

Railway Station *stands between the Moorish-style railway administration building and a modern glass tower. Modern freeways encircle the city.*

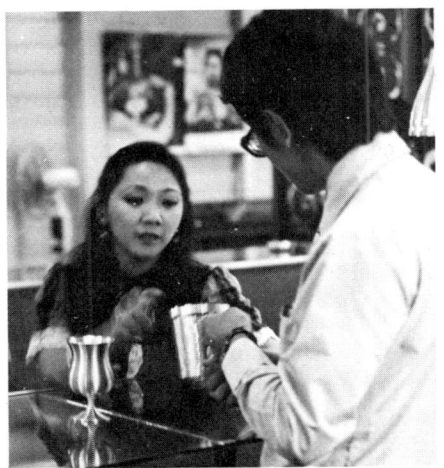

Pewter products, *produced in Malaysia, may be viewed and purchased in Pewter Showroom.*

Devout Muslims *pray at the Royal Mausoleum, located in the National Mosque in downtown Kuala Lumpur.*

town, offers pictures on bamboo and cloth, batik paintings and cloth, all under bright lights. The Chinese night market on Petaling Street offers everyday items and a good sampling of local fruits. Early risers might enjoy the Central Market, where tables overflow with vegetables, spices and sauces, and freshly butchered meats.

Department store hours are 10 A.M. to about 6 P.M. Shops are open from 8 A.M. until 7:30 or 10 P.M. Most places close Saturdays at 1 P.M., and almost all are closed on Sundays. Most of the large stores will accept travelers checks and credit cards. They will handle packing and shipping arrangements if you wish.

Contrasting city sights

A leisurely full day tour around the city ties together the main sights of Kuala Lumpur and points up its contrasts.

Masjid Jame, at the junction of the Klang and Gombak rivers, is the city's old mosque. Surrounded by palm trees, the domed, Moorish-style structure is ornamented with alternating bands of red and white on its minarets. Muslim men and their modestly dressed women, often veiled, answer the muezzin's calls for prayer.

National Mosque (Masjid Negara), south of the old mosque, seems to float up out of its 13 acres of fountained pools and vast lawns. Since it was opened in 1965, the National Mosque has become a landmark, a building of grand yet simple lines executed in concrete, marble, and tile. Dominating the main dome is a graceful, 245-foot spire from which the faithful are called to prayer over a public address system. Muslims pray here five times a day, but Friday is the busiest. During major celebrations, the Royal Malaysian Police march in formation to the mosque for prayer.

Visiting hours are 8 A.M. to 5 P.M. daily except Fridays.

Railway Station is a prime example of KL's Moorish-inspired architecture, similar in design to the palatial railway administration building, post office, and secretariat. All mix a profusion of pointed domes and towers, porticos and arches, pinnacles, and intriguing nooks and crannies.

The Railway Station was built in 1910—about 24 years after the first train puffed into town from Port Klang.

Merdeka (Independence) Stadium, east of the Railway Station, is the site where the Malaysians celebrated their independence as a nation on August 31, 1957. Actually a huge earth amphitheater for 30,000 people, the arena has a regular program of outdoor sporting events and also serves as a stage for national and international ceremonies. Nearby on Jalan Davidson stands Stadium Negara, an indoor sports stadium.

Giant stairway leads to sacred shrines in the Batu Caves. Thousands of people make the pilgrimage here annually at Thaipusam.

Petaling Street is a fascinating place to explore, offering little Chinese shops and businesses of every description jammed into a few blocks' space. Visit the See Yeah Chinese Temple, the city's oldest, tucked in among the shops and alleys off Jalan Rodger near the Central Market.

Pineapple Hill (Bukit Nanas), a forest reserve right in the middle of KL, is served by a fleet of barrel-shaped gondola cars carrying visitors up its 750-foot slope in two minutes. You can enjoy a view of the city en route and from atop the hill and then come down the other side. Facilities here include a handicraft center, a walk-in aviary, jungle walks, and a restaurant.

Lake Gardens, a mile west of downtown, is the setting for a collection of stunning buildings: the modern white Parliament House; the National Monument, a massive bronze sculpture honoring Malaysia's freedom fighters; and at the south end, the National Museum (Muzium Negara).

Largest of KL's 33 public greens, Lake Gardens offers twin lakes surrounded by rolling manicured lawns, neat flower beds, and natural forest. Malaysians stroll among the trees, enjoy weekend lawn picnics, row boats on lake waters, and rendezvous with loved ones on Saturday nights.

Parliament House, at the northernmost edge of the lake, houses the Senate and House of Representatives in a large, white rectangular building, overshadowed by an 18-story office block. When Parliament is in session, visitors may obtain passes to the public gallery.

National Museum (Muzium Negara), on Damansara Road at the south entrance of the gardens, deserves a visit of several hours for studying the displays depicting Malaysian life styles. Huge mosaic murals, representing the history and crafts of Malaysia, form the building's facade.

One of the most stunning buildings in Kuala Lumpur, the museum has a fascinating history. During the single Japanese air raid on the capital during World War II, the original National Museum was the only building totally destroyed. Industriously and imaginatively, KL's planners have rebuilt it as a major city attraction.

The National Museum is open daily from 9:30 A.M. to 6 P.M., except on Fridays when it is closed between noon and 2 P.M.

National Art Gallery, on Jalan Ampang, northeast of the central district, has an excellent collection of works by Malaysian artists. Its exhibition hall also frequently displays works by international artists. Admission is free; the hours are Monday through Sunday, 10 A.M. to 6:30 P.M. It is closed on Friday from noon to 2 P.M.

Day-long excursions

Out toward the jungle-clad hills yet still within the city, you'll find the residential area called Kenny Hill (dubbed the Beverly Hills of KL) and, further on, the planned satellite city of Petaling Jaya. The

Giant top spinning—a rural Malaysian sport

Spinning tops *attract gallery of locals and visitors on the peninsula's east coast.*

What the western world considers a children's game is often adult recreation in other parts of the world.

To the rural Malays, top spinning is a highly skilled sport taking years to master. Though sizes and shapes of the "toy" vary, the largest tops are found in Trengganu and Kelantan.

Competitive top spinning follows the rice harvest, when men and youths have leisure time for contests which may last all day. Village festivals were once spontaneous events, but since the advent of towns and two rice crops yearly, most festivals are arranged through local recreation departments. As in the past, most festivals occur at local playing fields and are announced by gongs and drums.

Among the contests are "knock out," in which one team tries to topple the tops of their opponents, and "long spinning," the object of which is to see who can spin a top the longest time. To the east coast farmer, hurling spinning objects is an excellent excuse for a lively village get-together.

latter, merging with the 700-acre University of Malaysia campus, began as a low-cost housing area 20 years ago but is now an industrial center and high-priced suburb.

Since the countryside is never far beyond the city, sidetrips to Batu Caves, Mimaland, the zoo, and Templer Park provide glimpses of village life, rubber estates and tapping processes, and even some tin mining dredges at work.

Batu Caves, 8 miles north of KL on the road to Ipoh, is a 400-foot limestone outcrop featuring a series of vast caverns. It's a 272-step climb to a shrine in one of the caves (or a short ride by funicular railway if the temperature and humidity seem too much). The recently opened and newly explored Dark Caves, forming a part of Batu, has a quarter-mile, two-way footpath to guide you through the limestone caves. Colored spotlights dramatically highlight the limestone and crystal formations.

Near the Batu Caves, you'll find an art gallery exhibiting statues based on Hindu mythology and culture.

The caves are open to visitors from 9 A.M. to 6 P.M. daily except Wednesday.

Each February, Batu Caves is the scene of the Thaipusam—one of the most important festivals of Malaysia's Hindu community. On festival morning thousands of devout Hindus climb the 272 steps to the shrine cave. Penitents stagger up the steps in a trancelike state carrying heavy tongue, chest, and back-piercing *kavadis* (metal skewers) to the shrine, where priests remove the pins of torture.

Mimaland (Miniature Malaysia), located 11 miles from KL on the road to Kuantan, contains gardens of native plants and jungle trails. This 100-acre complex offers recreational facilities for swimming, boating, hiking, golf, hunting, and fishing. A shopping arcade sells local arts and handicrafts.

Overnight accommodations are available in motel units or in *bagans*—stilt houses built over the water. The 30-acre lake contains a floating restaurant featuring both eastern and western cuisine.

National Zoo, 8 miles southwest from KL on the road to Ulu Klang, covers 42 acres of tropical jungle. The zoo and its peaceful green gardens encircle a small lake. You can view a cross-section of Malaysia's wildlife—brightly plumed birds, wild buffaloes, tapirs, crocodiles, gibbons, pythons, tigers—and wildlife indigenous to other lands. An aquarium contains tropical and fresh-water fish. Children will enjoy riding on the elephants, camels, and ponies. For refreshments or lunch, the Lakeview restaurant is nearby. The zoo is open from 10 A.M. to 6 P.M.

Templer Park, some 14 miles from KL on the North-South Trunk Road, is a retreat of tumbling cascades, towering trees, and green hills rich in native flora and wildlife. The park is named after Sir Gerald Templer, who wanted to bring the jungle to the city. You'll find well-marked hiking trails and lagoons for swimming.

Rubber plantations and tin mines form the basis of Malaysia's prosperity, and you can see rubber plantations along the main roads out of KL. On the road to the zoo, about 5 miles north of the city, you pass through a plantation. By 6 A.M. each day, tappers start their rounds, tapping the latex from

Water jet *bombards tin outcroppings in placer-type mining of country's main mineral export. Pipeline carries ore sludge uphill for processing.*

the neatly lined-up trees. Around 11 A.M. they return, collect a full cup of white latex from each tree, and bicycle or walk to the factory where the latex is processed into rubber sheets.

Opposite this rubber plantation and along the road to Batu Caves, you can see large open pits of tin dredging. The world's largest open-cast mine is located at Sungei Besi.

Penang, pearl of the Orient

The evergreen island of Penang, Malaysia's principal holiday resort, marks the northern end of the Strait of Malacca. Located two miles off the northwest coast of Peninsular Malaysia, Penang is a small, hilly, tropical island—just 15 miles long and 9 miles wide. A 46-mile-long road encircles the island, skirting between green jungle and golden sand beaches broken by rocky promontories.

Penang is known for its miles of beaches edging calm blue waters, a multiracial population, varied temples and mosques, and good shopping. Year round temperatures range from 74° to 90° F. during the day, and nights are unexpectedly pleasant.

In people and scenery, Penang is a miniature Malaysia. Of its almost 800,000 people, more than half are Chinese; the remainder are Malays, Indians, and Europeans. Each group has stamped its ethnic imprint on Penang's architecture, style of dress, cuisine, and life style.

George Town, the busy port-city, occupies the island's northeast corner, facing the mainland town of Butterworth. Highest point on the island is 2,270-foot Penang Hill, southwest of George Town; you ascend by funicular railway.

Penang's international airport at Bayan Lepas 12 miles south of George Town, is served by daily flights on air routes between Bangkok and Singapore. The Malayan Railway has daily express service to Butterworth from Bangkok, Singapore, and intermediate Malaysian cities; from Butterworth, it is an easy 2-mile ferry ride to Penang's Weld Quay. Ocean freighters, cruise ships, and trading vessels also make frequent stops.

A British trading port

Often called Pulau Pinang (island of the betel nut tree), Penang's history was based on trade. The British settlement at George Town was founded by Captain Francis Light in 1786, mainly as a base for the China opium trade. It was Light who suggested that Penang become a free port, and he served as its first superintendent until his death in 1796.

When Penang settlement was founded, the island was practically uninhabited, except for a few Malay fishermen and Chinese and Indian traders. Within six years the population soared to 10,000 people in the British-protected port. Soon small coastal traders bypassed Dutch and other Malaysian ports in favor of Penang.

Hotels and beach resorts

For many years Penang had only one good first-class hotel in George Town (the stately, ocean front Eastern & Oriental Hotel), but recently the island has had a hotel building boom. More than a dozen city hotels are strung along Penang Road. More are located along the north shore beaches, 8 to 10 miles outside town; these hotels are particularly suited to visitors who prefer the leisurely life of sand, surf, and sun on uncrowded, palm-fringed beaches.

City hotels favored by tourists include the Ambassador, Continental, Eastern & Oriental, Malaysia, Merlin, and the Penang Hill Hotel. Of the beach hotels (more under construction), these are popular: Casuarina Beach, Golden Sands, Lone Pine, Palm Beach, and the Rasa Sayang.

Food and drink

With Penang's multiracial heritage, you're assured of a wide range of cuisines. All the hotels serve Eastern and Western dishes, but the food stalls offer the adventurous gourmet a real bargain in Chinese, Malay, Thai, and Indonesian foods. You'll find a variety of food stalls with charcoal braziers selling satay, peanuts, and fresh crabs and prawns. Local drinks include iced coconut water and *see koe th'ng*—a mixture of shaved ice, coconut milk, nuts, various jellies and additional ingredients.

Getting around the island

Island taxis are inexpensive and metered. You can have your hotel phone in advance for one or you can engage a taxi from one of the many taxi stands. Five local bus companies provide inexpensive transport around the island.

The best bargain (if you haggle) is still the trishaw. George Town's light traffic and well lighted streets make this a safe and convenient way to tour the town day and night. In Penang's version of the three-wheeled trishaw, you sit up front with the bicycle rider in the rear.

For drives around the island and extended stays, rental cars are available from several firms.

Shopping bargains

Though Penang's free port status has been modified, the island's stores and shops still offer attractive prices on transistor radios, cameras, binoculars, perfumes, and cosmetics, along with a wide variety of handcrafted Malay, Indian, and Indonesian carvings, brassware, silver, and pewter.

You can shop in hotel shopping arcades, in stores along Penang Road, or in the Tun Abdul Razak complex. Local products of Penang and Malaysia—especially batiks—are the best buys. Several batik factory showrooms are located on the island (see Around the island drive, page 89). The shops offer bargains in batiks.

One shopping area you should be sure to visit is the Pasar Malam (night market), where you bargain for trinkets or batik sarongs, sample the local foods, and enjoy watching the people. It moves to a new location every two weeks (call the Penang Development Corporation for information).

Stores displaying the emblem of the Penang Development Corporation assure you of quality merchandise at fair prices.

Penang's city-port

When Captain Francis Light and his crew landed at George Town 200 years ago, they found the green island overgrown with dense jungle and underbrush. To encourage his men to clear the land, he loaded a cannon with silver dollars and fired it into the jungle.

Today, George Town is a city of nearly a half million people. Where jungle once stood you now see Fort Cornwallis, surrounded by the green expanse of its park, and the two-story colonnaded City Hall. Bordering the fort and public buildings on the ocean side is the Esplanade, a seafront road continuing some two miles further as Gurney Drive, a spacious tree-lined road edged with mansions set behind stone walls and ornate iron gates.

Primarily a Chinese town, George Town has red-tiled roof tops, Chinese character signboards, colonial-style buildings, ornate red-lacquered temples, hundred year old mosques, and lightly traveled streets carrying trucks taxis, and trishaws. Inside a traffic circle, a clock tower dedicated to Queen Victoria softens the impact of stark, modern high-rise buildings.

Along Weld Quay, passenger ferries shuttle vacationers from the mainland. Small boats transport goods from anchored ocean-going freighters to godowns (warehouses). Further south along the waterfront are villages of the water people extending over the sea.

Within walking distance or a short drive from the clock tower are these sights:

Fort Cornwallis, guarding the northeast approach to Penang, stands on the spot where Captain Francis Light first landed in 1786. Originally a wooden structure, the fort was rebuilt of stone in 1810. You can walk the ramparts and examine the cannons that were never fired against an enemy. The fort's inner area is now a garden and children's playground.

Goddess of Mercy Temple, on Pitt Street, is a Chinese temple belonging to the street people: the noodle makers, trishaw drivers, and the housewives who shop in the markets. Amid burning joss sticks, they burden the goddess with their problems or thank her for answering their prayers.

Kapitan Kling Mosque, further down Pitt Street, is Penang's major mosque. Built about 1800, the whitewashed, red-tiled building topped by domed minarets is probably the island's finest example of Mohammedan-influenced architecture.

Khoo Kongsi (clan house), located on Pitt Street just before it ends in Cannon Square, is a miniature Chinese imperial palace surrounded by cobblestone courtyards. The clan house serves as a center for worship and welfare work for people with the same surname. Stone lions chiseled from green granite guard the entrance; the roof-beams, pillars,

British cannon at Fort Cornwallis guards Penang's offshore waters. The seaside Esplanade passes the attractive George Town City Hall.

MALAYSIA 87

Pit vipers, *coiled in branches above the vase, have entranced this visitor to Penang's Snake Temple.*

Penang's Reclining Buddha, *clothed in a golden robe, dwarfs elephant tusks on the shrine below it.*

and walls record legendary episodes carved, painted, and polished by experts from China.

Clan piers, located south of Weld Quay, are the village stilt-houses extending over the sea. Fishermen and boatmen with the same surname live here in row dwellings of plank and attap. Each clan pier is modeled after a land village, complete with its own temples, stores, electricity, and running water.

Penang Museum and Art Gallery, on Farquhar Street, has exhibits depicting the history and cultural heritage of the island. You can view a 19th century Chinese bridal chamber, a room hung with paintings and etchings, and a showcase of jeweled *krisses* (a daggerlike weapon). The Art Gallery upstairs displays batik paintings, oils, graphics, and Chinese ink drawings.

Penang Buddhist Association, on Anson Road facing the Dato Kramat playing fields, occupies a fairly modern (1929) unpretentious building. You'll find no joss-stick hawkers or paper-money burners here—prayer is the main activity. Inside the great hall is a surprising mix of Czechoslovakian chandeliers, carved tables from old China, and marble statues of Buddha and his disciples.

Wat Chayamangkalaram, a Thai temple on Burmah Lane, houses the third largest reclining Buddha in the world. Within the meditation hall of this monastery and spiritual retreat, saffron-robed monks, worshippers, and visitors are dwarfed by the 108-foot lifelike statue of Buddha.

Sidetrips from George Town

Just southwest of town, in the Penang Hill area, are several sights worth a visit.

Penang Hill, dominating the northern part of the island at 2,270 feet, provides a pleasant, cool respite from the city below—temperatures are usually 10° cooler. You ride up the steep incline to the summit by funicular railway, enjoying the unfolding view of jungle and blue sea. At each substation, tree-shaded paths wander through cool forest or gardens of private bungalows on the terraced slopes. Atop the summit you can visit a small Hindu temple and a mosque or spend a quiet night in the Penang Hill Hotel.

Kek Lok Si Temple, above Ayer Itam village outside the city limits, is the largest Chinese temple in Malaysia. Split in three tiers on the slope of a rocky hill and dominated by its seven-tiered Pagoda of 10,000 Buddhas, the temple attracts Chinese pilgrims on weekends. They stroll through the tunnel-like corridors, pray before statues in nooks and crannies, climb the hundred or so steps to the top of the pagoda, and feed the fish and tortoises in the split-level pools.

The Botanical Gardens, known as Penang's "waterfall gardens," are set in a naturally forested, bowl-shaped site southwest of town. In the Japanese-style gardens, a small stream runs beside foot paths shaded by native tropical plants and trees. Hundreds of monkeys scamper about the grounds, especially in the morning and early afternoon.

Around the island drive

The road around the island unfolds a travelogue of rubber and spice estates, coconut plantations, padi fields of rice, kampongs of Malay houses on stilts, and stretches of lovely beaches. The road is winding and mountainous at times, with occasional dirt side roads leading to remote villages on the coast or inland. Heading south out of George Town, the main sights include the following:

Tuanku Abdul Rahman Aquarium, at milestone 4 on the road south of town, displays tropical marine life found in Southeast Asian waters. Winding, one-way corridors are lined with glass-fronted tanks, housing giant Indian carp from inland rivers and spotted eels found in offshore coral reefs. The marine museum contains exhibits, models, and charts explaining the life cycle of fish and crustaceans and the development of Malaysia's fishing gear and fish products.

Outside, you'll find a combination patio restaurant-amusement park with Chinese cooks and children's rides. The aquarium is open from 10 A.M. to 6 P.M. daily except Wednesdays.

Kampong Batu Uban, a mile south of the aquarium, is one of the island's typical Malay fishing villages. Life revolves around the sea—villagers fish with nets from small boats in the early morning, sell part of the catch in town, mend nets on the beach, and repair boats pulled up under swaying palms. The fishing families live in wooden, stilt houses with many window openings; some dwellings have attached verandahs shaded by coconut trees and surrounded by flowering plants and bushes. Wives and young girls keep the compound spotless, constantly sweeping and raking the sand around the houses.

Snake Temple (Temple of Azure Cloud), at milestone 9, is an ornate building where pit vipers are lulled into a stupor by clouds of heavy incense. Reached by a flight of steps lined with refreshment and souvenir stalls, the gold-leafed, red-lacquered temple contains many of the poisonous Wagler's pit vipers. They hang from the ceiling; wrap themselves around table legs, chandeliers, candlesticks, and vases; wind through the branches of small trees; and lounge on the altar shrine. In the annex room to the right, photographers will take your photo with a "nonpoisonous" snake or two coiled about your arms or neck.

Batu Maung, on a side road about two miles from Bayan Lepas Airport, is another Malay fishing village. Further on, a small shrine marks the sacred footprint of Admiral Ho, the Chinese discoverer of Malaya. Families picnic along the beach and enjoy the Batu Maung Garden Photo Studio—reminiscent of Tiger Balm Gardens in Hong Kong and Singapore. For a few Malay dollars you can be photographed with concrete dolphins, a giant frog or ostrich, an elephant, and even a live horse.

Back on the main road and a few miles west of the airport, you pass another interesting fishing kampong; then the road bears north and inland, climbing past rubber trees and green rice fields.

Titi Krawan, about two-thirds of the way up-island, is a pleasant rest-stop, with waterfalls and freshwater pools where you can take a refreshing swim.

Batik factories, located at several points on the island circuit, offer bargains in batik material and clothing. In several batik factory-showrooms, you can watch the process from hand stamping to drying the colorful yards of fabric. The showrooms sell batik cloth, as well as ties, shirts, dresses, beach hats and bags, and even batik bikinis, at lower prices than in town.

Muka Head Lighthouse, sitting on a rocky promontory, can be reached only by a trek along the isolated beach.

Sandy beaches, popular for swimming and sunbathing, are found primarily along the northern tip of the island. Most of the beaches are secluded between rocky promontories and shaded by swaying palms. You'll pass Telok Bahang (good fishing area), Batu Ferringhi (where most of the beach hotels are located), and Tanjong Burgah.

Most of the beaches are uncrowded; some have hotels and restaurants. On a day trip you can stop at one and use its changing and showering facilities, go swimming, water-skiing, skin diving, or horseback riding on the beach.

From Batu Ferringhi the road returns to town along the coastline, dipping down to small, rock-edged beaches and climbing over low headlands.

West coast islands

During the 1800s, pirate strongholds on Malaysia's Pangkor Island and in the Langkawi group pro-

Trees shade *fishermen repairing their boats at Kampong Batu Uban. You can visit Malay fishing villages on Penang's around-the-island drive.*

vided safe havens for sea-faring bandits. Little has changed here over the intervening years. The people still live in fishing kampongs perched on stilts above the water, depending on the sea for their livelihood.

But now, these same islands with their isolated beaches and protected coves lure visitors looking for a peaceful holiday resort away from the mainstream of other travelers. Calm waters invite skin diving and swimming; sandy beaches offer sun bathing and shell collecting.

Langkawi

The 99-island Langkawi group lies off the north coast of Kedah within sight of Thailand. The only developed island in the group, itself called Langkawi, offers jungles rich in wild orchids, colored cliffs, waterfalls, black sand beaches, blue lagoons, birds, butterflies, and brilliant flowers. You reach the island by ferry from Kuala Perlis, Kuala Kedah, or Penang.

Pekan Kuah, Langkawi's main village, sits along the beach about a mile from the concrete jetty where ferries and small trading boats unload. The town has a Government Rest House, two small hotels, a post office, and a few shops. Just south of town, sprawled over a 100-acre site along the beach, is the Pulau Langkawi Casino & Country Club. This international tourist complex has a 100-room Malaysian-style hotel with resort facilities, including a golf course and water sport opportunities.

Sixty miles of paved island roads pass through a countryside of rubber plantations, padi fields of rice, thick jungles, fishing villages, and isolated beaches. Pine-shaded, white-sand beaches can be found at Tanjong Rhu, on the northern side of the island. At Kampong Pantai Kok, boats can be rented for the hour-long ride to view the famous waterfalls at Telaga Tujoh.

Pangkor

Off the peninsula's west coast about midway between Penang and KL lies Pangkor Island, where fishing, swimming, and sailing are the main resort activities. Reminders of its pirate stronghold days are the jungle-covered stone walls of a 200-year-old Dutch fort and the coat of arms of the Dutch East India Company chiseled on a nearby rock.

Pangkor Island is presently reached via Ipoh, capital of Perak, a 2½-hour drive north of KL (40 minutes by air). From Ipoh it's a pleasant 56-mile drive through rural Malaysia to the river town of Lumut and from there a 40-minute ferry trip to Pangkor.

Presently two hotels—the Seaview and the Pantai Puteri Dewi hotels—and a small Government Rest House provide the island's accommodations. Most overseas visitors prefer the 55-room Pantai Puteri Dewi, sprawling on a large coconut plantation facing the Strait of Malacca. Its chalets and

---

The Sultanate of Brunei—oil-rich and independent

Only a handful of tourists a year visit the tiny, oil-rich Sultanate of Brunei, an independent British protectorate on the northern coast of Borneo. Tourism is not promoted—because it isn't really needed. Since oil was discovered in 1929, the country has been economically self-sufficient (there isn't even an income tax).

Golden dome of mosque dominates Kampong Ayer, the water village in Brunei's capital.

Brunei's riverside capital of Bandar Seri Begawan (formerly Brunei Town) is only a two-hour flight from Kuala Lumpur or a pleasant half-day stopover between Kota Kinabalu and Kuching. You might hear Texan or English accents in Seria, Brunei's oil city.

Sandwiched between the states of Sabah and Sarawak, Brunei today is a mere remnant of the large and powerful state that once controlled all of Borneo and the southern Philippines. Related to its neighbors by history, culture, and religion, Brunei has had a long tradition of independence. Its present ruler descends from a family of sultans who have ruled the country for 28 generations.

Life centers on the mosque. Five times a day the muezzin calls faithful Muslims to prayer from his high minaret perch on the Omar Ali Saifuddin; the mosque's gold-leafed dome dominates the city skyline. Other sights include the Brunei Museum, Churchill Memorial Aquarium, Royal Ceremonial Hall, the Mausoleum of Sultan Bolkiah, and the Jerudong Animal Farm.

From the capital, the major sidetrip is to the water town at Kampong Ayer. You travel by covered boat through the winding water streets. In the early morning, market boats paddle along the waterways from one street of pile-supported houses to the other.

Rubber tapper *makes a precise, diagonal cut in the tree, allowing the milky latex to flow.*

Seremban State Mosque, *on the road to Malacca, sits amid Lake Gardens, a favorite weekend recreation area.*

Malay-style bungalows curve along a mile-long beach of golden sand. Green headlands rise at either end of the beach, assuring a calm surf.

The around-the-island road from the Pantai Puteri Dewi to fishing villages on the east coast provides easy access to smaller Emerald Island lying just south of Pangkor. Skin divers and coral hunters prowl its offshore waters.

South of Kuala Lumpur

Endless vistas of forest, rice lands, and evergreen rubber plantations characterize the Malay Peninsula south of Kuala Lumpur. If you can spare two or three days—or longer—for a road trip between KL and Singapore, you can see some of the country's best rural landscapes and visit Malacca, one of Malaysia's oldest and most interesting cities. This stretch of countryside reveals homey aspects —native farmhouses and old towns hinting at a colorful history.

The most scenic route through this area is the West Coast Highway south from KL to Singapore —via Seremban, Port Dickson, Malacca, and then inland to Johor Baru. You travel about 250 miles over good, dust-free macadam roads by bus, rent-a-car, or chauffered car with driver-guide.

You can take along a box lunch from your hotel, make a lunch stop in Seremban, or buy fruit and satay from roadside stands and carts en route.

Towns to explore

Seremban, 42 miles southeast of KL, is the state capital of Negri Sembilan. Reminiscent of the quiet Malay villages once sprinkled across the state, Seremban is a typical Malay-Chinese town that sprang out of the tin mining boom 85 years ago. Set in a valley, the town's one main street is made more interesting by a maze of cluttered arcades and tiny alleys. On the hillside above town old colonial buildings house local government offices. Places worth a visit include an ultramodern mosque, the Lake Gardens, and the museum. In the gardens, you can see a traditional old Malay house built without nails, typical of the area.

Port Dickson, one of Malaysia's most popular seaside resorts, is located about 25 miles south of Seremban. Here you'll get your first view of the sea, framed by pillars of coconut trees. Coastal beaches of yellow sand (or sand and pebbles) curve 11 miles south to the old Rachado Lighthouse.

Basically a one-street town with a slow-paced harbor, Port Dickson's main attractions are its miles of beaches, the 16th century Portuguese lighthouse, and the nearby archeological dig at Pengkalan Kempas. You'll find beach houses, motels, and hotels scattered for six miles along the coast.

Malay kampongs

Thirty-five miles down the coast toward Malacca, you enter some of the richest rice country in Malaysia. Stately rubber trees give way to rice fields, coconut plantations, and numerous kampongs. Wooden Malay houses, inevitably shaded by coconut palms and other trees, perch on stiltlike foundations above neatly-swept, hand-packed earth yards. Numerous glassless windows let the breezes through the houses, creating a "see-through" effect. Often the houses are decorated with carved-wood

MALAYSIA **91**

Malacca's "river of history" *still flows leisurely through the ancient town. Four hundred years ago, great battles were fought here.*

Monks pray *in Malacca's Cheng Hoon Teng Temple, the oldest in Malaysia. Many of its stones came from China as ballast on ships.*

Red clock tower *attracts townspeople to the center of historic Malacca. Salmon-colored Christ Church stands in the background.*

Portuguese fish seller *offers his catch in Malacca's Portuguese settlement two miles south of town.*

pillars, elaborate front steps faced in colored tiles, cheerful window hangings of checkered fabric or coarse lace, and a profusion of flowers. A photo stop usually brings out curious children, who giggle and pose or shyly peek at you from behind a protective building or tree.

Historic Malacca

Sightseeing takes an historic turn in Malacca, a city lying 96 miles south of Kuala Lumpur and 155 miles north of Singapore. Before Columbus discovered America, China had trade agreements with Malacca, capital of a small Malay kingdom founded in 1402. A succession of European rulers governed this historic seacoast town; as a result, it is noted more for its churches than its mosques or temples. Though the Muslim faith entered Malaysia through Malacca, the city was also the home port of St. Francis Xavier on his missionary journeys through Southeast Asia.

A seafaring legacy

For centuries Malacca was the rendezvous port for sailing ships from many seafaring nations. Located on the Malacca River at the junction of the maritime route linking the Indian Ocean with the South China Sea, Malacca stood where the monsoon winds converge. Ships carrying the rich spices of the East—camphor, cloves, nutmeg, and sandalwood—unloaded in Malacca; silks, carpets, and porcelain were brought in from India and the Middle East. European merchants called at this port to purchase the riches of the Orient.

Once the greatest city in Southeast Asia, Malacca today has a medieval air, with narrow streets, quaint old buildings, and an often-bridged river cutting through its center. At the river quay where romantic square-rigged sailing ships once traded in exotic spices and silks, you'll now see cargo lighters loaded with charcoal and freight from offshore vessels.

Hotels and bungalows

Accommodations in Malacca range from small city hotels and government rest houses to beachside motels. Even though Malacca retains an air of being off the beaten path, you should make advance reservations.

Of the eight or so hotels and motels in Malacca, tourists favor the Shah's Beach Motel, with its chaletlike bungalows and swimming pool, and the government holiday bungalows and chalets. All are on the beach road west of town.

Malacca's shopping street

Jalan Gelanggang (formerly Jonker Street) is Malacca's most interesting street and shopping area. Its overflowing sidewalks are lined with shops, offering everyday items and unusual gifts. Here's where you'll find the cobbler and rattan furniture maker, the coffin shop and Chinese temples, antique and apothecary shops, wood carvers and metal craftsmen.

Specialties made from local wood include canes and intricate woodcarvings, all at reasonable prices. The signs along the street are in English, Chinese, Malay, Tamil, and Thai.

A look at old Malacca

The best place to start your tour of Malacca's historical sights is the Town Centre. As you cross the Malacca River bridge, you'll see the neat little square with its red stucco clocktower, salmon-colored Stadthuys, Christ Church, and—off to the right—the Malacca Tourist Information Office. Professional scribes (like Chinese letter writers) set up tables to hold their antiquated typewriters and send messages for those who never learned to read or write.

Stadthuys, believed to be the oldest Dutch building in the Far East—built between 1641 and 1660—has thick walls, massive hardwood doors, and studded wrought iron hinges. Now used for government offices, it once housed the Dutch Governor.

Christ Church, between Stadthuys and the post office, was built during the same period. Its pink bricks were shipped from Holland and faced with a local red clay by Malacca masons. Tombstones within the church tell a history of hardship and early death from disease.

Off Banda Hilir Road, east of the Town Centre, you'll find the following historical sights:

St. Paul's Church, overlooking the town from Residency Hill, was the burial place of St. Francis Xavier before his body was removed to Goa. Built in 1590 by the Portuguese, the church stands in ruins. Its interior is lined with Dutch tombstones, and the tower today is a lighthouse. In front of the church stands a statue of the saint.

Malacca Museum, housed in a 300-year-old Dutch building, contains exhibits covering the state's history—Portuguese costumes, Dutch weapons, Malay swords and shields, and British cannons. You can visit between 9 A.M. and 5 P.M., but no photographs are allowed within the museum. Across the street is the City Cross, erected in the 16th century and designating Malacca as a Portuguese colony.

Porta de Santiago, a single gateway, is all that remains of the old Portuguese fortress "A Famosa." Built in 1511, the fort withstood attacks until a Dutch bombardment in 1641 and destruction by the British in 1795.

St. John's Fort, built as a chapel, was converted to a fort by the Dutch. Steps leading to the top were once guarded by cannons. From here you can see the Strait of Malacca, the city, and the hillside Chinese cemetery on Bukit China.

Portuguese settlement, two miles out of town, houses about 600 descendants of the Portuguese. Their blue and green painted Malay kampong houses contrast sharply with the natural woods of the Malays. On the beach, you'll still find fishermen mending nets and repairing small boats as their forefathers did.

Bukit China (China Hill) on the northeast side of Malacca, forms one of the largest Chinese burial grounds outside of China. Weather-eroded gravestones and several preserved graves of Chinese nobles cover the slope.

Sultan's Well (Perigi Rajah), at the base of Bukit China, is probably the oldest well in Malacca. Legend has it that if you toss a coin into the well and drink of its water, you'll return to Malacca before you die. These days the well is screened for sanitation reasons, but the water is served by the cupful in the adjacent Poh San Teng Temple.

St. Peter's Church, on the road north to the airport, is the Church of the Portuguese Mission under the Bishop of Macau. Built in 1710, the church is a mixture of Eastern and Occidental architecture. Inside, you'll find a life-size reclining figure of Jesus Christ, beautiful stained glass windows, and several old tombstones.

Back across the Malacca River bridge, on the western side of town—and before heading for the beaches at Tanjong Kling six miles away—are three more interesting sights:

Cheng Hoon Teng Temple, on Temple Street in the center of Chinatown, is the oldest Chinese temple in Malaysia. Constructed in the 17th century by craftsmen from China, the intricately carved temple has hardwood roof ridges and crossbeams decorated with mythical figures, inset with colored glass and painted porcelain. Stone courtyards surround the temple on four sides.

Sri Poyyatha Vinayagar Moothi Temple, on Goldsmith Street, is Malaysia's oldest Hindu temple. The Indian community built it in 1781 and named it for Vinayagar, whom they believed could remove all obstacles. He is worshipped by all Hindus who ask his aid in business, marriage, and death.

Tranquerah Mosque, on Jalan Tranquerah Road behind a wrought-iron gateway, was built in typical Sumatran architectural design. For 150 years the foot-worn floor has born the weight of Malacca's Muslims, many of whom repose in the graveyard beside it.

For golfers

Eight miles from Malacca, at Ayer Kroh, is the 18-hole Ayer Kroh Country Club. The 6,988-yard championship course is laid out in a setting of lakes, rolling hills, and tall trees.

Sidetrip from Malacca

A 30-mile trip inland from Malacca takes you to Mount Ophir—called Gunung Ledang in Malay—the mountain with a legend. Its cone-shaped summit seems much higher than 4,187 feet because it rises so abruptly from the lowland rubber plantations. According to legend, the mountain is the home of a fairy princess.

From the road near its base you can wander through gardens of tropical flowers and fruit trees and alongside clear pools of water brightened with silver and gold fish. Hikers wishing to try the trail to the summit should allow about five hours for the trip.

South to Johor Baru

The coastal road dead ends about a hundred miles south of Malacca, but Singapore-bound traffic turns inland at Batu Pahat to pick up the main north-south route. From Malacca south, you pass rubber plantations, rice fields, and Malay farm houses set back from the road.

Malaysia's southernmost town is Johor Baru; it serves as the gateway to Singapore, to which it is joined by a causeway. You first see Johor Baru, backed by a row of hills, from the long coastal road sweeping into this seaside town along the Johor Strait.

Atop one hill is Bukit Serene, the Sultan's private residence; its 106-foot tower is a city landmark, offering vistas of Singapore and the surrounding seas. Looking east from this point you see the Istana Gardens enclosing the Sultan's Palace. You can visit the palace from 9 A.M. to noon except on Fridays and public holidays. Nearby is the Johor Zoo, once the Sultan's private game reserve. Farther along the road, high on a hill, stands the Abu Bakar Mosque—a spacious building lined with marble colonnades and large enough to hold 2,000 worshippers. Just before you reach the causeway, you'll see the fortresslike old colonial government offices.

About 25 miles northeast, less than an hour's drive, the Kota Tinggi Waterfalls provide a favorite picnic area with self-contained chalets, eating stalls, and a restaurant.

Malaysia's east coast

Separated from western Malaysia by a rugged mountain chain, the peninsula's eastern seaboard is a land of sandy beaches, thick jungles, Malay villages, and many offbeat sights for the adventurous traveler. Here you may see adult farmers competing in top spinning and kite flying and giant turtles lumbering across lonely beaches to lay their eggs. The more popular destinations on the east coast—from south to north—are Kuantan in the state of Pahang, Kuala Trengganu in Trengganu, and Kota Bharu in Kelantan.

On this quiet side of Peninsular Malaysia, the people are predominantly Malay, and Islam dominates their daily lives. Life in the kampongs moves at an unhurried pace, and the beaches are quite deserted, except during fishing and turtle seasons. Curved prow boats with bright coats of paint rest on sandy shores. In many sleepy villages, going to

Giant Kelantan kites *are works of art. When airborne, they make a tuneful humming sound.*

Malay fishing villages *border the country's east coast; livelihood comes from the sea.*

market is the most exciting event. Traditionally dressed women deal with hawkers selling coconuts, yams, bananas, bamboo shoots, and other jungle and marine edibles.

The east coast also has many lovely islands to visit and miles of narrow jungle roads to follow. Temperatures average 76° to 85° F. during the dry season from February to April—the most pleasant time to visit.

Traveling to the coast

From Kuala Lumpur you can reach Malaysia's east coast by air (the three main towns) or by railway (to Kota Bharu), but it's road travel that reveals the best of the coast. If you leave KL early in the morning, you'll drive over a winding mountainous road across colorful Genting Pass and arrive in Kuantan—162 miles away—in time for lunch.

From Singapore and Johor Baru, you can drive up the east coast via Mersing all the way north to Kota Bharu. An east-west highway, now under construction, will connect Butterworth with Kota Bharu. A selection of small hotels and other modest accommodations is available in each of the three main towns and nearby beach areas.

Kuantan's beach world

The capital of Pahang, Kuantan (population 38,000) is the center of a beach world. Accommodations are available at the Kuantan Merlin, Hotel Kuantan, Hotel Samudra Kuantan, and the Titik Inn. All accommodations have dining room facilities.

Besides its beaches, Kuantan offers other touring possibilities. By prior arrangement, villagers perform *wayang kulit* (shadow plays), top spinning, *bersilat*, the Malay art of self defense, and *rodat*, the traditional fishermen's dance. Handicraft centers to visit include a batik block printing center and demonstrations of *kris* (dagger) making and straw weaving. At Sungai Ular you can hire a boat for a 15-minute cruise to the uninhabited tropical island of Pulau Ular.

For daytime sports, skin diving is best near Kuantan in April and May and again in September and October. Golfers are welcome at the nine-hole Royal Kuantan Golf Course.

Animal watchers can see crocodiles in the Cherating River on the coast between Kemanan and Kuantan, and you can visit a turtle nursery at Chendor Beach, 32 miles north of Kuantan. If you want to experience typical village life, some villages on the Cherating River are willing to accommodate visitors.

Kuala Trengganu

In Trengganu, the state just north of Pahang, you'll find many more miles of sandy white beaches.

East coast fishermen *mend their nets on the palm-fringed beach at Kota Bharu. Visitors can bask on the area's uncrowded beaches and shop for superb woven fabrics and batik at local shops.*

Taman Negara *National Park is accessible only by river craft or light plane. Visitors travel along jungle trails or by small river boats. Overnight accommodations are available in a rest house*

Kuala Trengganu, the capital of the state, offers all the typical activities of the east coast. The area has several hotels and motels.

Along Trengganu rivers, you can see Malay houses clinging to the banks and witness traditional rural life. Inland from the coast are orchids, rice fields, jungles, mountains, and waterfalls. Sekayu waterfall, 35 miles west of Kuala Trengganu, is known for its cool mountain air and natural swimming pools.

Kota Bharu

Only a few miles from the Thai border, Kota Bharu, capital of Kelantan, is the northernmost town on the east coast. The city is best known as a good shopping center for arts and crafts, especially batik and silver.

Other attractions include the market square, mosques and minarets, and a fantastic strand known as the Beach of Passionate Love.

East coast islands

All along the eastern seaboard lie a scattered and broken chain of lovely islands, many of which are only beginning to become tourist destinations. Just offshore from Mersing, in the southern state of Johore, are Tioman and Rawa islands. Tioman, whose prominent features are twin peaks on its southern shore, offers good skin diving in its clear offshore waters. Delightful accommodations are provided at the Merlin Samudra Hotel. Pulau Rawa has about a dozen chalets for guests.

In the north off the Trengganu coast are Pulau Perhentian and Pulau Redang, two quiet, friendly islands noted for swimming and skin diving around the coral reefs. Perhentian has a rest house. Both islands are accessible from Kuala Trengganu.

Peninsular Malaysia's national park

River roads cover the 1,677 square miles of Taman Negara National Park, a vast virgin rain forest on the east side of the dividing range. Rich in animals, birds, and insect life, the preserve offers a memorable look at Malaysia's tropical wildlife and plants. On the western edge of the park is the peninsula's highest peak, 7,184-foot Gunung Tahan.

From Kuala Lumpur your best route to the park is through Kuala Lipis (about a 5-hour drive). Here you'll transfer to a river boat; the 5-hour river trip should be started early in the day so you can arrive at park headquarters before nightfall. A rest house with cottages provides park accommodations.

Throughout the park are salt lick hides, designed for day and night close-up viewing of big game. Animals that sometimes come within photographic distance include elephants, tapirs, sambars, tigers, barking deer, black panthers, and wild dogs.

Insular Malaysia

On the northern rim of the island of Borneo, are the states of Sabah and Sarawak. Separated by the South China Sea from Peninsular Malaysia, and closer to Manila than to Kuala Lumpur, these two states are not areas of instant spectacle and entertainment.

This part of Malaysia is sparsely settled, its landscape characterized by jungle-covered mountains and swampy, river-cut lowlands. Main towns and regional centers of business and government are Kota Kinabalu (formerly Jesselton) in Sabah and Kuching in Sarawak. Night life and cultural events are not readily available.

Like Peninsular Malaysia, Sabah and Sarawak are multi-racial. Malays, Chinese, and Europeans mix with the varied indigenous people of the island —such as the Ibans and Bidayuhs—many of whom retain distinctive ways of life, housing, and dress.

You can fly in to Kota Kinabalu and Kuching from Kuala Lumpur and other cities, or you can board a ship of the Straits Steamship Company in Singapore for a leisurely journey.

Weather

Insular Malaysia possesses an unvarying, equatorial, hot-and-humid climate, with temperatures in the 72° to 88° range. Afternoon showers occur regularly; evenings are somewhat cooler. The months from February through April are generally drier (and the best months to visit). The northeast monsoon brings rain to the coast from October to February, but the region's inland areas receive their heaviest rainfall from April to October.

Kota Kinabalu

Sabah's Kota Kinabalu is a compact seafront town built along a narrow strip of hill-backed land facing Gaya Bay. A string of coral islands dots its natural harbor. During World War II the town was almost completely destroyed, but it has been rebuilt as a well-planned capital.

Kota Kinabalu is an easy town to explore on foot. The downtown area has plain multistory, concrete buildings lining streets planted with trees and shrubs. Many fine homes rise on the woodsy hillsides behind the town. Along the shore, Malay villages are built on stilts over the water or tidal flats.

Of Kota Kinabalu's seven hotels, those most favored by tourists are the Capital, Ang's Hotel, and Kinabalu International, all located along the seawall; Jesselton, in the center of town; and Borneo, 3½ miles southeast of town on a beach.

City sights. The central market and transportation center are the busiest areas of Kota Kinabalu. Hawkers and shoppers, wreathed in the smoke from stands of charcoal-cooked beef satay, spill out over the street near the seafront. Good market buys include woven baskets and mats, brass gongs, native hats, and tropical fruits. Many of the sellers and colorfully dressed shoppers arrive by launch

Colorfully printed batik *is hung out to dry. Later, this distinctive fabric will be made into shirts, blouses, hats, bags, bikinis, and dresses*

To see the Sabah countryside, charter a rail car

An interesting way to see the countryside south of Kota Kinabalu is on a rail car trip. The Sabah State Railways maintains 96 miles of track serviced by rail cars (a snub-nosed, 15-passenger bus on rails). The line passes through unusual jungle terrain and along scenic rivers, terminating in Tenom. A group of five or more passengers can charter a rail car any day.

On an hour's trip, the rail car passes through jungle and along rivers to the small river town of Papar. A 45-minute stop allows you time to poke about a shop or two and people-watch (the Kadazan girls in this area are considered among the most beautiful in Sabah). Sunday is the big market day in the country.

For a longer look at the countryside, especially on market day, you can charter a rail car and arrange for a Malay feast and entertainment (check with the Sabah Tourist Association in Kota Kinabalu).

The regular rail car continues from Papar on to Tenom (a 4-hour trip) through a series of spectacular gorges. This is the heart of the Murat country.

from outlying islands, docking at the seawall.

On a short tour around town, you can visit a small museum, take a short drive to the beach area at Tanjong Aru (good swimming except when jellyfish are in season), stop to see the flowers at Prince Philip Park, and ride a boat across the harbor to visit lovely Gaya Island. Sports-minded visitors will find a yacht club, golf course, and monthly pony races at the Sabah Royal Turf Club.

A lively country market

The main countryside excursion from Kota Kinabalu is the full-day trip to Kota Belud for viewing Mount Kinabalu and visiting the *tamu* (Sunday market).

From padis, plantations, and forests, the rural people come to town, dressed in their traditional finery for a day of fun and games. On market days a field is laid out with open-front stalls or impromptu arrangements of produce and handicrafts. Suddenly it comes alive with color and activity—bartering of produce, bargaining for water buffaloes, handicraft exhibits, folk dancing, cockfights, buffalo races. Colorful Bajau cowboys, renowned for their horsemanship, occasionally demonstrate riding skills and dexterity.

Kinabalu National Park

Southeast Asia's highest peak, 13,455-foot Mount Kinabalu, dominates Kinabalu National Park, a 265-square-mile wilderness area ranging from mossy rain forest to subalpine scrub. Most visitors are content to view the mountain from afar, but the mountaineer wishing to challenge this once revered "place of the dead" can make arrangements in Kota Kinabalu.

From the city it's a 58-mile jeep ride or a 25-minute flight to the town of Ranau, followed by a 15-minute jeep ride to park headquarters. The base camp at 4,500 feet has a hostel, restaurant, and visitors' cottages and cabins.

Next morning a short jeep ride takes you to the 6,000-foot level where the climb starts. Terraced stairs cover the first 2,000 feet. You'll find aluminum shelter huts spread out about every 2½ hours' walk, the last one at 12,500 feet, an hour from the summit.

For the less ambitious, paths are provided through certain areas where you can enjoy the natural setting. April and May are the best climbing months.

Sarawak's Kuching

Sarawak's state capital, Kuching, spreads out along the north and south banks of the Sarawak River, some 20 miles inland from the South China Sea. Kuching is a picturesque old city with an interesting mixture of people and architecture; it offers unusual tour possibilities.

Most of Kuching's half dozen hotels have air conditioning and dining rooms, and some have nightclubs. Most tourists stay at the Aurora, Borneo, Longhouse, or Odeon hotels, or at the Holiday Inn.

The main part of town is located on the south bank of the river. Here, you'll find the government offices, State Mosque, churches, temples, wharves, and dockyards. On the riverfront you can see the law courts, including the Supreme Court Building erected by the second Rajah in 1874. Bold and imaginative local art forms were incorporated in its roof panels, door, and window grills.

On the north bank stands the State Capitol, the former White Rajahs' Palace, and an old fort. But Sarawak's real fascinations are the story of the last of the white rajahs, the Ibans (Sea Dyaks) and their unique longhouses, and the Niah Caves with human bones more than 50,000 years old.

White Rajahs' reign. Sarawak's history has long been romanticized by tales of three "White Rajahs" (rajah means prince or king), members of an aristocratic English family who ruled the area for 105 years.

The first Rajah, James Brooke, arrived in 1839. He was a British adventurer with a knack for exploring and pirate-fighting. By 1841, after settling rebellions and driving off the enemies, he became ruler of an uncharted land famed for its headhunters. The family reign continued with his nephew, Rajah Charles Brooke, and Charles' son, Charles Vyner.

Sir Charles Vyner Brooke, the last white rajah, enacted a new constitution in 1941 as a move toward self-government. After the Japanese occu-

Bajau cowboys *are one of the sightseeing attractions at Kota Belud, where they demonstrate their horsemanship upon caparisoned mounts.*

Kuching, *Sarawak's capital, follows the banks of the Sarawak River. Fishing boats work the nearby South China Sea.*

Kota Kinabalu, *Sabah's capital, appears clean and modern today. The city was severely bombed during World War II.*

White Rajahs' former palace, *now the official residence of the Governor of Sarawak, graces the river's north shore in Kuching.*

Sunday Market *at Tuaran, south of Kota Belud, finds turbanned women bartering for fruits and vegetables under the midday sun.*

MALAYSIA 99

pation, Sarawak became a British colony in 1946. Less than 20 years later—in 1963—it joined the Federation of Malaysia.

Kuching sights. You should allot at least two days to see Kuching and its environs. Your stay should include visits to the excellent Sarawak Museum (well worth a longer look); the State Mosque; the architecturally modern, open-air St. Joseph's Cathedral; the settlement of Malay stilt houses; and the open-air markets and street bazaars.

If time permits, you can climb aboard a river launch and cruise down the Sarawak River to an interesting fishing village near the river's mouth. In the north part of town, you can see the former White Rajahs' Palace and nearby Fort Margherita. You can obtain special permission to cross the river for a closeup look at the palace, now the Governor's residence.

The Sarawak Museum houses a collection of artifacts including indigenous tools, fine weaving, carving, burial paraphernalia, and an exhibit on Stone Age excavations from the Niah Caves. Several rooms of a longhouse have been recreated allowing you to see inside a Land Dyak house. On the museum grounds, the Sarawak Arts Council has a display of native crafts—carvings, masks, weavings, baskets, mats, and ceremonial items—made by the various tribal groups. Each item sold carries a warranty from the museum curator testifying to authenticity of style, form, and material used.

Sarawak's longhouses

Out-of-town excursions offer an opportunity to see pepper and rubber plantations, and you can arrange to visit a Dyak longhouse.

Within a half day's road trip from Kuching, you can visit a longhouse of the Bidayuhs (Land Dyaks). To see a Sea Dyak longhouse, you take a 30-minute flight from Kuching to Sibu (Sarawak's second largest town), followed by a day's excursion by motorized longboat on a tributary of the Rejeng River. The Ibans actually live along interior rivers.

The longhouses are communal villages under one roof, some housing more than a thousand people. The Dyaks live much as they did centuries ago. Many of them—men and women alike—are heavily tattooed and have drooping earlobes extended by heavy weights. Men wear their hair in a traditional cap cut, short in front and long in back. Barebreasted women are still evident in many villages.

You can even arrange for an overnight stay in a longhouse (men sleep on the verandah and women inside). In the evening you are entertained by the *ngajat*, a dance traditionally performed after a successful head-hunting expedition.

Festivals and events

Malaysia's many ethnic groups and religions celebrate an exciting variety of festivals and special events throughout the year. Each group lives by its own annual calendar, celebrating according to their traditions and religions. Chinese, Muslim, and Hindu festivals fall on varying dates of the Western calendar, so you'll have to check with the Tourist Development Corporation of Malaysia for the exact dates. The following list covers some of the country's major celebrations.

Hari Raya Puasa. Held on the first day of the tenth month in the Mohammedan calendar, this day of prayer, feasting, and visiting marks the end of a month-long Muslim fast.

Chinese New Year. Chinese families decorate their houses, dress in their colorful best, visit Buddhist temples, and celebrate with feasting and fireworks (see page 13).

Thaipusam. Hindu devotees honor the birthday of Lord Subramaniam by carrying *kavadis*, wooden frames decorated with flowers and skewers that are pinned into the back and chest of the carrier. Main celebrations take place at the Waterfall Temple in Penang and at Batu Caves outside Kuala Lumpur.

Birthday of the Deity of Chor Soo Kong. Annual February celebration at Penang's Snake Temple.

Goddess of Mercy Birthday. In Kuala Lumpur, Penang, and Malacca, Chinese temples dedicated to the goddess are the scene of celebrations, including theatrical shows.

Hari Raya Haji. Muslims throughout Malaysia celebrate their *haji*, the pilgrimage to Mecca, with mosque services and home entertaining.

Mauloddan Nabi. This national holiday marks the birthday of Prophet Mohammed (see page 13).

Wesak Day. Held in May, this countrywide event commemorates Lord Buddha's birthday with re-

Land Dyaks *perform native dances for visitors on a day excursion from Kuching. Traditional dress is worn only in the rural parts of the country.*

Practical information for visitors to Malaysia

To help in trip planning, here are some important details you will want to know:

Entry requirements. Citizens of the United States and other countries recognized by the Malaysian government do not need a visa for a visit of three months or less, but you must have a valid passport to enter Malaysia.

You will need an international health certificate showing inoculation against smallpox. If you are arriving from an infected area, cholera and yellow fever shots are also required. The U.S. Public Health Service recommends that you have cholera, typhoid, paratyphoid, tetanus, and gamma globulin shots. If your plans include a jungle safari, check with your doctor for antimalarial treatment.

Arriving visitors must present a clean general appearance, and male visitors must have hair no longer than shoulder length.

You pay an airport tax of about U.S. $3 on departure at Kuala Lumpur.

Customs. You may bring in one quart of liquor, 200 cigarettes, and a half pound of tobacco or cigars. If you enter with too many cameras, watches, or other expensive items, you may be required to post an import duty deposit, refundable on departure with the items.

Currency. The Malaysian dollar is the unit of currency, and the rate of exchange is U.S. $1 to M $2.40. You are allowed to import and export M $500. Money can be converted at any bank or licensed money-changer. Hotels charge a small fee to change money.

Traveler's checks and credit cards are accepted at hotels, restaurants, and stores in the larger cities. Have your passport handy when cashing traveler's checks.

Health conditions. Hospital and medical services are good, with many English-speaking doctors. Medicines and toiletries are available at many large hotels and drug stores throughout the country. In most large hotels, the water is safe for drinking; in the country, use boiled water.

Tipping. Throughout the country, tipping is not encouraged. Major hotels and restaurants in the cities add a 10 percent service charge to your bill. At air, rail, or ship terminals, tip M $1 for one or two bags. Taxi drivers normally do not expect a tip; if you have a number of bags, prepare to tip M $0.10 per piece.

Climate. Malaysia is warm, but it's not as hot as its position near the equator suggests. Days are sunny and very humid; nights are fairly cool. The best months to visit Malaysia are from February through October.

Average temperature in the lowlands ranges from 72 to 90°F. It's cooler in the hill country, at elevations from 2,000 to 5,000 feet, with temperatures between 50 and 70°. Although the country has no marked wet or dry season, short downpours occur throughout the year. Malaysia's heaviest and most frequent rains fall from July through December.

For more information. Your best source on travel in Malaysia is the Tourist Development Corporation of Malaysia, MPI, Wisma Building, P.O. Box 328, Kuala Lumpur; or their U.S. office at 600 Montgomery Street, 36th Floor, San Francisco, CA 94111. Offices of Malaysian Airline System are located in Los Angeles, New York, Chicago, and San Franciso. Consulates are located in San Francisco, Los Angeles, and Honolulu; the embassy is in Washington, D.C. In Kuala Lumpur, the U.S. Embassy is located in the A.I.A. Building on Jalan Ampang.

Special note. Some attractions charge an additional fee for visitors carrying cameras.

---

ligious rites and lantern processions at temples in Kuala Lumpur and Penang (see page 13).

Kadazan Harvest Festival. This Sabah holiday in May celebrates a successful harvest with a traditional ceremony and dances (see page 12).

Gawai Day. Several traditional Dyak festivals are combined on June 1 for Sarawak festivities and dancing.

Feast of the Hungry Ghosts. Chinese ancestors traditionally return to earth for one day to visit their descendants. Paper money, fruit, and other offerings are burned in small fires to appease the ghosts of the ancestors.

National Day. August 31 is a public holiday marking Malaysia's birth as a nation. It is celebrated in the principal cities and towns of the country with parades, music festivals, and outdoor shows.

Festival of the Emperor Gods. One of the biggest Chinese festivals, it reaches dramatic peaks at Penang—a procession winds up Pava Terubong Hill to the temple to celebrate the heavenly return of the nine celestial kings—and at Ampang Village, 5 miles outside Kuala Lumpur, where a fire-walking ceremony is featured.

Deepavali. The Hindus celebrate the victory of Lord Krishna over an enemy (see page 13). The day begins with prayers at the temples, followed by visits to friends and relatives. At night, Hindu homes are lighted by oil lamps.

Pesta Pulau Pinang. During the month of December, George Town holds a water carnival with speed boat races, marathon swimming, and dragon boat races.

Modern office buildings and hotels soar skyward overshadowing the harbor's sampans **(top)**. Chinese letter writer **(right)** does a steady business on Sago Street. Sidewalk stall **(far right)** offers Chinese noodles and prawns.

Singapore

A dazzling showplace of Asian progress

Waves of progress have rolled across the island and city-state of Singapore, leaving in their wake a dazzling, modern city with towering office blocks and new hotels set in a garden paradise. The "new" Singapore is most evident as you drive along the tree-lined highway from enlarged and modernized Paya Lebar Airport, and along Orchard Road with its huge shopping complexes and impressive array of modern hotels. Dozens of skyscrapers, clustered at the harbor's edge, appear heavy enough to flip the island over into the sea.

Singapore has counterbalanced its building boom by remaining an attractive and open parklike city. A series of government enforced programs have transformed sidewalks, gas stations, traffic circles, and public squares into miniature parklands with flowering and fruit-bearing trees and shrubs. This vale of green sweeps through the city like a flood.

Beneath its western facade, Singapore is strongly oriental, one of the largest Chinese cities outside China. Its intermingling races—Chinese, Malay, Indian, and a smattering of Eurasians and other minority groups molded into an amalgamation of Singaporeans—touch most of Asia's peoples and cultures. Yet each group maintains enough of its own customs and life styles to give Singapore a special magnetism.

Within the city, vestiges of a colonial past remain: Victorian-style government buildings, a cricket club, an esplanade, street names. Yet around countless corners or a few minutes into the countryside, Singapore's Asian and multiracial aspects zoom into sharp focus—Buddhist and Hindu temples, crowded Chinese shophouses and colorful markets, streets of Indian shopkeepers and moneylenders, *kampong* stilt houses in forest clearings, and roadside fruit stalls.

Because Singapore thrives on commerce, its free port provides shoppers with a bargain center for southeast Asian handicrafts and the world's products. On any given day of the year, hundreds of ships—from 200,000-ton supertankers to old tramps to water taxis—ride at anchor.

The island reigns as a showplace of Asian progress. Vast industrial estates rise on drained swampland, impressive low-cost housing estates loom across the island, and its population enjoys the second highest standard of living after Japan.

Although the island is known as a city-state, Singapore City occupies only about a quarter of the island. Low hills and coral reefs mark the western shore; sandy beaches line the eastern boundary. The island's highest point, 581-foot Bukit Timah (Hill of Tin), rises above a central plateau surrounded by reservoirs and forests. Elsewhere, the island supports rubber and coconut plantations, vegetable farms, and orchards.

In the past decade, satellite towns, built on the neighborhood principle, resettled people away from the burgeoning city center to towering housing units in the less developed areas of the island. About two-thirds of Singapore's 2.3 million people reside in these high density blocks, mainly to preserve Singapore's open parks, reservoirs, and watershed areas.

Modern development and industrialization, urban renewal, and satellite towns have changed Singapore more in the past five years than during the preceding 140 years after the island was ceded to the British.

Singapore—then and now

The island republic of Singapore, once a British colony, lies at the southern tip of Malaysia at the narrow end of the Strait of Malacca. West of Borneo, and east of Sumatra, Singapore is dwarfed by its neighbors but gains significant stature from its strategic location along world trade routes, its vast harbor, and its free port.

Only 85 miles north of the equator, the republic consists of a tropical island (209 square miles) and about 54 islets. Singapore's total area covers about half the area of Los Angeles. A road/rail causeway reaches ¾ of a mile north across the Johor Strait, linking the island to the Malaysian state of Johor.

An island of low, undulating hills, Singapore reaches 26 miles from west to east and extends 14 miles from the strait to the island's southern tip. The city of Singapore covers the south side of the island, arcing around a 36-square-mile harbor. Some 40,000 ships visit the busy waterfront each

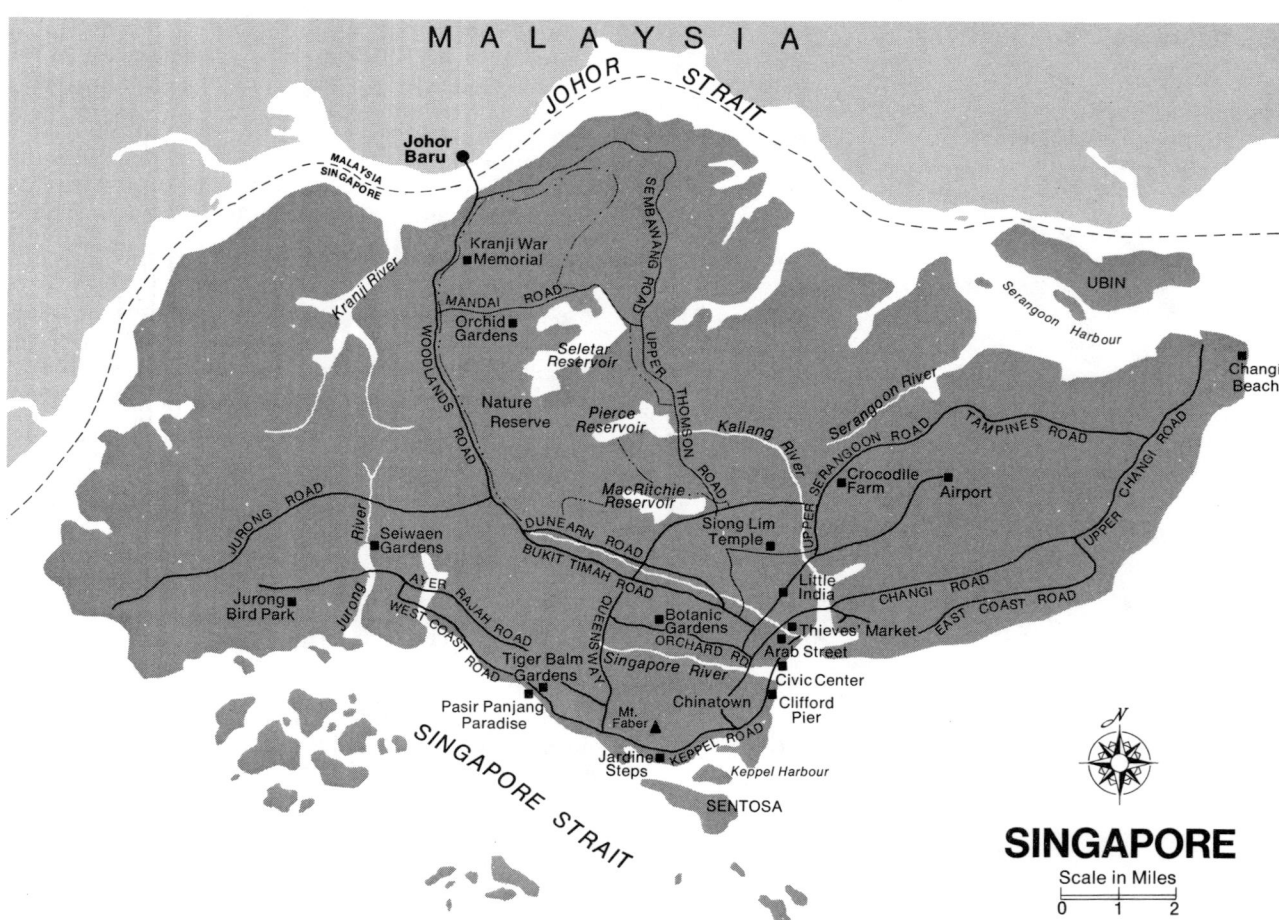

year, making it the fourth ranking shipping port in the world.

Olde Singapore

When Sir Stamford Raffles landed near the mouth of the Singapore River in 1819, jungle and swamp covered the island. In those first months, a thousand men (mostly Indian convicts) worked at clearing the dense vegetation.

The oldest part of the city, near the river's mouth, follows Raffles' planning scheme: a grid pattern of streets with the main roads running parallel to the harbor and secondary roads crossing at right angles.

During the first years, thousands of men from the Middle East and Asia flooded the trading center, and each ethnic group was allotted space. The Arabs and Bugis settled the area between the coast, Rochore River, and the outlying swamps. The Chinese concentrated in the area south of the Singapore River, forming what became Great Chinatown. Early Indian traders clustered along the river's south bank, near what became Chulia, Market, and High streets. Malay fishermen lived on boats or built stilt houses over the water. For more than a hundred years, population remained densely concentrated near the harbor and river, and visible traces of their existence remain today.

Colonial rule to nationhood

Even before the Christian era, Singapore's history was closely allied to trade. Malay sea gypsies (Orang Laut) and pirates visited the island first, followed by Chinese traders. By the 4th century, Arabs sailed into Singapore harbor en route to the Molucca Islands in eastern Indonesia. Later, Chinese Buddhists and monks arrived.

In the 8th century, the island—known as Temasek (Sea Town)—became part of the flourishing Hindu-Sumatran kingdom of Sri Vijaya. During this era its name was changed to *Sing Pura*, Sanskrit for the City of the Lion. This later evolved to the name Singapore.

The town was destroyed in the 14th century, when Majapahit's powerful Hindu-Buddhist-Javanese state eradicated the rival Sri Vijaya kingdom. Even today, Malays claim that Singapore's laterite clay takes its red color from that bloody massacre.

Colonial rule. Singapore's modern era dates from 1819, when the British East Indian Company established a trading post at the mouth of the Singapore River. The legendary Sir Stamford Raffles (see page 107) immediately declared Singapore a free port; he set up a code of law and established trading regulations, a town-planning scheme, a magistracy, and a police force.

Five years later, the Sultan of Johore ceded Singapore—together with nearby islands—to Great Britain in perpetuity, along with Penang and Malacca (known as the Straits Settlement). Singapore became a British Crown Colony in 1867.

Throughout the 19th century, emigrants from

Sir Stamford Raffles' *statue overlooks a landscaped plaza at the mouth of the Singapore River, near the spot where he stepped ashore in 1819.*

India settled in Singapore, competing as merchants and shopkeepers with the already well-established Malays and Chinese.

Independent republic. At the beginning of World War II, the Japanese attacked across the Johor Strait. Singapore surrendered in 1942 and was occupied by Japanese troops until 1945, when it was returned to British control.

In 1959 Singapore became an internally self-governing state within the British Commonwealth. Four years later, it joined the Federation of Malaysia; but in 1965, Singapore separated from Malaysia, becoming an independent sovereign state. Since that time, though, the two countries have maintained defense and trade ties.

On December 22, 1965, Singapore became a republic headed by a president.

Parliamentary democracy

Singapore's parliamentary system of government is based on full adult suffrage with voting compulsory for every citizen 21 years of age or older. A speaker, elected by parliament, presides over the 69-member parliament. Although Malay is the national language, parliament members also may address the body in Chinese (Mandarin), Tamil, and English; simultaneous translation is provided.

Elected for a term of four years, Singapore's president appoints a prime minister who advises him on the selection of 12 cabinet members. No local city government exists in Singapore. The judicial power of the republic is vested in the Supreme Court and several lower courts.

Singapore's people

Like Malaysia, its sister-nation to the north, Singapore's multiracial population is a melange of Chinese, Malay, Indian, and other ethnic groups, though most citizens consider themselves Singaporeans. Large segments of the population still follow traditional customs in dress, religion, and festivals.

Singapore's population now exceeds 2.3 million people. More than 76 percent are Chinese, mostly Straits Chinese (second and third generation Chinese born in Singapore). Malays account for 15 percent, Indians and Pakistanis for another 7 percent, and Eurasians make up most of the balance.

Dress. The varied and colorful clothing worn by its people emphasizes Singapore's multiracial society. Most men wear western-style clothing: white shirt, dark trousers, and sometimes a jacket and tie. Some of the hotel doormen appear as resplendently garbed and turbaned Indian Sikhs. In Chinatown, men wear a white T-shirt with baggy pants; trishaw drivers favor loose-fitting shorts with their T-shirt, and some sport pith helmets.

But it's Singapore's women who display the brightest costumes. Though many women wear the latest western fashions, a large number still prefer their national dress. Malay women wrap themselves in the *sarong kebaya*, a long skirt with transparent blouse. Indian women glide through the markets dressed in flowing *saris*.

Chinese shoppers appear in tightly fitted *cheongsams*, slit to the thigh, buying goods from other Chinese women wearing the *sam foo*, a loose-fitting tunic and trousers. Around the city, construction sites harbor another breed of women, called *Sam Sui*. Working as laborers, they belong to a Chinese celibate order; you can recognize them by their costume of red headdress, similar to a nun's, and dark blue tunic and trousers.

Language. Many residents—particularly the younger generation—speak several languages and dialects. Though the official language is Malay, English is used as the language of commerce and administration.

In government schools, parents may choose to have their children instructed in any of four recognized languages—Malay, Chinese (Mandarin), Tamil, and English. Virtually all of the educated people of Singapore speak English.

Religion. Most Chinese are Buddhist, Taoist, Confucianist (often a mixture of all three), or Christian. Most of the Malays are Muslim. Indians follow the Hindu or Muslim faith.

Tropical plants and wildlife

Until 150 years ago, Singapore was covered with thick vegetation. Tropical forest concealed nearly two-thirds of the island, and mangrove swamps edged the coast.

Today, the island's only remaining virgin forest is the 163-acre Bukit Timah Nature Reserve, marked by its three artificial lakes. The mighty leopards and tigers that once menaced jungle workers are now extinct, but numerous smaller animals and reptiles still survive, including mouse deer, flying lemurs, flying squirrels, and porcupines.

Among the most commonly seen birds are the yellow-vented bulbul, pied triller, tree sparrow, crows, and doves.

Some 2,000 species of plants flourish on the tropical island. In the forest you can spot a scattering of delicious exotic fruit—durian, breadfruit, mangosteen, and mango. Coconut and rhu trees are found both inland and along the seashore.

Roadside flowers, such as blue giant thunbergia and yellow black-eyed Susan, bloom year round. Singapore rhododendrons and orchids are also common; the Botanic Gardens contain some 500 orchid species.

Though crocodiles have disappeared, water monitors (up to four feet long) can still be found in watershed areas. The chichak—the tiny gecko-like house lizard—will be seen clinging to suburban Singapore ceilings and walls.

Singapore's surrounding waters abound in marine life: prawns, lobsters, crabs, fish, oysters, and green turtles.

Chinatown's streets *are a kaleidoscope of colors and sounds; here locals can buy fresh vegetables, a tasty snack, or new shoes.*

Getting there and getting settled

Easily accessible by air, sea, and land, Singapore lies almost 8,500 air miles west of the United States—a trip requiring about 18 hours from California. The time difference is 15½ hours between the U.S. west coast and Singapore. When it is 8:30 A.M. Tuesday in Singapore, it's 5 P.M. Monday in California.

Some 25 international airlines, including Singapore Airlines, serve the country's Paya Lebar Airport, one of the world's most attractive and modern facilities. Singapore is a regular port of call for many passenger ships and freighters.

Serving as the southern terminus of the Malaysian Railway, Singapore is linked by daily trains to Malaysia's capital of Kuala Lumpur and Butterworth (Penang). The International Express travels from Singapore to Bangkok, Thailand, three times a week, with passengers changing trains at Butterworth, Malaysia's northern border station.

City and island transport

Singapore's complex street pattern, originally planned during the 1800s for pedestrians and bullock carts, may be somewhat confusing to the newcomer; streets and alleys have been converted to one-way traffic. Vehicles move faster—if not always in a straight line. You can choose from many kinds of transportation: taxis, buses, private hire cars, trishaws, and bicycles.

Taxis operate day and night. Metered taxis are black and yellow or solid blue-grey (all have SH on their license plates). Fare for the first kilometer is S $0.30; each additional kilometer costs S $0.20. If three or more persons share a taxi, each extra person pays an additional S $0.10. You can also rent a taxi by the hour.

The Singapore Bus Service (SBS) provides bus transportation over a network of roads that crisscross and circle the island. Fares start at S $0.20 and are collected by a conductor. For timetables and information on routes and fares, consult the Singapore Tourist Promotion Board (see page 123).

Your hotel or travel agent can arrange for a rental car or a hire car and driver. Traffic keeps to the left. If you plan to drive, you'll need an International Driver's License.

The trishaw (bicycle with sidecar) provides leisurely paced transport through the city's narrow streets, especially in Chinatown. Fare is S $0.40 per kilometer, but establish the price before you roll off.

Sir Stamford Raffles—foresighted shaper of Singapore

One man's foresightedness, political shrewdness, and administrative ability propelled Singapore from a swampy fishing village to an independent republic. The man: Sir Stamford Raffles, who founded Singapore in 1819 as a trading settlement and free port.

Raffles' early career proved uneventful, giving no promise of his later fame. Born the son of a thriftless sea captain in 1781, he started as a clerk for the East India Company at the age of 14. After spending ten years educating himself, Raffles joined the governor of Penang (Malaysia) in 1805 as an assistant secretary. During the sea voyage to his first foreign post, he taught himself Malay. After his arrival he learned the Malays' history, customs, and traditions and studied the peninsula's plant and animal life.

Eventually the Governor-General of India appointed him as special political agent for the Malay states. After Java's conquest in 1811, led by Raffles, he became that island's lieutenant-governor.

During the ensuing five years, Raffles established a name for himself in administration; he exercised this same ability and energy at his next station, in Bencoolen, Sumatra, in 1818.

After a period in England, where he was knighted by King George IV, Raffles returned to Southeast Asia. With permission from the Governor-General of India, Raffles set off to establish a station that would guarantee the southern entrance of the Strait of Malacca and provide a supply base on the India-China trade route.

On January 28, 1819, he anchored off Singapore with two East India Company warships. Being aware of the Johore family succession dispute over Singapore and knowing the Sultan of Johore was pro-Dutch, Raffles recognized the elder brother Tengku Long as the legal ruler and made him the sultan of the island. On February 6 they signed an agreement allowing the East India Company to establish a supply station at the mouth of the Singapore River.

Though Raffles visited the settlement only three times—for a total of nine months—during the next four years, the plans and arrangements he made and enforced decided Singapore's future. Within two years the settlement generated enough income from trade to pay for its existence.

But Raffles died from a brain tumor in 1826—unrewarded. During his last years, the East India Company made some heavy monetary demands on him and harrassed his widow for all past debts. For many years England remembered the man buried in Hendon Courtyard only as the founder of the London Zoo.

It was left to Singapore to recognize Raffles' role in shaping the country's destiny. His statue (see page 105) stands at the mouth of the Singapore River, a silent tribute to the man and his ideas.

Harbor tours (by sampan or motorboat) leave from Clifford Pier. Water tours of the harbor and adjacent islands can also be made by motorized/sail Chinese junks. Several companies operate morning, afternoon, and evening tours.

Hotels and more hotels

In the past few years, Singapore's hotel count has boomed. Modern structures have soared skyward; hotel building has moved away from the waterfront. In a few years, the number of hotel rooms has increased tenfold, with ample accommodations available in a wide range of prices. Singapore's grand old lady, the Raffles Hotel, should remain on the scene for years to come; the hotel, renowned for its old-fashioned elegance, was recently designated an historical landmark.

Singapore's "hotel row"—Orchard Road—was formerly a nondescript boulevard. Now, burgeoning hotel construction is attracting shopping centers, banks, airline offices, and commercial headquarters.

Most Singapore hotels provide standard international facilities; many also offer swimming pools, health clubs, shopping arcades, and group facilities. All tourist hotels add a three percent government tax, and most impose a 10 percent service charge.

Among the numerous large tourist hotels located along or near Orchard Road are the Phoenix Singapore, Mandarin, Hyatt Singapore, Goodwood Park, Holiday Inn Singapore, Singapore Hilton, Singapura Forum, York, Ming Court, Ladyhill, Shangri-La, and Marco Polo; further north are the Royal-Ramada and Equatorial hotels. Cockpit and Oberoi Imperial hotels are located between Orchard Road and the business district.

Near the Civic Center, major tourist hotels include the large Peninsula Hotel. The Apollo, Miramar, and Kings hotels are located in a residential area south of the Singapore River. Popular smaller hotels are the Grand Central, Bencoolen, Orchid Inn, Negara, Metropole, and Queens.

Dining and entertainment

You'll find foods representing a fascinating array of national cuisines in Singapore, making the city a diner's delight. In addition to Chinese food you can sample dishes from Malay, Indonesian, and Indian cuisines. Japanese, Russian, and European restaurants also abound. You'll want to take an evening stroll through at least one of the open-air restaurants where vendors set up their pushcarts and peddle popular local dishes. For more on Singapore's varied cuisines and restaurants, please turn to page 118.

If you want a night on the town, you can choose from nightclub entertainment, theater revues, or dancing to live rock music. Or you can join the Singaporeans at an amusement center or night bazaar. Music and dance programs offer glimpses of Malay, Chinese, and Indian culture (see page 121).

Duty-free shopping

As a duty-free port, Singapore offers bargain shopping for goods from all over the world; most imported items—as well as local products—are duty-free. It's still the practice to bargain, except

Duty-free *cameras, watches, and electronic goods, often cheaper than in their country of origin, are sold in Singapore's shops and stores. You can bargain in smaller shops (but know your prices).*

Workman polishes *a gleaming pewter tray. Hand-engraved Malaysian scenes are popular decorations on pewter vases and pitchers. Many stores can also engrave your initials or family crest.*

in very large shops and department stores where prices are fixed. For shopping suggestions, obtain a copy of *Singapore—Our World of Shopping* from the Singapore Tourist Promotion Board. Shops approved by the STPB display the organization's official window decal, a gold merlion (half fish, half lion) on a circular red background.

In addition to the usual duty-free goods (cameras, watches, transistor radios, hi fi and stereo equipment), the best buys include Oriental antiques, batik, hand-loomed silks, jewelry, Malayan silverware, pewterware, and Malayan handicrafts.

Many of the city's major hotels have shopping arcades; prices are often a little higher than in other shops, but the quality and selection are excellent. Popular shopping areas include Raffles Place, High Street, North Bridge Road, and Orchard Road. Robinson's and C. K. Tang are the city's major department stores. Merchandise from mainland China is sold at Chinese Emporium stores. A vast array of goods is offered at the night bazaars *(pasar malam,* see page 112), Thieves' Market (see page 114), and Change Alley (see below).

The Singapore Handicraft Centre, a 26-unit complex of shops and demonstration areas, features handicrafts representative of many Asian countries. The center is located at the corner of Tanglin and Grange roads.

Downtown sightseeing

A walking tour provides the best way to savor Singapore's luxuriant greenery, its Victorian buildings, and its tropical weather cooled by sea breezes. A three-hour stroll, beginning in the city center, allows plenty of time to visit sights along the way and browse through the shops.

Before beginning your walk, however, get your bearings and enjoy a panoramic look at the city and its harbor from the observation lounge atop the Mandarin Hotel on Orchard Road. Take along a map to help you locate city landmarks.

Merlion Park and Change Alley

Merlion Park, at the tip of a promontory on the south bank of the Singapore River, offers a splendid harbor viewpoint before you stride forth on your city walking tour. Centered around a 26-foot, water-spouting merlion, the landscaped park offers benches overlooking the busy harbor.

From the park, walk south, crossing Collyer Quay by Clifford Pier. Continue along the waterfront to Change Alley, a famous lane lined with motley shops selling everything from pots and pans to cottons and silks, from handicrafts to antiques (some real, some instant).

Change Alley received its name from the Indian money changers who congregated here yelling "money change." These walking, gesticulating bankers are still legal money changers, but check their rates.

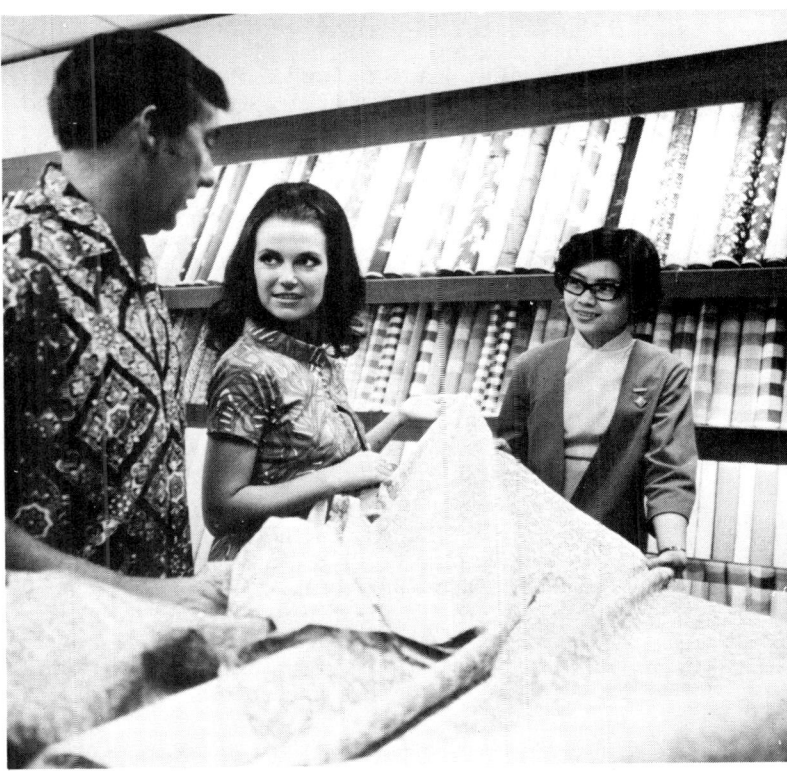

Chinese Emporium *offers a wide selection of fabrics, porcelains, household items, handicrafts, and other merchandise from mainland China.*

Malaysian weaving *is demonstrated at the Singapore Handicraft Centre. The complex's shops sell a variety of Asian handicrafts.*

Raffles Place and the civic center

Change Alley leads to Raffles Place and Park (a pedestrian mall), heart of city-state Singapore and one of the busiest commercial districts. Shops and department stores nudge banks, law firms, and shipping companies; tiny side streets lead to old-style offices of import and export houses, dealers in tin and rubber. While modern Singapore now overlays most of the old colonial atmosphere, some of the city's Victorian past lingers here in street names and turn-of-the-century buildings.

Heading north across Raffles Place, walk toward one of the two bridges crossing the Singapore River near its mouth. On your left, where the river widens inland, is Boat Quay, mooring place for a welter of junks, sampans, and launches that carry cargo to and from ships anchored in the harbor.

The north bank. Along the river's northern bank is Empress Place, named in memory of Queen Victoria and dominated by a statue of Sir Stamford Raffles (see page 105), commemorating his nearby landing site. North of Empress Place are the attractive civic center—City Hall, Victoria Memorial Hall, Parliament House, the Supreme Court—and St. Andrew's Cathedral, spaced amid wide lawns dotted with trees.

Some of the buildings in the civic center overlook the beautifully maintained greens of the Padang (plain), where for more than a century Singaporeans have played cricket and enjoyed the sights and sounds of passing parades. Weekend matches at the Singapore Cricket Club add a strong British flavor.

At the northwest corner of the Padang stands St. Andrew's Cathedral, seat of the Church of England in Singapore. The Gothic-style cathedral, circled by traffic on four sides, is surrounded by a large lawn shaded by tropical trees. Indian convicts completed work on the cathedral in 1863.

Along Queen Elizabeth Walk

To enjoy a leisurely seaside stroll, cross Connaught Drive on the Padang's east side. Continue across the Esplanade, once the tenting ground of English and Indian troops, until you reach Queen Elizabeth Walk. This half-mile-long expanse of trees, flowers and benches follows the water's edge within view of the ship-filled harbor. Here you can breathe deeply of sea air, mingle with Singapore's strollers, and perhaps watch an itinerant snake charmer.

At the far end of the Esplanade, bordering Connaught Drive, you'll find the sprawling Satay Club (see page 121)—a collection of stalls selling satay and other local dishes. A block further north, where Connaught Drive curves into Beach Road, the famous old Raffles Hotel provides a pleasant excuse to stop and relax with a Singapore Sling, another old Singapore favorite.

King George V Park

The rolling green lawns of King George V Park, marked by flowerbeds, shade trees, and neat walkways, provide a garden setting for the Van Kleef Aquarium and the National Theatre. River Valley Road borders the park on the south, while Clemenceau Avenue provides the western boundary. Overlooking the scene is Fort Canning, once the site of Raffles' bungalow; in 1895 the house was armed with cannons and the area was renamed Fort Canning Hill.

National Theatre. Built in 1963, the starkly modern building provides a striking setting for theatrical and musical performances. The theater is actually an amphitheater built against a sloping hill. Check the *Weekly Guide* issued by the Singapore Tourist Promotion Board for current performances.

Van Kleef Aquarium. Set back from River Valley Road among the park's trees, the aquarium contains more than 4,600 specimens of marine life, ranging from sea anemones to octopuses and king crabs. The aquarium is open daily, including public holidays, from 9:30 A.M. to 9 P.M.

Several other sights are located near the park:

Chettiar Hindu Temple. One block west on Tank Road stands the Chettiar Hindu Temple, built in the 1850s by Nattukkotai Chettiars (moneylenders). The temple is dedicated to the six-headed Indian god, Lord Subramaniam.

If you can, visit the temple during the Hindu religious festival of Thaipusam; at this time, processions of penitents, skewered with needles and blades, congregate here (see page 122).

Armenian Church. The oldest Christian church in Singapore is the Armenian Church on Hill Street; its proper name is the Armenian Apostolic Church of Saint Gregory the Illuminator. Only 12 Armenian families lived on the island when the church was built in 1835.

Although the Armenian congregation is dwindling, the handsome church, shaded by lofty trees, is being preserved as an historic landmark.

National Museum. Located in a white, two-story, domed building on Stamford Road, the National Museum was started in 1823.

Although originally the museum was small, a new art gallery and theater have been added to the complex. Here you can see a good collection of Indonesian and Bornean ethnology (houses, brasswork, burial jars, weapons, implements). Check the local newspapers for current theater performances. Visiting hours are 9 A.M. to 5:30 P.M. weekdays, 10 A.M. to 1 P.M. Saturdays.

The ethnic communities

Singapore's major ethnic groups tend to congregate in their own sections of the city. Chinatown is one of the largest in Southeast Asia; many of the older generation maintain old China's mode of dress and way of business.

The Indian population will be found on Serangoon Road, and settlers from the Middle East have set up their shops on Arab Street.

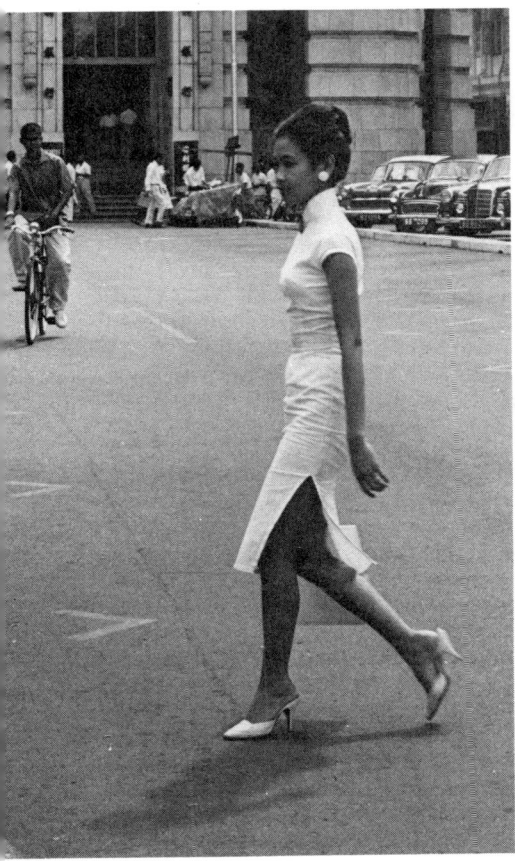

Queen Elizabeth Walk, *inviting with its trees, flowers, and benches, follows the water's edge and offers views of the ship-filled harbor.*

Exotic dress styles *reflect Singapore's cosmopolitan population. This young Chinese woman wears the distinctive* cheong-sam.

Singapore's Padang, *backed by the domed Supreme Court and the columned City Hall, provides a refreshing green expanse and play field.*

St. Andrew's Cathedral, *erected more than 100 years ago, stands on a grassy, tree-shaded corner of the Padang.*

SINGAPORE

Provincial Chinatown

Chinese laborers, merchants, and traders began gravitating to Singapore in the 1820s, and today 76 percent of the island republic's population is Chinese. They developed the area south of the Singapore River as a Chinatown, retaining provincial characteristics with people of specific trades living on certain streets.

Over the years this "Great Chinatown" spread inland and north across the river, creating "Little Chinatown." The square mile of Great Chinatown, containing some 100,000 people, provides a quick glimpse into the past and present. The area extends south from the Singapore River, bounded by Anson Road and Telok Amoy Street on the east and New Bridge Road on the west.

Shophouses. Hundred-year-old shophouses, two and three stories tall, line the narrow streets of Chinatown. Once these shophouses served as spacious working and living quarters, but since they first appeared in the mid 1800s, they have been divided and subdivided. Today uncounted numbers of people crowd into curtained-off rooms, some people renting beds by the night.

The first floor of a shophouse usually serves as the family business area: coffee shops, coffin makers, sheet metal workers, wrought iron fabricators, noodle shops, and fish sellers. Awning-covered street stalls display rolls of cloth and batik, squealing pigs and gasping fish, glazed candies, bunches of fragile flowers, unusual meats, and pans of sizzling seafood.

Market places. To submerge yourself in high-pitched voices, exotic sights and smells, brightly colored merchandise, and tasty foods, stop at the market place on Trengganu Street, bounded by Smith Street on the north and Sago Street on the south. Here the locals can buy anything from fresh fruits and vegetables to plastic laundry baskets.

A contrast now emerges from the old face of the city—the new air-conditioned People's Park shopping complex on New Bridge Road. A pace setter with more than 350 shops and 70 offices, the complex has 28 stories. Here, from 10 A.M. to 10:30 P.M., you can rub elbows with Chinese shoppers in a variety of shops, restaurants, and emporiums.

Don't forget to visit the restored and renovated Old Telok Ayer Market on the street of the same

---

Singapore's night markets—portable, open-air bazaars

When evening sea breezes fan the streets, Singapore residents and visitors often head for the open air. Every night of the week, lorries and pushcarts rumble through the city, transforming parking lots, alleys, streets, and other open spaces into a *pasar malam*, or night market. These unique markets begin setting up after 6 P.M.; many stay open through the night. They provide daytime workers and night owl shoppers with their own portable "department stores," offering a vast array of goods.

On Wednesday nights you can visit the Tanglin Road pasar malam, located in a quiet, tree-lined area not far from the major hotel area on Orchard Road. But throughout the week, the market (actually several markets) moves from one neighborhood to another. On any given night they may be held in some half-dozen different sites in the city. Check with the Singapore Tourist Promotion Board (see page 123) for current market locations.

Under the glittering light cast by bare bulbs and acetylene lamps, hundreds of sellers—some noisy, others calm—vie for the shoppers' attention. Most of the sellers speak English, and haggling over the price provides part of the fun. But remember to compare prices at a number of stalls before closing a deal.

Even if you don't intend to buy anything, you'll be surprised at the range of trinkets displayed along the length of the open-air market; often the stalls continue on for a mile.

Typical goods at the market are batik-printed shirts, bolts of cloth, oil paintings, glazed China ornaments, Moorish brass candlesticks, leather sandals, shoes, slippers, plastic appliances, perfumes, toys, children's wear, linens, costume jewelry, kitchen utensils, Thai woodcarvings, bronze incense urns, and the latest records.

Youthful shoppers *gaze upon the trinkets offered for sale at the night market.*

Street "pharmacist" in Singapore's Chinatown offers passers-by a bowl of brew to cure real or imaginary ailments. Many of the residents' needs are purchased from portable stalls and carts.

Chinese hawker sells live fish from his portable market on Trengganu Street in Chinatown. Part of the fascination is watching shoppers make selections and haggle over prices.

name. Sir Stamford Raffles initiated the octagonal Victorian building, framed in cast ironwork, when he visited Singapore in 1822.

Craft streets. Certain streets shelter traditional crafts and family cottage industries. You'll find lantern makers on South Bridge and Circular roads, noodle shops on China Street, image makers on Club Street and Gemmill Lane, clog makers on Temple Street, paper-model makers and letter writers on Sago Street, fortune tellers on South Bridge Road, death houses (Chinese funeral parlors) on Sago Lane, and the itinerant storyteller by Boat Quay. The medicine man appears wherever he can gather a crowd to listen to his timeworn pitch.

Temples. One of the oldest places of worship in Singapore is the Wak Hai Cheng Bio (bio means temple) on Phillip Street. The present temple dates from 1852; the fairies, pagodas, and porcelain animal figures were added when the temple was redecorated in 1896. Formerly, a tiny shrine had marked the site since the days when trading ships on the China-Malacca run anchored here to take on water.

Chinese Hokkiens (natives of southeast China) favor the Thian Hock Keng (Temple of Heavenly Happiness) on Telok Ayer Street, identified by its granite pillars and ornamental stone work. Built in 1821, the joss house is also noted for its wooden carvings and the statue of the Mother of Heavenly Sages, brought from China by worshippers in 1840.

Narcis Street has two interesting temples. The Kim Lan Beow (Golden Epidendrum Shrine) was built in 1830; its main god is Chen Sui Chor Soo, but several lesser deities are also honored. Further down Narcis Street is the Poh Toh Temple, famed for its numerous statues of Chinese gods and deities.

The city's oldest Hindu place of worship, the Sri Mariamman Temple, is also located in Chinatown on South Bridge Street. Its much-photographed archway is a sculptural masterpiece of Hindu deities and mythical themes, depicted in brilliant colors. On festival days the temple is the scene of such ritual ceremonies as firewalking or the releasing of hundreds of pigeons.

Little India

Markets and eateries redolent of spices signal your arrival in Little India. Though only 7 percent of Singapore's residents can claim Indian descent, this minority has maintained its culture in art, dance, and literature.

Serangoon Road, center of the Indian colony, is lined with shops selling Bombay silks, Madras

Turbaned Sikh *serves as a school warden, protecting children as they cross Singapore's busy streets.*

Shopkeeper *and friends stay cool under the awning of this variety store in Little India section of the city.*

cottons, and gold jewelry. Most visible examples of Singapore's Indian heritage are its turbaned money lenders, Indian temples, and sari-clad women found throughout the city.

From Little India you can visit the Temple of 1,000 Lights on Race Course Road. The temple was named for the lights surrounding a 50-foot image of Buddha. You'll also find a footprint carved in teakwood and inlaid with mother of pearl, believed to have been left by Lord Buddha on a mountain in Sri Lanka (Ceylon).

Along Arab Street

You'll find a potpourri of goldsmiths, florists, textile tradesmen, and dealers in semi-precious stones along Arab Street, a thoroughfare linking Beach Road and the Rochore Canal Road. Every shop harbors a haggling merchant, anxious to make a quick sale.

The lofty, majestic domes of the Sultan Mosque rise on North Bridge Road near Arab Street. Built in the 1920s, it is one of Singapore's oldest Muslim mosques. Five times a day the muezzin calls the faithful to prayer with the cry "Allahu Akbar." Surrounding the mosque, tiny shops offer colorful bolts of Indian silks, sari cloth, and batiks.

North of the city

The northern part of Singapore island is surprisingly open—with stretches of virgin forest, reservoir recreation areas, and orchid gardens. You can visit Chinese temples, a crocodile farm, Singapore's zoo, and other attractions on a half-day trip north of the city.

The island road ends at the Johore Causeway, the rail and highway link connecting Singapore to the Malaysian Peninsula.

Thieves' Market

The maze of alleyways north of the Rochore Canal, from Sungei Road to Kelantan Lane, shelter a hodge-podge of several hundred shops selling everything from priceless antiques to plastic flowers and fresh fruit.

This area is known as the Thieves' Market; rumors claim an article stolen one night is offered for quick, cheap sale here the next day. Shops are open every day of the week, with action beginning about noon.

When it started about 50 years ago, the market carried only secondhand goods; now its shops offer a broad range of new goods as well. You can find army survival gear and canned peaches, Japanese cigarette lighters and rusty spanners. Some stalls specialize in brassware—ancient coal-irons, lamps, urns, and trays.

Another daily activity is the fruit auction. Hawkers stand behind their overburdened stalls, trying to attract passers-by with fantastic deals. Bargaining might start at 12 apples for S $1 and increase to 20 apples before a buyer steps forward. Fresh crabs selling for S $0.80 attract the most enthusiastic buyers, with pushing housewives usually cleaning out the stalls in less than an hour.

Soochow Gardens

Landscaping designs based on the famed ancient Chinese city of Soochow provided the inspiration for Soochow Gardens. You'll find them on the grounds of the Siong Lim Temple, the city's largest Buddhist temple, on Kim Keat Road (near the Toa Payoh Housing Estate).

Footpaths link the temple to the 2-acre gardens, where you walk under flowering shade trees, past small streams and a carp-filled pond with fountain, and across a sculptured marble bridge. At night, lights illuminate the gardens.

Inside the temple you'll see a magnificent statue of Kwan Yin, Goddess of Mercy, and other art objects.

Crocodile farm

Some 500 snapping crocodiles, imported from Indonesia and the Khmer Republic, are bred on the crocodile farm on Upper Serangoon Road. It is open to visitors Monday through Saturday from 9 A.M. to 6 P.M. An adjacent shop is filled with reptile skin shoes, bags, and belts.

Reservoirs and the zoo

From the city's outskirts, Upper Thomson Road winds north through the Bukit Timah Nature Reserve. West of the road are three large reservoirs that not only supply the island with water but have become public parks and recreation areas for Singapore residents.

MacRitchie Reservoir, nearest the city, offers peaceful walks through tropical greenery, band concerts on some Sundays, and a floating restaurant and bandstand over the water. Virgin forests surrounding Pierce Reservoir offer a safe haven for birds and flying lemurs.

At Seletar Reservoir, recreational facilities include boating and canoeing, fishing, jungle pathways, and a children's playground. Singapore's Zoological Gardens here cover 80 acres of rolling forest land; about 300 animals are confined behind water-filled moats.

A vast orchid display

Cutting through the preserve north of Seletar Reservoir, Mandai Road links Upper Thomson Road with Woodlands Road (the highway leading to the Johore Causeway). West of the reservoir, the Mandai Orchid Gardens cover about 10 acres of sloping hillsides.

You'll see both ground and climbing orchids. Dedicated orchid fanciers will enjoy visiting the seedling houses, where new hybrids are nurtured. The famous Black Orchid from Sumatra, with its four-foot-long trailing sprays, blooms in July. In September and October you'll see the Tiger Orchid, with its impressive 5-foot spikes of richly marked flowers.

The gardens are open daily. Keep your admission ticket; its value can be credited on purchases of orchid blooms, postcards, or flower seeds.

Kranji War Memorial

A hillside overlooking the Johore Strait is the site of the Kranji War Memorial, honoring those who died during World War II. Four thousand white memorial stones are arranged in a geometric pattern; a stark white, wall-less memorial honors some 24,000 who have no graves.

West of city center

Singapore's West Coast Road runs within sight of the sea, past ornate Chinese mansions and Malay kampongs. A half-day drive to the western end of the island allows time for an overview of the island from Mount Faber and a visit to Tiger Balm Gardens before you arrive at Jurong Town, an industrial estate with parklands and green belts.

To the top of Mount Faber

The green-capped heights of Mount Faber (335 feet) serve as a lookout point for views of Singapore's city skyscrapers, the ship and island-filled harbor, and nearby Indonesian islands; the mountaintop is also a favorite weekend retreat for tourists, families, and lovers.

The narrow, tree-shaded Mount Faber Road

Thieves' Market *offers an astounding variety of items old and new. The bazaar got its name decades ago, when many of the articles were stolen goods.*

Tiger Balm Gardens *contain a bewildering array of colorful figures, animals, and historical scenes—fascinating to children of all ages.*

winds up to the mountaintop viewpoint and to the station where you take a cable car to the resort island of Sentosa (see below).

Tiger Balm Gardens

Fat laughing Buddhas and bright-eyed animals greet visitors at the flamboyant Tiger Balm Gardens (Haw Par Villa) on Pasir Panjang Road, some 5 miles west of the city center. Open to visitors without charge daily from 9 A.M. to 5 P.M., the garish attraction was built primarily to advertise Tiger Balm oil, a preparation claiming to cure aches and pains.

Once through the red Chinese archway, you find yourself surrounded by giant, colorful sculptures set in a Chinese landscape. Children delight in the plaster and concrete snakes, oversized rhinoceroses, white polar bears, and Chinese mythological characters representing the joys and pains of life and death.

The daily "Instant Asia" show (see page 121) is held nearby at Pasir Panjang Paradise.

Jurong Town—parklands and industry

Singapore's largest industrial estate (nearly 7,000 acres), Jurong Town was also planned as a pollution-free recreation area. Its hundreds of factories

Across the harbor from Singapore—unspoiled Sentosa Island

To the south of Singapore, visible from the city's towering skyscrapers, the resort island of Sentosa rises from the tranquil blue sea. Its 700 acres of unspoiled beauty—rolling, wind-swept hills, narrow tree-lined roads, and a network of winding walkways—offer an enticing respite from the city's busy pace. About 2½ miles long and a mile at its widest, the island encloses the southern half of Keppel Harbor, only ¾ mile from Singapore's waterfront.

You reach this refreshing island by ferry or aerial cable car. The 10-minute trip by cable car travels from the summit of Mount Faber to the Jardine Steps on the waterfront and then swings across the harbor to Sentosa's Mount Serapong.

At the island station's information center, you can pick up a brochure and map detailing the island's natural and manmade features. Fares are about S $4 round trip from Mount Faber to Sentosa Island, about S $3 round trip from Jardine Steps to the island.

Present island attractions include a palm-shaded swimming lagoon and adjoining boating lagoon for canoes and pedal boats, an 18-hole seaside golf course, barbecue and picnic groves, a coralarium featuring displays of coral and shells, and restored Fort Siloso and its firearms museum. Overnighters can stay in a renovated colonial administration building, shaded by angsana trees and guarded by cannons.

Ongoing plans call for several modern hotels, a variety of beach cottages, restaurants, transport by horse carriage or monorail, a Malay-Chinese village featuring local handicrafts, a maritime museum, an Olde Singapore shopping center, and an amphitheater for cultural performances.

Cable cars *travel from the shady heights of Mount Faber to the resort island of Sentosa.*

Jungle-edged lakes, *tree-shaded walkways, tropical plants, and roaming monkeys await visitors to Singapore's Botanic Gardens. The orchid collection is outstanding. Grounds are floodlighted at night.*

export goods to all parts of the world. Scattered within the estate you'll find a series of parklands, largest of which is 900-acre Jurong Park. It includes a 200-acre lake with three large islands, a bird park, oriental gardens, and a recreational center for bowling and ice skating.

Jurong Bird Park. One of the most unique natural history attractions in all of Southeast Asia, Jurong Bird Park spreads over a 50-acre landscaped site. Numerous display aviaries are dominated by a vast walk-in aviary backdropped by a 100-foot man-made waterfall. The water cascades down granite rocks, then flows into a stream crossed by several bridges. Bird varieties in the 73-foot-high aviary range from the familiar to the exotic, from the tiniest owls to such giants as the flightless cassowaries, from birds of brilliant plumage to fierce-looking predators.

You can see the park's main features on a 15-minute, mile-long tram car ride. From the tram route, footpaths branch off to the various display aviaries and a restaurant. The park is open from 9 A.M. to 6:30 P.M. on weekdays, and until 7 P.M. on weekends.

Seiwaen Garden. An island in the middle of Jurong Lake has been transformed into a 32-acre Japanese-style garden. Footpaths lined with bamboo and cherry trees wind through the garden past weathered boulders, massive stone lanterns, a pair of carp-filled ponds linked by streams, a waterfall, and traditional Japanese-style guest houses. The garden is open daily from 9 A.M. to 9 P.M.

A new garden recreating the look of old China occupies the lake's northern island. Another park is planned for the lake's eastern bank; it will include part of an 18-hole golf course, with some of the course holes on the lake's third island.

Jade and botanic gardens

Two other interesting attractions lie northwest of the city center, within easy distance of many of Singapore's newest hotels. Take Orchard Road northwest to visit the excellent display of Chinese art at the House of Jade and Singapore's outstanding Botanic Gardens.

House of Jade. At the junction of Tanglin and Nassim roads, a 50-year-old mansion houses a priceless Chinese art collection of jade and quartz. Antique glass cases shelter jade pieces from the early Sung and Ching dynasties—mythical figures, dragons, phoenixes, gods, and goddesses. The house is open daily from 9 A.M. to 6 P.M. Free passes are available from the Singapore Tourist Promotion Board.

Botanic Gardens. Continuing west on Tanglin and Napier roads, you come to the entrance of Singapore's Botanic Gardens. From the main gate on Cluny Road, the gardens spread over 80 acres of rolling green lawns. Planted here are some 3,000 species of native and exotic plants, including an extensive orchid collection. Among the most famous plants introduced by the gardens were 22 rubber trees, brought from the Kew Gardens in

SINGAPORE 117

Deeply lined and tanned *from the tropical sun, this fisherman returns to his home near Changi Point from a day of working nearby shallow waters.*

Brazil in 1877; the rubber industry of Singapore and Malaysia developed from these plants.

Lakes and landscaped walks make strolling pleasant, and the grounds are floodlit at night. Sunday evening band concerts attract large crowds to the parklike gardens.

East to kampongs and beaches

Singapore's east coast, with its stretches of white sand beaches, mixes recreation areas with Malay villages. Though most Malays have moved into government housing estates, some still prefer to live in the traditional wooden slat houses built on stilts. You can enjoy this rural side of Singapore on a drive to the beaches at Changi Point.

About 7 miles east of the city center, along the Changi Road, you drive through the urbanized area of Geylang, where a number of Malay families live in kampong-style homes. The whine of jet engines at the airport mingles with the babble of bartering and trading at the marketplace. On the way to Changi, tucked away under groves of palm trees, you'll still find the traditional wooden stilt houses with their *attap* (palm leaf) roofs.

At Changi Point, palm trees shade some five miles of sandy beaches along Nicoll Drive. Offshore, *kelongs* (rows of stilts) rise above the sea, designed to lure marine life into underwater nets. Early morning fishermen take pomfret and garoupa by the basketful.

Swimmers, boaters, and picnickers congregate here on weekends. Several small beach stalls sell snacks and soft drinks.

Dining and entertainment

When you want a change from sightseeing and shopping, you'll find plenty of other activities to keep you busy. In Singapore you can sample cuisines as varied as the city's cultural potpourri. Night life also offers many options, ranging from sophisticated revues to the carnival atmosphere of an amusement center or outdoor bazaar. Golf and water sports attract both visitors and residents. Sightseeing tours by limousine and motor coach are offered by several Singapore agencies.

Varied food experiences

Singapore's cuisine offers experiences as varied as the Lion City's population. You can dine on classic European dishes in elegant hotel dining rooms or sample local food favorites at open-air stalls. Asian and oriental restaurants abound, but if you insist, you can even find a passable hamburger.

Though Singapore is a free port, liquor is one of the few imports that is taxable. Liquors and beers from around the world are available, and the local brewery produces a good beer and stout of its own.

The Singapore Tourist Promotion Board publishes an excellent food and restaurant guide, *Singapore—Our Gourmet World,* listing many of the best restaurants in various categories and offering menu suggestions.

Here are just a few of Singapore's food specialties and dining spots:

Chinese. With a population that is 76 percent Chinese, Singapore's predominant cuisine is Chinese—with seven different regional styles represented. Literally hundreds of excellent Chinese restaurants —ranging from tiny noodle shops to elegant banquet halls—offer a fascinating variety of dishes. A lunch favorite is *tim sum* (steamed or fried bite size morsels of pork, chicken, beef, prawns, or vegetables).

• Mayflower Restaurant, DBS Building, Shenton Way, offers Cantonese specialties in a large, noisy, colorful room.

• Dragon Room Restaurant, 5th floor of Specialist Centre, Orchard Road, serves Shanghai dishes amid traditional Chinese wall paintings. The restaurant is known for its braised meats, fish dishes, and casseroles.

Malay-Indonesian. The basis of many Malay-Indonesian meals is *nasi* (rice) with side dishes of meat, fish, prawns, and vegetables. Spicy curries and *sambals* (based on hot chilies, replacing salt and pepper) come from Indonesia, while curries with a thinner gravy originated in Malaysia. *Rijsttafel* (rice table), a Dutch creation, consists of numerous dishes, eaten with rice and amply sprinkled with peanuts and coconut. Most famous, however, is *satay*, a skewered meat preparation on a stick. Similar to shish kebab, satay is made from mutton, chicken, or beef and barbecued, then dipped in a hot chili-peanut-tomato sauce.

• Da'tuk Rajah Restaurant, 24 Raffles Place, Clifford Centre, features a hot food counter where 12 dishes are displayed. It is noted for Penang (Malaysia) food—spring roll, baked fish in banana leaf, and roast mutton dishes.

• French Restaurant, the Cockpit Hotel, 6-7 Oxley Rise, serves rijsttafel; waiters wear Javanese costumes. The choice is wide—from spicy dried beef, mild chicken curry, or prawn curry to a variety of sliced vegetables cooked in hot sauce.

Northern India. Food representative of Northern India includes a variety of curries and *tandoori* chicken—the latter marinated in yogurt, lemon, lime, and spices and then grilled in an oven surrounded by hot coals.

• Kashmir, 9-11 Tomlinson Road, around the corner from the Singapore Tourist Promotion Board, serves delicately spiced barbecued tandoori chicken and crispy *naan* bread in an opulent Moghul atmosphere.

• Omar Khayyam, 55 Hill Street, opposite the American Embassy, offers dishes ranging from tandoori chicken to *luziza* (prawns soaked in honey and sour spices). The restaurant has a relaxed ambience; Indian art and quotations from Omar Khayyam decorate the walls.

Japanese. Most travelers are familiar with the well-known Japanese dishes of *sukiyaki* and *tempura*, and with *sashimi* (raw fish dipped in a tangy sauce and horseradish paste) or *sushi* (little balls of vinegared rice with raw fish).

• Fujiya Japanese Restaurant, 2nd floor, Shenton House, Shenton Way, serves the usual Japanese dishes in a cozy atmosphere.

• Yamagen Japanese Restaurant, 19th floor, Yen San Building, Orchard Road, opposite the Mandarin Hotel, serves such favorite dishes as sushi and sukiyaki.

Korean. Typical Korean dishes include *polgogi* (barbecued beef, chicken, pork or prawns dipped in special sauces), chicken, ginseng soup, and *kimchee* (pickled and highly spiced cabbage).

• Korean Restaurant, 4th floor, Specialist Centre, Orchard Road, offers a set menu that will satisfy your curiosity for Korean food. Decor is unpretentious.

Western restaurants. Singapore's hotels are the best places to seek Western foods. You can find American prime rib, Russian borsch, or Swiss fondue. Most hotels feature entertainment in their larger restaurants.

Floating restaurants. Singapore's floating restaurants provide over-the-water dining with splendid views of the city's skyline and harbor activity. You have a choice of dining aboard the *Fairwind*, a Chinese junk; the *Oasis*, a floating restaurant complex; or two *kelong*-type establishments (Malay fish traps built on pilings over the water)

Hugo's Grill, *at the Hyatt Singapore, is one of dozens of fine international restaurants in the city. Hotel dining rooms serve a wide range of cuisines prepared for many tastes.*

Singapore's "steamboat" *is a chafing dish over a charcoal fire with a chimney up the middle, similar to the Mongolian hot pot. You cook small pieces of meat, fish, and vegetables in the broth.*

Chinese noodles, *chicken, and turtle soup are among popular choices at outdoor food stalls. Modest prices and a good variety have made these al fresco restaurants a way of life in Singapore.*

Delicious satays *simmering over an open flame attract hungry office workers and avenue strollers to the open-air Satay Club.*

Dining al fresco

Another Singapore activity is dining al fresco. In many sections of the city, open-air food stalls, brimming and steaming with special foods, beckon the hungry. These tiny food stalls, both informal and inexpensive (complete meals for S $3.00), give visitors a chance to taste a wide variety of Singapore's national food.

Popular dishes are Chinese noodles and prawns, pork, chicken, and duck dishes; Malay satay; and Indian curries. Genuine turtle soup, clams, mussel soup, *nasi goreng* (fried rice), and *pisang goreng* (banana fritters) might also be included in the menu.

To order, all you do is point at whatever looks tempting—the chef takes care of the rest. Most open-air restaurants are open until 2 A.M.

One al fresco dining experience can be enjoyed at the Satay Club, located on Connaught Drive along the Esplanade (see page 110). Stalls in the row of pyramid-roofed outdoor units sell sticks of satay for S $0.10 to 0.30 each.

The Rasa Singapura Food Centre behind Tudor Court on Tanglin Road has 29 food stalls under one roof. Here you can try chili prawns, roast duck, and all kinds of satay. Ethnic specialties include Chinese, Malay, and Indian dishes. This indoor complex replaces the famous open-air Orchard Road Car Park which was recently edged out by a high-rise development.

You can also get inexpensive meals from street stands at Newton Circus, near the intersection of Clemenceau Avenue and Bukit Timah Road. Numerous neat tiled hawker stands serve Malay, Indian and Chinese dishes.

Restaurants in Serangoon Road offer authentic Indian meals, while Chinese food is the main offering in Albert Street, Koek Road, People's Park, and Bedok End Street.

Nighttime entertainment

Visitors planning a night on the town can choose from hotel nightclubs, music for dancing, amusement centers, and the evening street parade.

The Tropicana, Scotts Road, features international shows and revues on a revolving stage in its theater restaurant. The Neptune, Overseas Union Building, Collyer Quay, seats 1,200 people for spectacular shows while you dine on Cantonese food. The Oasis, Kallang Park, caters to "nighttime bachelors" with 200 attractive hostesses.

If you prefer live rock music, places to try include the Lost Horizon at the Shangri-La Hotel, the Kasbah at the Mandarin Hotel, or the Penthouse at the Imperial Hotel.

Singapore has three amusement centers—Gay World in Geylang, New World on Serangoon Road, and Great World on Kim Seng Road. These parks offer an inexpensive way to spend the evening among Singaporeans.

You can climb aboard ferris wheels and spinning rides, visit shooting galleries and horror houses, try your luck in penny arcades or games of chance, and sample local food favorites at any of dozens of food stalls. The amusement centers are open from 6 P.M. to midnight.

An interesting late stop on your tour of Singapore night life is Bugis Street. Lighted by a string of lights, the street is packed with food stalls, tables, and attractive young women sporting the latest revealing fashions (actually most of these women are men). The nightly street parade is free, but drinks are overpriced.

Cultural shows

Local groups have preserved indigenous dance and musical forms of China, India, and the Malayan archipelago; you can enjoy performances at daytime or evening shows.

A 45-minute "Instant Asia" show is presented mornings daily at the Singapore Cultural Theatre located adjacent to the Singapore Handicraft Centre at the corner of Tanglin and Grange roads. The traditional performance includes the Chinese lion dance, Malay welcoming dance, and Indian classical love dance, among others. For details and reservations, contact the Singapore Tourist Promotion Board.

The Malayan Night Revue at the Raffles Hotel includes dinner and a show (at 9 P.M.) of Malay dances, sword fighting, and the *bersanding* (a mock marriage ceremony). After the show (about 10:30 P.M.) you can take the Raffles "trishaw tour of Chinatown." Some nights as many as a hundred trishaws roll along the route for a late evening tour of Singapore's Chinatown. Inquire at the Raffles Hotel reception desk for more information about evening entertainment.

A Malay show and dinner at the seaside Villa Saujana are part of an evening group tour. Hin's Heavenly Cookhouse, Hilton Hotel, features a cultural "happening" as part of the dinner fare.

The sporting life

Singapore's tropical climate affords opportunities for a full roster of active and spectator sports including golf, water sports, tennis, bowling, horse racing, cricket, soccer, hockey, squash, and auto racing.

Golfers will find some 12 courses, including the prestigious Singapore Island Country Club. If you plan to play golf, arrange for your local club to provide an introduction to a member (most local hotel and travel agency managers are members). Visitors are restricted to one day's play per month, and Saturday afternoon is closed to visitors.

The warm waters around Singapore's offshore reefs and islands offer game fish for spear fishermen, coral gardens for viewers and photographers,

Snake charmer *thrills the audience during the "Instant Asia" show at Pasir Panjang Paradise. Other acts include dancing and sword fighting.*

Tropical waters *surrounding Singapore are perfect for sailing, canoeing, swimming. Sea breezes cool the island year round, tempering the equatorial heat.*

Wild-eyed lions *wiggle and lunge during a Singapore parade in celebration of National Day. The Lion Dance signals a time of victory and joy.*

shells for diver-collectors. The best diving season is between April and August, and wet suits are never needed. Visibility is generally 30 feet. No rental equipment is available, but Singapore sport shops carry various lines for sale.

Boats are available at Collyer Quay, virtually in the center of Singapore, and at Jardine Steps a few miles out of town.

Festivals and events

In Singapore's multiracial and multicultural society, nearly every week brings some holiday or festival. The city-state's biggest events occur from Christmas through Chinese New Year in January or February and on National Day in August.

But almost any day during the year you can see a Malay wedding in the kampongs, a Chinese street opera in Chinatown, or orchestras and dramas at the Victoria Theater.

Most of Singapore's festivals fall on different days in succeeding years, so check local newspapers or the Singapore Tourist Promotion Board's *Weekly Guide* for exact dates. Here are some of Singapore's many annual festivals:

January-March

Chinese New Year. The Chinese community celebrates the New Year at the end of January or beginning of February by opening their homes to visitors and giving children new clothes and *ang pows* (money in red packets). Firecrackers and dragon parades are also part of the celebration.

Hari Raya Haji. Muslims celebrate the completion of their *haji* (pilgrimage to Mecca) the first week of January. You can see this festival in early morning at the Sultan Mosque, North Bridge Road.

Chap Goh Meh. Chinese New Year festivities end on the 15th day of the year; at night the young seek out places of entertainment. Look for the "sugar lion" festival at the Wak Hai Cheng Bio Temple on Philip Street.

Thaipusam. This Hindu festival is celebrated at the Sri Mariamman Temple on South Bridge Road and the Chettiar Temple on Tank Road. Devotees carry *kavadis* with thin steel rods piercing their chest and skewers hooked in their cheeks (see page 13).

April-June

Cheng Bang. During April the Chinese celebrate "All Saints Day" by visiting their ancestors' graves. Sacrificial offerings of incense, candles, drinks, and food are presented in their names at grave sites.

Songkrat. During April the Thai "water festival" is celebrated in Thai Buddhist temples where people splash each other with water (see page 12). You can join the festivities at the Ananda Metyarama Thai Buddhist Temple on Silat Road or the Sapthapuchaniyaram Temple on Holland Road.

Practical information for visitors to Singapore

Here are some important details in planning your trip to Singapore:

Entry requirements. Citizens of the United States and other countries recognized by Singapore do not need a visa for visits of three months or less. However, you do need a valid passport to enter Singapore.

Cholera, yellow fever, and smallpox inoculations are required for visitors entering from an infected area. The U.S. Public Health Service recommends cholera, typhoid, paratyphoid, tetanus, and gamma globulin shots.

Visitors arriving in Singapore, especially males, must be well groomed with hair not reaching below the collar or covering the ears.

On departure from Singapore, you pay an airport tax of about U.S. $0.90 for flights to Malaysia, U.S. $4.80 for flights to other destinations.

Customs. Besides your personal items, you may bring in the usual 200 cigarettes, 50 cigars, and 1 quart of liquor. Prohibited items include firearms, explosives, narcotics, and pornographic materials.

Currency. The unit of currency is the Singapore dollar; the rate of exchange is U.S. $1 to S $2.15. Singapore has no restrictions on the amount of foreign currency you can bring into the country, but when entering you are allowed only S $500 in Singapore, Malaysian, and Brunei currency. It is legal to change money with licensed moneychangers, but first it is advisable for you to check both the bank and hotel exchange rates.

Traveler's checks and credit cards are accepted at hotels, restaurants, and larger stores. You'll need your passport to cash traveler's checks.

Health conditions. Hospital and medical facilities are excellent; many English-speaking doctors are available. Medicines and toiletries may be purchased at Singapore's drug stores and large hotels. Tap water is safe for drinking.

Tipping. Light tipping is the rule, and most hotels and restaurants add a 10 percent service charge to the bill. At rail or ship terminals, tip S $0.50 per bag and S $1 for any piece requiring two persons to carry. At the airport, tipping is optional (porters are paid by the government). Taxi drivers do not expect a tip, but S $0.10 per bag is standard. Tipping is optional for guides, beauty and barber shop personnel, and cloakroom attendants.

Climate. Though Singapore is close to the equator, its climate is mild. Temperatures in the daytime average 85° F.; at night, about 75° F. Sea breezes cool the generally hot and humid climate. The drier period of March through mid-October is the best time to visit Singapore.

The island has no well defined wet or dry season. Afternoon showers are likely to occur throughout the year, but they last only briefly. Singapore's annual rainfall averages about 95 inches, most of it coming during the northeast monsoon—mid-October through February; December is the wettest month. The island of Singapore escapes typhoons and hurricanes.

For more information. Your best source on travel in Singapore is the Singapore Tourist Promotion Board, Tudor Court, Tanglin Road, Singapore, 10. Their U.S. offices are located at 251 Post Street, San Francisco 94108 and 342 Madison Avenue, Suite 1008, New York 10017. Singapore has an embassy in Washington D.C. In Singapore, the U.S. Embassy is located at 30 Hill Street.

Vesak Day. Held in late May or early June, this festival celebrates Buddha's birth, death, and enlightenment (see page 13).

July-September

Festival of the Hungry Ghosts. The Chinese believe that during the seventh moon their ancestors' souls are released from purgatory to roam the earth. Food and "ghost money" are offered at their graves, and stall owners pile their tables with food for the spirits. The celebrations include Chinese theatrical performances and puppet shows.

National Day. On August 9 Singapore celebrates its 1965 independence from Malaysia with a giant parade and festivities on the Padang.

Moon Cake Festival. Held in mid-September, this festival commemorates the overthrow of the Mongol overlords by Chinese who hid messages in moon cakes (see page 13). Poets, women, and children celebrate by exchanging and eating moon cakes.

October-December

Festival of Nine Emperor Gods. In mid-October, Chinese Taoists make pilgrimages to their temples (Serangoon and Tai Seng roads), and vegetarian food is served for nine days. Spirit mediums, possessed by the emperors, climb sword ladders or flog themselves with spiked iron balls. Open-air *wayangs* (Chinese operas) are staged.

Kusu Festival. This month-long festival is held in October and November. Chinese Taoists make a pilgrimage in decorated boats to Tua Pek Kong Temple on Kusu Island, four miles south of Clifford Pier. Weekends are especially colorful.

Deepavali (Festival of Lights). In early November, Hindus commemorate the slaying of the tyrant King Naragusura by Lord Krishna (see page 13). Hindu homes are lighted with oil lamps or candles during the festival. At the Sri Mariamman Temple, South Bridge Road, you can see a demonstration of fire-walking men crossing a bed of hot coals.

Wat Arun (top) towers above the Chao Phraya River across from the Royal Palace. Democracy Monument **(right)** stands midway along Bangkok's grandiose and busy Rajdamnoen Avenue. Burning incense sticks **(far right)** create a mystical atmosphere in this Chinese spirit house.

Thailand

Exotic land of golden-spired temples

Visitors to Thailand discover an exotic, varied land. The new hotels, department stores, office blocks, and neon-lit night life of modern Bangkok barely hide the city of the *klongs* (canals) and the meandering Chao Phraya River, a waterway lined with stilt houses and overshadowed by extravagant *wats* (monasteries). Throughout Thailand, thousands of towering, gold-leafed wats provide visible evidence of Buddhism's ever-present influence. Saffron-robed monks are a constant reminder of the people's faith.

Romanticized by tales of Anna and the King of Siam and of the infamous bridge over the river Kwai, Thailand offers some intriguing travel sights. To the north is Chiang Mai, home of the hill tribes and ageless elephants working teak forests; to the west, Nakhon Pathom, birthplace of Buddhism in Thailand; to the east, Pimai, marked by ruins older than those of Angkor in Cambodia; to the south, a few hours' drive from Bangkok, summer resorts and miles of palm-fringed beaches edging the Gulf of Thailand.

Further south, along the Thai-Malaysian peninsula, are fishing villages, numerous sheltered swimming coves, miles of sandy beaches, and uninhabited tropical offshore islands.

This is the country of Thai silk, resplendently gowned Thai dancers, colorfully-garbed Buddhist monks, lush green flatlands covered with rice fields, lumbering water buffaloes, clear mountain streams, tumbling waterfalls, and best of all, the smiling and friendly Thai people.

Proud and nationalistic, the Thais call their country *Muang Thai*—"the land of the free." Unlike other nations of Southeast Asia, Thailand has never been subject to colonial rule by a Western nation.

The universal greeting is "Sawasdee," meaning "hello," "good morning," or "good evening." Thais accompany this salutation with the *wei*, made by placing the hands and palms together, raising them to the face, and bowing slightly.

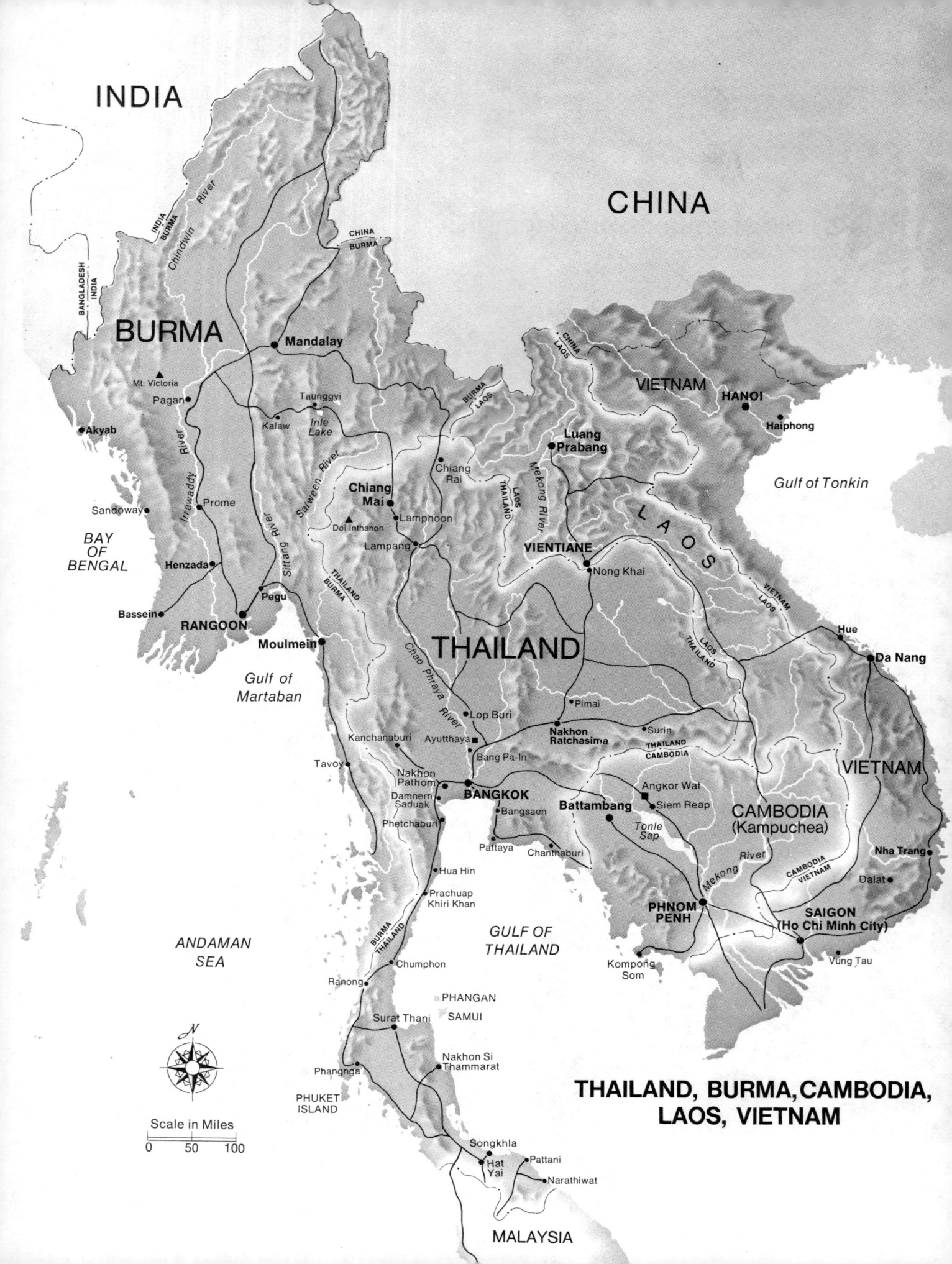

Thailand—past and present

Thailand's tropical kingdom lies in the heart of Southeast Asia, its forested mountains and wide plains interlaced with rivers and klongs. Somewhat larger than California, it covers an area exceeding 200,000 square miles, stretching more than a thousand miles from north to south.

Thailand shares borders with four countries: Burma on the west, Laos on the north and northeast, Cambodia on the southeast, and Malaysia on the extreme south. China lies only 75 miles from Thailand's northern boundaries. In its southern region, Thailand shares a narrow isthmus with Burma, separating the Gulf of Thailand on the east from the Andaman Sea on the west. Small islands are sprinkled along the country's 1,625-mile coastline.

A broad central plain, irrigated by the Chao Phraya River and its tributaries, forms the nation's rice bowl. It supports most of the country's 45 million people, and throughout Thailand's history, it has been the site of the nation's political development.

In the north, broad valleys separate lofty mountain chains, carpeted with forests of teak; logs are harvested with the help of trained elephants and floated down the Chao Phraya River. Rubber estates and tin mines extend down Thailand's southern peninsula.

An ancient history

Historians believe the Thai people originated in China's vast southeast region, migrating south about 4,500 years ago to the area now known as Thailand. Independent for seven centuries, Thailand was officially known as Siam in English-speaking countries before 1939.

Royal wars. Thailand's early history remains somewhat uncertain, since all official records disappeared when the Burmese destroyed the city of Ayutthaya in 1767. Modern Thailand dates its history from 1350, when this ancient capital was founded by a new line of Thai kings. The new kingdom grew strong and prosperous by the 15th century, and its ambitious warlords started a series of long and indecisive wars. Invading Khmer territory, they captured Angkor but failed to hold it. Wars also developed in Chiang Mai—then a Lao state—and later with Burma.

When the Burmese captured Ayutthaya in the 1700s, they razed and burned the city, leaving in the ruins some 1200 bronze and gold Buddha images. These statues were rescued and, after Bangkok was established as Thailand's new capital in 1782, were restored with lacquer and gold leaf. Today they can be seen in Bangkok's monasteries; the largest collection is at Wat Po.

Colonial influences. In the 16th century, the Portuguese became Thailand's first European visitors. They set up trading posts at Ayutthaya and on the Malay Peninsula. In the 17th century, when the Dutch and English replaced the Portuguese as major powers, both countries opened trading posts in Thailand.

In an attempt to convert Thailand to Christianity, the French soon followed, sending missionaries, ships, and soldiers. Troubled by these new influences, Thailand expelled most of the foreigners in the late 17th century and closed its doors to the western world for more than a hundred years.

By the mid-19th century, Thailand developed an enlightened line of absolute kings who, despite the loss of some territory to the British and French, retained political independence and initiated programs of partial modernization. King Mongkut, crowned in 1851, reopened Thailand to western trade and introduced western learning and science. The book *Anna and the King of Siam* is a fictionalized account based on this period.

The first United States trade treaty with Thailand was signed in 1833.

Wartime occupation. Japan occupied Thailand at the outset of World War II, and a short time later Thailand declared war on Great Britain and the United States. Many Thais who opposed the Japanese established an effective underground, winning the country moderate treatment by the allies after the war. In fact, the United States refused to acknowledge Thailand's war declaration.

As a member of the United Nations, Thailand serves as a regional center for various U.N agencies.

Constitutional monarchy

Thailand became a constitutional monarchy in 1932; previously it had been an absolute monarchy. Its present ruler is King Bhumibol Adulyadej, officially known as King Rama IX. The king was born in Cambridge, Massachusetts (where his father was engaged in public health research), and received his education in England.

At present, the National Administrative Reform Assembly, composed of 300 to 400 members appointed for 4-year terms by the King perform legislative functions.

Responsibility for local government rests with the Ministry of Interior, which appoints governors for each of Thailand's 71 *changwad* (provinces). A changwad is subdivided into *amphur* (districts), *tambol* (sub-districts), and *muban* (villages). Thailand's major cities, such as Bangkok and Chiang Mai, are headed by local mayors assisted by a municipal assembly.

Plants and animals

Lavished with warm sunshine, abundant rain, and gentle winds, Thailand's forested lands and shallow waters teem with plant and animal life. In many areas, cultivated crops encroach on the jungle, but forests still cover more than half the country.

Bears, tigers, leopards, black panthers, wild boar, and several varieties of wild buffalo and deer

Buddhist monks *assemble under the three-tiered yellow roof of Wat Benchamaborpitr. Courtyard is paved in white marble.*

Fisherman *dips his bamboo-framed fishing net into one of many klongs crisscrossing the countryside. Marine life grows prolifically here.*

Push cart vendor *serves soup and noodles to Chiang Mai's residents. If you like, you can dine al fresco on a wide selection of foods.*

Woman *poles her sampan piled with bananas, pineapples, and melons along Bangkok's klongs during the morning market hours.*

still live in Thailand's jungles. Monkeys and civit cats share trees with honeysuckle birds. Many kinds of snakes, including the poisonous banded krait and cobra, slither across the jungle floor. The forest overflows with insects—including some 800 species of butterflies and moths—and smaller creatures, such as bats and the gecko lizard.

Northeast Thailand supplies the country with some 7 million water buffalo, 5 million oxen, and about 12,000 tame elephants.

Edged by mangrove swamps and warm, shallow waters, the Thailand peninsula provides a haven for crocodiles, crabs, fish, rock lobsters, prawns, and the amphibious pig-tailed monkey. In the Gulf of Thailand, fishermen harvest schools of mackerel, herring, mullet, pomfret, sole, bass, anchovies, and sharks. Inland rivers, marked by fishing traps, nets, and bamboo fishing poles, enrich the farmers' diet with fresh minnow, carp, catfish, and dappled murral.

Thailand's valleys, mountains, plateaus, and alluvial plains support more than a hundred varieties of trees. In the north, tall, straight teak forests supply the world's markets. Coconut, areca, and sugar palms grow in the central lowlands. Rubber trees are cultivated on the southern peninsula, and trained monkeys pick ripened coconuts from tall palm trees.

The Thai people

The Thais are descendants of southeastern Chinese who migrated south in the 12th century after being driven out of China by Kublai Khan. Generally small, slight, and delicately built, the hospitable Thai people have courtly manners and friendly smiles. They account for almost 90 percent of Thailand's 45 million people.

The largest minority group is Chinese—some 3 million people. Over half of Bangkok's population is Chinese; for centuries they have dominated Thailand's commerce and retail trade. Other minorities include almost a million Malays, clustered near the southern border, as well as Indians, Pakistanis, Khmers, and Vietnamese.

As in other Southeast Asian countries, Thailand's people migrated into territories inhabited by primitive Negrito tribes, sometimes called Aborigines. These hill tribes—Meos, Karens, Lisus, Yaos, Akhas, and Lahus—live in mountains north of Chiang Mai. Each tribe has its own language and observes many primitive ancestral customs.

Dress. In Bangkok and other urban areas, western clothes and the latest continental fashions dominate local dress. But in rural areas—where 85 percent of Thailand's population lives—people dress in a cool and comfortable fashion.

Thai farmers wear loose cotton shirts and trousers and wide straw hats. Their most indispensable item is a *pakaoma*, a piece of cotton cloth used as a bathing robe, decorative waist sash, or all-purpose bundle wrapping.

Country women wear the traditional *pasin*, a colorful piece of cloth wrapped tightly around the hips and draped to the feet. On the rural klong tour out of Bangkok, you'll notice both men and women using their garments to hide themselves while bathing in the canal.

Language. Thailand's language, phonetically related to some Chinese dialects, uses written characters derived from the Khmer alphabet, which in turn is based on the ancient Sanskrit of India.

When the Thai language is written in Roman script, multiple spellings abound. It is scarcely phonetic, therefore difficult for westerners to pronounce. Thai is a tonal language, and challenging for a foreigner to master. In the main cities, English is widely understood and spoken, especially among professional and business people.

Religion. Approximately 93 percent of Thailand's people follow Theravada Buddhism. However, the king traditionally protects all religions, so the country also has Muslims, Taoists, and Christians, as well as hill tribesmen who continue their ancient spirit and animist worship.

Buddhism, adopted by the Thais in the 13th century, provides inspiration for their social system, art, and literature. Through its influence, Thais develop a carefree attitude, flexibility, and a lack of tension—qualities characterizing their national image.

As part of their religious practices, the Thai Buddhists pay respect to their country's 23,000 *wats* or monasteries (sometimes called temples). Devotees purchase gold leaf and apply it to the thousands of Buddha images. Buddhists also venerate roadside shrines (spirit houses) with flowers, incense, and candles. Performance of these and other deeds—such as alms giving and filling the rice

Piled with fresh fruit, *roadside stalls are a tempting stop on many countryside journeys. Vendor wears a typical woven conical hat.*

bowl of monks—is considered a privilege, helping to earn reward in the Thai Buddhist "merit system."

Many Thai men gain merit by becoming *bhikkus* (monks) in the Sangha, Brotherhood of Monks. This usually occurs before a man marries and starts raising a family. Considered as laymen, they may enter or leave the order at any time.

Visiting Thailand

Thailand lies some 8,300 air miles west of the United States, a flight requiring some 22 hours from California. The time difference between the U. S. west coast and Thailand is 15 hours. When it's 10 A.M. Wednesday in Bangkok, it's 7 P.M. Tuesday in San Francisco.

More than two dozen international airlines—including Thai International—serves Bangkok's Don Muang Airport. Several steamship companies offer regular service—both passenger cargo and cruise ships—from the U.S. west coast to Klongtoey, Bangkok's port 20 miles south of the city, or to Sattahip, former U.S. military port also to the south.

Bangkok is also the northern rail terminus of the International Express; the train leaves Singapore three times a week.

Taxis and samlors

The best way to get around Thailand is by air or rail, reserving the bus for day trips. Public bus lines provide service to some parts of the country, and tour operators run air-conditioned coaches to many destinations outside of Bangkok. Several steamship companies operate coastal service.

Buses and trams traverse Bangkok's streets, but taxis and took-tooks (three-wheeled motor scooters) are convenient and low priced.

Although taxis are metered, always negotiate with the driver in advance and agree on the price (a ride across Bangkok should not cost more than B40). Some hotels have their own taxi services, where you pay in advance, avoiding the delay and expense of haggling.

You should also agree on rates before taking a samlor ride, which generally costs about two-thirds of the taxi fare; soon these small vehicles will be banned from Bangkok's busy main thoroughfares. Hire cars with chauffeurs are also available in Bangkok.

In Thailand traffic moves on the left, and you'll need an international license if you want to drive. If you plan to rent a car, consider hiring a driver; traffic careens along at an unnerving pace, and Bangkok's street names are confusing.

Thai-style boxing, a national sport

The high pitched wail of flutes and the resounding beat of drums signal the start of a Thai boxing match. From the red and blue corners step the gloved fighters. Circling gracefully, as in a slow motion ballet, the boxer in blue trunks unleashes a high kick. "Thump!" The blow is quickly followed with a series of snapping elbows, thrusting knees, and short jabs to the body, head, thighs, and kidneys. The three-minute rounds seem to last an eternity, the two-minute breaks flash by, and five rounds prove physically damaging and tiring to even the most skilled fighters.

Thai boxing dates from the medieval ages when bows and arrows, swords and pikes decided a battle. For close-in fighting, the military devised a method of turning an unarmed soldier into a human battering ram, using all his skills and contact points to disable an enemy. In 1560, King Naresuen, captured by the Burmese, regained his freedom with Thai boxing, defeating that country's best fighters. Upon returning to Thailand, the king became a hero, and Thai-style boxing a national sport.

Though the matches are highly secular (the Thais are enthusiastic betters), the fighters prepare for a fight in a deeply religious manner. They kneel on the canvas, face the four corners, face the direction of their birth, and bow in fervent prayer. Often Thai boxers wear a sacred headband or a charm around the upper arm for good luck.

Throughout the country, 1,500 training camps teach Thai boxing. In Bangkok you can attend boxing matches several nights a week at either Rajdamnoen or Lumpini stadiums.

Thai boxers *unleash high kicks and elbow jabs during daily exhibitions at the Rose Garden.*

Choice of hotels

Many new hotels have gone up in Bangkok during the past decade, and several of the older hostelries are undergoing remodeling. Service is generally excellent, performed cheerfully by a willing and friendly Thai hotel staff.

At the other major tourist destinations—Chiang Mai, Pattaya, and Phuket Island—you'll find luxury hotels and small resorts. Pattaya Beach offers high-rise hotels and beachside bungalows; resort hotels cater to guests with an array of water sports and equipment rentals.

All hotel prices are subject to a 10 percent service charge and an 8¼ percent government tax.

Thailand's cuisine

Influenced by Chinese, Indian, and Malay cookery, Thailand's cuisine achieves a unique blending of tastes and styles, resulting in some hot and spicy dishes. Though the country's hotels and restaurants frequently offer Westernized versions of Thai dishes, they specialize in other cuisines—Chinese, Muslim, Korean, Japanese, and Western cooking. To experience real Thai food, you'll have to visit a genuine Thai restaurant, preferably in the company of Thais.

A typical Thai meal consists of four to five courses, served with rice and ending with *khong wan* (a dessert) or fruit. When dining in a Thai restaurant, you sit on large pillows and eat from a low table, using a fork and spoon. Since meat is cut into bite-size morsels, knives are unnecessary. Shoes are never worn inside Thai restaurants.

Among local dishes, you might try *gang pet*, a hot curried sweet-tasting dish made from pork, chicken, beef, fish, or prawns. Another Thai favorite is *khao pat*, fried rice flavored with bits of crab, chicken, pork, onion, egg, and saffron. Frequent Thai condiments are garlic, chili, and *nampla*, an amber-colored fish sauce.

Almost every meal contains one of the dozens of Thai curries based on chicken, beef, or shellfish, frequently flavored with coconut milk or lime juice. The taste runs from sweet and sour to bitter and peppery. Those hot, small, red or green peppers have been known to cause tears for many a Western diner; to smother the burning sensation, take a spoonful of rice or sugar rather than water.

Thais finish their meals with a special dessert called *khong wan*, which may resemble jello, cake, custard, or pudding; or some of Thailand's succulent fruit—mangoes, oranges, melons, bananas, rambutans, and papayas. National drinks include the full-bodied Singha beer and Mekhong or Thai whisky. Many visitors adopt the pleasant oriental custom of drinking hot or iced tea with the meal.

Varied entertainment

Thailand's urban areas have a remarkably large number of nightclubs, discotheques, cocktail lounges, and hostess bars. Hotels, theater restaurants, and supper clubs feature local and international shows, with music provided by Thai bands.

Several Thai restaurants and some hotels feature performances of Thai classical dance, one of the most cultivated art forms in the world.

Souvenir shopping

Although Thailand is neither a manufacturing power like Japan nor a duty-free port like Hong Kong, it does offer some unusual souvenir buys for visiting shoppers.

Bangkok's most famous product is Thai silk. An American, Jim Thompson, brought this soft, handwoven fabric to the attention of leading fashion designers just after World War II. Stores and shops sell it in a variety of colors, patterns, and weights. You can buy ready-made (or custom-made) Thai silk suits and dresses or silk and cotton by the yard for draperies and wall hangings. Though lacking the sheen and glamour of silk, Thai cotton is popular for dresses, blouses, and suits.

Other favorite items are Thai jewelry (especially star sapphires and princess rings); silverware; nielloware (silver inlaid with a black alloy); Thai celadon (a high-fired stoneware); bronze tableware; antiques; lacquerware; temple bells. Thai dolls; Khon masks; teak, rattan, and bamboo products; and temple rubbings (motifs in bas-relief).

Dining in Thailand *can range from a four to five-course, typically spicy Thai meal to continental cuisine served in international restaurants.*

The sports scene

Thailand's popular spectator sports generally involve a form of fighting, using agility, skill, and endurance. These sports include Thai-style boxing, kite flying, fish fighting, bull fighting, and sword fighting.

One of the leading national sports is *takraw*, played by two teams using a hollow, braided rattan ball. Team members keep the ball in the air by kicking or hitting it with their heads or shoulders—using any part of the body except the hands. Horse racing and soccer are also popular sports.

The country's dozen golf courses are plush and rich in vegetation. Most clubs have caddies (usually girls), and greens fees are inexpensive. The Thais prefer playing with a crowd, rather than a foursome, giving rise to the term "alligators"—a string of six, seven, or more golfers teeing off together.

Exotic Bangkok

Often called the "Venice of the East", Bangkok sprawls along both banks of the curving Chao Phraya River some 20 miles inland from the Gulf of Thailand. Brightened by many gleaming spires, temples, and walled palaces and cut by a network of *klongs* (canals), Bangkok serves as Thailand's capital and center of business, industry, and transportation.

Of the city's more than 4 million inhabitants, fully one-fifth live on or near the water. The flat alluvial region around Bangkok, extending 200 miles inland, forms the Central Plain—the heart of Thailand's rice growing area.

A modern and prosperous capital, Bangkok presents a number of contrasting and confusing images. Laced by its shadowy, boat-clogged klongs, the city mixes Thai and western-style architecture—sleek glass and concrete office buildings and hotels rise beside ancient and extravagant Buddhist *wats*. The city's exhaust-clouded avenues seem to be perpetually jammed with traffic.

To get an idea of Bangkok's layout, imagine the city as an upturned left hand with its fingers spreading east. The Chao Phraya River flows from north to south, running from the tip of the thumb and curving across the wrist. The Grand Palace is located on the river's eastern bank, where the hand joins the wrist. The palm holds the city's burgeoning center, and the radiating fingers represent the main avenues reaching out toward Bangkok's eastern suburbs.

The Royal Capital

In 1782 King Rama I moved his government from Thonburi on the west side of the river over to the eastern bank, marking the beginning of Bangkok. In those early days, the city's mud flats supported a Chinese trading community and a few Buddhist wats, with floating Thai houseboats tied up along the river. Rama I built Bangkok to resemble the former capital at Ayutthaya, complete with a network of klongs.

The city's klongs are manmade branches of the Chao Phraya River which winds past the city and empties into the Gulf of Thailand. The klongs formed the city's first streets, and several were constructed wide enough for boat races, a sport still popular today. Not until the 1840s, when horse-drawn carriages entered the city, did Bangkok start filling in some of its klongs, turning them into tree-shaded avenues.

During the reigns of the early kings, the enclosed Grand Palace on the bank of the river was a complete, self-contained world—the symbolic center of Bangkok and Thailand. Thrust into the 20th century, the city moved away from the palace; yet the palace remains the ceremonial center of Bangkok.

A city of contrasts

On the drive into Bangkok from Don Muang Airport, 12 miles north of the city, you ride along a four-lane highway past boxy, concrete office blocks, garish billboards, flooded rice fields, ambling water buffaloes, and pastoral scenes of fishermen dipping their nets into murky roadside klongs.

Bangkok has no distinctive downtown center or metropolitan skyline. (Because the city rises from

Chakri Hall, *part of the Grand Palace, is a mixture of Western and Oriental styles with its spires, tile roof, central balcony, marble facade.*

mud flats, the erection of tall structures is expensive and sometimes dangerous.) Instead, it is a cluster of ground-hugging districts, each unique, yet each having similar characteristics. Thais, Thai-Chinese, Indians, and Pakistanis are sometimes intermingled in the same area, at other times separated into ethnic districts. Throughout the city you'll find new international hotels, modern shopping centers, local shops and markets, restaurants, and entertainment areas.

Just behind the main thoroughfares are calm residential streets laced with small watery klongs and narrow *sois* (lanes). Moving through the city, you'll glimpse cool tropical gardens splashed with flowering bougainvillea, processions of monks carrying brass offering bowls, small fields of rice greening the city, and the soaring lines of new highrise buildings.

A wide choice of hotels

Bangkok now offers the visitor some 70 international standard hotels, supplemented by a variety of smaller establishments. Most of the hotels are tourist and convention-oriented, with emphasis on service, cuisine, and entertainment. All the major hotels offer rooms with private bath and air conditioning; many have restaurants, shopping arcades, and swimming pools.

Though Bangkok's hotels are scattered across the city, many are found on or near Rama I Road and its continuation, Ploenchit Road (a main east-west thoroughfare). Another hotel district is located further south, toward the river, along or near Suriwong and Silom roads.

Only the Oriental Hotel has a riverfront setting. Among other favorite tourist hotels are the Amarin, Ambassador, Dusit Thani, Erawan, Hyatt Rama, Montien, Narai, Indra Regent, Mandarin, Sheraton-Bangkok, and the Siam Inter-Continental.

For the tourist on a limited budget, the city offers a number of smaller hotels, including a YMCA and a YWCA.

Dining in Bangkok

In Bangkok hotels and restaurants you can sample dishes from various parts of the world. You'll also find many restaurants offering Thai-style dinners. Milder forms of local dishes—as well as western favorites—are featured in many hotel restaurants and coffee shops.

If you want to try some authentic national foods, here are some of Bangkok's popular, moderately priced Thai restaurants:
• Baan Keo Ruen Kwan has two branches, one at 414/6 New Petchburi Road, near the Bangkok Hotel, the other at Soi 12, Sukhumvit Road. Popular with Thais, both are recommended for large parties wishing to try genuine Thai food.
• Chitr Pojana, catering mainly to Thais, also has two locations. The restaurant at 1082 Phaholyothin Road is in a multi-story building seating thousands.

Classical Thai dancing, *music, and sword fighting are part of the evening entertainment at the Baan Thai theater-restaurant in Bangkok.*

The original, smaller version is located at 52 Soi 20 Sukumvit Road. Both have open-air and air-conditioned rooms.

Theater-restaurants. Bangkok also has many theater-restaurants where you can enjoy favorite national dishes in a traditional setting. These restaurants usually provide more interesting decor and offer menus tempered for visitors tastes. Programs feature Thai cultural entertainment—classical and folk dancing, music, and sword fighting.
• Baan Thai, Soi 32, Sukhumvit Road, is one of the most beautiful tourist restaurants. Traditional in decor, the Thai-style building is set in a lovely garden that is floodlighted at night.
• Piman, 46, Soi 49, Sukhumvit Road, offers a set Thai menu. Decorated in the Sukothai style of ancient Thailand, the restaurant is furnished in authentic antiques and elaborate woodcarvings.
• Sala Norasingh, Soi 4 (South Nana), Sukhumvit Road, has a set menu of Thai meals.
• Sukhothai, Dusit Thani Hotel, Saladaeng Circle, observes traditional style in everything—decor (carved teak woodwork), music, and food.

Bangkok nightlife

After dark, Bangkok offers entertainment to suit every taste. The city's major hotels, restaurants, and nightclubs offer a choice of local performers and international shows.

You can spend the evening in a quiet supper club or cabaret, visit the cinema, or watch a performance of Thai classical dancing. Bangkok also has a gaudy array of discotheques, small nightclubs, bars, and massage parlors in the Patpong area. As in most Asian and oriental cities, many of Bangkok's nightclubs provide hostesses.

The city has six main nightlife areas: the Gaysorn area is located amid some of the city's best shops and hotels on Rama I Road, between the Siam Inter-Continental and the President hotels. Patpong Road has only one large cabaret—the Cafe de Paris—but numerous unusual small clubs. Discotheques vibrate noisily on New Road and New Petchburi Road. Other nighttime activity centers on Rajdamnoen Avenue and Sukhumvit Road.

Classical dance performances

For many visitors, Bangkok's most fascinating entertainment is the Thai classical dance-drama, characterized by intricate steps and gestures. Dressed in heavily embroidered silk costumes, dancers convey varying emotions by the movement of their hands; many performers adopt long brass fingernails.

In addition to the dinner performances listed above, several hotels offer regular shows. One, the Oriental Hotel, stages an outdoor show on Thursday and Sunday at 11 A.M. For about U.S. $2, you can watch Thai boxing and swordfighting displays, as well as classical and folk dancing. Staged on the lawn beside the hotel, the performances provide an ideal subject for photographers.

The serious viewer of classical dance can attend full-length theater performances at the National Theater, near Pramane Ground. Usually held on weekends, these shows are performed by national dance groups. Check with your hotel or local newspaper for current performances.

You can also see performances of classical dancing at the Pakavali Institute and the Buddhai Sawan School of Fencing.

On a half-day excursion out of Bangkok, you can visit the Rose Garden Village show for demonstrations of dancing, boxing, and swordfighting. The Ancient City also features Thai dancing.

Thai souvenirs

The best buys in Bangkok are Thai handicrafts (see page 131). Several large stores specialize in Thai silk and cotton; here you can buy material by the yard or the latest ready-to-wear fashions.

In this sprawling city, there's no defined shopping district. Generally, shops are found near the hotels, at one of the big shopping centers such as Rajaprasong or Ploenchit Arcade, or at one of the city's markets.

The Weekend Market, one of Asia's largest, occurs each Saturday and Sunday at Pramane Ground. Here, under flapping canvas tents set up around the field's inside perimeter, you can buy anything—sarongs, men's and women's clothing, antiques, leather belts, shoes, house plants, caged birds, and fresh produce and fish.

Other markets include the Thieves' Market (Nakorn Kasem), situated between the north ends of Yawarat and New Road (see page 136); the Buddhist Market, near Wat Sutat; the Jewelry Market

Saffron-robed monks *cross the inner courtyard of Wat Phra Keo, which houses the Emerald Buddha. The wat is the temple for the Grand Palace.*

around Banmoh; the Flower Market on either side of Klong Theves; and the Cloth Market, found in the Indian section on Pahurat Road.

Most stores and arcades open early and close at 7 or 8 P.M. Bargaining over the price is expected, except in the larger, fixed-price stores.

Sightseeing in Bangkok

With so many dazzling wats visible from almost any vantage point in the city, your sightseeing problem in Bangkok is one of selectivity. To sample the capital's attractions, you may want to visit a few of the finest wats and tour the Grand Palace, then vary this exotic architecture with a look at Bangkok's other attractions.

Start with the palace

First stop for most visitors is the Grand Palace in Bangkok's oldest section. Covering a square mile on the east bank of the Chao Phraya River, the palace grounds are entered from Na Phralan Road. Inside this once forbidden city, the main attractions include the Amarin Vinichai Hall, a T-shaped structure used as the coronation room; Dusit Palace, its four stepped roofs crowned at the corners by gilded spires; and Chakri Hall, distinctive for its unusual mixture of European and Thai architecture.

After passing through the Gate of Supreme Victory (arched high enough to admit caparisoned elephants), you follow a cobblestone walkway leading to the inner palace grounds—a world of stone spires studded with chips of colored glass, *chedis* (bell-shaped spires), stylized animals, galleries and cloisters decorated in lacquerwork and mother-of-pearl inlays. The first structure you'll see is the Chakri Hall (great palace), its classical marble facade topped with a series of upturned, stepped roofs.

You can visit the Grand Palace daily from 8:30 to 11:30 A.M. and 1 to 4 P.M. The Palace is closed on holidays. Admission is free on both Saturdays and Sundays.

Viewing the wats

Before touring the city's wats, you should familiarize yourself with some of the terms used and the proper viewing etiquette.

Buddhist *wats* are actually monasteries, the enclosed grounds containing dormitories for monks and students and other facilities necessary for a monastic life. Housing an image of the Lord Buddha, the *bot* is the main chapel or shrine where ceremonies are held. Sacred objects are kept in the *viharn*. The tall, bell-shaped spires rising above the *wat* grounds are called *chedis*. A *prang* is more massive than a chedi, usually with a rounded top.

Simple rules of the country suggest you remove your shoes before entering a *bot*. Women should refrain from standing too close to or touching a monk.

Here are some of the city's most important *wats:*

Wat Phra Keo (Emerald Buddha Chapel) is located in the northeast corner of the Grand Palace. Topped by a golden, three-tiered roof, the multi-storied bot contains the Emerald Buddha, a 31-inch statue carved from translucent green jasper. Frescoes depicting the earthly life of Lord Buddha decorate the interior of the bot.

Wat Po (Monastery of the Reclining Buddha), surrounded by a low wall, is just south of the Grand Palace. Main attraction of the complex is the massive statue of the Reclining Buddha, stretching 160 feet long and rising 39 feet high. Resting on its right side, the Buddha is overlaid with gold leaf except for the soles of the feet, which are inlaid with mother-of-pearl.

Wat Arun (Monastery of the Dawn) stands on the west bank of the Chao Phraya River, almost opposite the Grand Palace. Its dominant feature is the 242-foot prang, surrounded by four smaller prangs. Constructed of brick-covered stucco, the prangs were built by Rama II in 1809. From the top of the central prang, reached by a narrow flight of steps, you have an overall view of the boat-clogged river and the city beyond.

Wat Sraket (the Golden Mount) is an artificial hill near Chakra Padi Pong Road, just east of the old city wall. When completed in 1868 by King Mongkut, it was the highest point in Bangkok. Reached by a circular staircase, its upper platform is some 260 feet high and has a gilded chedi in the center. November is the time of the Wat Sraket Fair, when pilgrims climb the steps to offer homage to the relic of Lord Buddha enshrined atop the hill.

Other wats of special interest are Wat Trimitr, housing a literally priceless golden Buddha; Wat Sutat, known for its giant, red-lacquered swing; and Wat Indra, dominated by the standing Buddha.

Chinatown and a thieves' market

Encompassing a maze of narrow lanes in the southern part of central Bangkok, Chinatown stretches along the parallel streets of New Road and Yawarat

Wat Sraket *rises some 260 feet above relatively flat Bangkok. Extensive views of the city and environs are possible from its upper platform.*

THAILAND

Road. The original Chinese settlement clustered on the site of the present Grand Palace.

Like the rest of the city, Chinatown rises from mud flats, a beehive of squat, century-old shops selling tea, jewelry, rattan, cure-all medicines, and items for everyday use. Streets are jammed with honking cars, overloaded trucks, fragile-looking trishaws, noisy motor scooters, and thousands of Chinese, Thai-Chinese, Indians, and other nationalities flooding the narrow sidewalks.

The Thieves' Market spreads over the north end of Chinatown. Though it was once primarily an outlet for stolen goods, today you'll find many displays of industrial machinery—power and hand tools, air compressors, and pumps. Scattered through the area, however, are shops offering reproductions of Thai antiques (where experts occasionally unearth a rare sculpture, bronze, or porcelain) and small stores selling Chinese character stamps (called *chops*) and polished bronze incense bowls.

Northern Bangkok

The northern section of Bangkok resembles a garden city, marked by broad tree-shaded avenues, meandering klongs, and modern houses brightened by small gardens. Rajdamnoen Avenue, a Thai adaptation of Paris' Champs Élysées, leads north to the National Assembly, Dusit Zoo, palatial palaces, and public parks.

National Assembly Hall, at the northern end of Rajdamnoen Avenue, is a white Italian marble structure, topped by a cupola, where Thailand's parliament used to conduct its official business. Dating from 1907, the hall was designed by Rama V as a throne room. An equestrian statue of the king dominates the large square in front of the hall. Inside, murals depict Thai history. The hall is currently being renovated and is closed to the public.

To the left of the square, fronting the Assembly Hall, is Amphorn Gardens, part of Dusit Palace.

Dusit Zoo, adjacent to the Assembly Hall, is entered from Rama V Road. Containing some 150 acres, the zoo is noted for its large boating lagoon and network of connecting canals. Tree-shaded paths border the water. A favorite weekend destination of Bangkok families, the parklike zoo includes a collection of exotic animals, a children's playground, and various souvenir and snack stalls.

Chitr Lada Palace, across from the zoo on the east side of Rama V Road, is the residence of the reigning monarch (Rama IX). Though the palace is not open to the public, take time to drive around its circumference. Enclosed by a stone-lined moat and wrought iron fence, the palace grounds feature a grassy lawn shaded by hundreds of trees.

Wat Benchamaborpitr (Marble Monastery), on Sri Ayutthaya Road southwest of the royal palace, was built in 1899 by Rama V. One of the finest examples of Thai architecture, it is constructed of white Italian marble and houses a famed collection of 52 life-sized bronze Buddha images.

Across the klong from the bot are the monks' quarters, frequently guarded by young boys selling caged birds. For a few cents, you can purchase a bird—setting it free brings good luck.

Eastern Bangkok

Many of the city's new hotels, elegant shops, embassies, office buildings, and shopping centers are located in the eastern section of Bangkok, bounded by New Petchburi Road on the north and Rama IV Road on the south.

Some of the city's wealthiest residents live on the *sois* (lanes) branching off Sukhumvit Road. Among the diverse attractions open to visitors are Jim Thompson's Thai House, the Snake Farm, and Lumpini Park.

Jim Thompson's Thai House, located at 6 Soi Kasemsan 2, north of Rama I Road opposite the National Stadium, is actually a composite of six old Siamese houses. The houses were dismantled in Ayutthaya, brought downriver, and rebuilt to form Thompson's main home and servants' quarters.

Floors, ceilings, columns, wall panels, and roof timbers are made of teak. Italian marble paves the entrance hall; antique green Chinese tiles—originally brought from China as ballast on rice boats—were used for the terrace parapet.

Thompson's house contains some fine stone and bronze statutes, porcelains and paintings, beautiful chinaware, and Thai furnishings. At the rear of the house, a terraced garden borders a tree-shaded klong.

Mr. Thompson—who popularized the Thai silk industry (see page 131)—mysteriously disappeared in the 1960s while on a hunting trip in Peninsular

Dusit Zoo *has a good collection of such animals as the popular hippopotamus. Families congregate here on weekends to enjoy the shady, parklike setting.*

River excursions on the Oriental Queen focus on the life of Thailand's water people. Stilt houses and barges line the distant shore.

Malaysia; since that time, a special trust has maintained the house. It is open to visitors Monday through Friday from 9:30 A.M. to 3:30 P.M.

Saowapa Snake Farm, on Rama IV Road, is part of the Red Cross Institute. Every morning at 11 A.M., attendants extract venom—used for vaccines—from the cobras, king cobras, kraits, vipers, and other snakes. The farm is closed on holidays. A small admission charge includes a handbook (in English) on the institute and its work.

Lumpini Park, farther east on Rama IV Road opposite the Saladang traffic circle, is Bangkok's largest park. Rectangular in shape, the tree-shaded green contains lakes and waterways, a restaurant, and picnic areas.

Museums and art galleries

Bangkok has an excellent museum and numerous small, interesting galleries featuring the work of Thai artists, most of whom concentrate on Thai subjects. Check with local papers and the Tourism Authority of Thailand (see page 151) for current shows and times.

National Museum, occupying a former 18th century palace near the river, recalls the nation's history and past glories. Built in 1782, the building is located on Na Phrathat Road, west of Pramane Ground.

Here you'll see a fine collection of traditional Thai paintings, as well as exhibits of porcelain, coins, weapons, textiles, royal thrones, traditional garments and dance costumes, and elaborate cremation chariots. The museum is open every day except Monday, Friday and holidays from 9 A.M. to noon and 1 to 4 P.M. Admission is free on Saturdays and Sundays.

More traditional Thai art is on display at Jim Thompson's Thai House (see page 135) and at the Suan Pakkad Palace.

Located at 352 Sri Ayutthaya Road, the palace is owned by Princess Chumbhot. It features a formal garden with a lacquer pavilion, decorated with 17th century gold leaf and carvings depicting the life of Buddha. The palace is open from 9 A.M. to 4 P.M. daily Monday through Saturday. It is closed on Sundays. Tours are conducted by English-speaking guides.

Excursions out of Bangkok

If you venture beyond Bangkok, you can see the rural life in the countryside, cruise the klongs and rivers on sightseeing and dinner excursions, visit floating markets, climb the steps of Thailand's largest pagoda, and wander through a capsulated version of the country's historic monuments, temples, and palaces.

Many of these sights are included in half-day and full-day trips from Bangkok, or they can be visited independently. You can arrange sightseeing trips through your hotel or city tour operators.

Cruising the waterways

Thailand's waterways are a dominant feature of the country, serving as its highways and lines of communication and setting the tempo of life with their leisurely flow. Though many filled-in klongs are only remembered in street names, others still survive.

Several specialized vessels take visitors on waterway excursions, maneuvering amid the rice barges, log rafts, sampans, and fishing boats for a memorable look at the life of the water people.

Through the klongs. The most popular (and therefore most congested) klong trip is the early morning excursion by launch departing from the Oriental Avenue landing and cruising to the floating market within Bangkok's city limits. With so many boats fighting for space on the narrow waterways, this trip has lost much of its charm.

A better trip is the three-hour rural klong trip on a *hang yao* (a long-tailed boat designed for shallow waters). You board at Prakanong Bridge on the southeast side of the city. Your boat takes you from the larger klongs into smaller ones and finally out into the padis, where you see farmers at work and vendors in sampans loaded with fruits and vegetables. On the way you move past a colorful array of sawmills, schools, wats, and typical houses. You stop at a Thai farmhouse near Hua-Pa, then board a converted 40-passenger rice barge for the return trip to Bangkok.

Thai dinner cruise. A converted teak barge makes nightly dinner cruises along the Chao Phraya River,

THAILAND **137**

departing from the Oriental Avenue landing at 6 and 8 P.M. Resplendent with carved and oiled teak paneling, polished bronze fittings, and handwoven fabrics, the *Tahsaneeya Nava* has a rich and traditional look.

Aboard the dining barge, you'll cruise past such Bangkok landmarks as Wat Arun (Monastery of the Dawn), the Royal Palace, and the king's barge house, with its carved and brightly painted royal river craft. Along the banks are gracious old colonial mansions, now housing embassies and banks. You'll also see life along the river—fishermen with hand nets, boats carrying farm produce to riverside markets, and tiny sampans loaded with containers of noodles and rice for people living along the river's banks.

Dinner aboard the barge offers a sampling of Thai cuisine, its normal spicy seasoning muted for tender palates. On the menu are mild curries of chicken, beef, and seafood served with rice and a variety of side dishes. You also have a selection of the country's fruits and other Thai desserts and sweets. Full bar service is available.

Aboard the Oriental Queen. An interesting part of Bangkok's cruise fleet is the 200-passenger *Oriental Queen*. Departing from the Oriental Hotel pier, the sleek, white cruiser makes day tours to Bang Pa-In and the ancient ruins of Ayutthaya and offers a candlelight dinner cruise every Wednesday night.

The first day tour leaves the Oriental Hotel at 8 A.M., cruising up the Chao Phraya River past elaborate temples and landmarks. Along the river's length you'll see Thai stilt houses, small sampans, and long lines of towed barges. By noon the vessel arrives some 35 miles north of Bangkok at the Summer Palace of Bang Pa-In. Lunch is served aboard before you visit the palace.

An air-conditioned bus takes you to the Summer Palace, country residence of a succession of kings. Star attraction is the 300-year-old Royal Palace, where the court formerly resided part of the year. You continue by bus to Ayutthaya (about 43 miles north of Bangkok). The city was Thailand's capital for 417 years until the Burmese sacked and destroyed it in 1767.

Some of the city's magnificent ruins have been restored; others are undergoing archeological excavation. Huge chedis, fine stone carvings, remains of temples, and Buddha images abound, giving a hint of the early splendor of this former city of a million people. In a shady garden, the small museum displays various Buddha images, hand-carved door panels, Buddha altar sets, and other works of art. You return to Bangkok by bus, through scenic green farm lands and padi fields, arriving in the city by 5 P.M.

The second tour reverses this schedule, leaving the city by bus for Ayutthaya and Bang Pa-In. You visit these sites during the cooler morning hours, then board the air-conditioned *Oriental Queen* for a buffet lunch and the cruise downriver, arriving in Bangkok about 5 P.M.

Markets, temples, and gardens

One of the more popular day trips out of Bangkok visits the rural klong and floating market of Damnern Saduak, stops briefly at Nakhon Pathom

In Surin ... Thailand's elephant roundup

Wild elephants *are rounded up and caught by slipping a loop around one leg.*

Each November, the annual "Elephant Roundup" takes place in Surin, about 280 miles northeast of Bangkok. Visitors see how elephants are captured and trained and then watch some compelling performances: elephant races, a parade of caparisoned war elephants, traditional dance ceremonies, and a tug of war between a mature elephant and 100 men.

A specially chartered, all-sleeper "express" train with dining car transports visitors from Bangkok to Surin in 8 hours for this event. You can also reach Surin year round by train or road (a six to seven-hour drive), with overnight accommodations provided in a rustic rest house.

Throughout Thailand's history, many invaders have been repelled by warrior kings mounted on battle-trained elephants. During the U.S. Civil War, Thailand offered to send President Lincoln trained war elephants, a foreign aid offer that was politely refused. In many parts of Thailand today you'll still see these massive beasts hauling teak logs from the forest as they have for several hundred years.

Crumbling chedis, *headless Buddhas, ruined palaces mark the remains of Ayutthaya, former Thailand capital sacked by the Burmese in 1767. Some ruins are still undergoing excavation.*

to view its chedi, and winds up with lunch and a cultural show at the Rose Garden.

Floating market. Damnern Saduak located about 60 miles southwest of Bangkok, presents an alternate to the capital's crowded, commercial floating market. To reach the market at the height of the activity, plan to get an early start. You should arrive between 7 and 10 A.M. because by 11 or so the action is over.

At the Damnern Saduak boat landing, you board a hang yao for the short ride to the small side klong where the floating market is located. On both sides of the klong, boardwalks in front of the buildings allow you to get close to the commercial activity.

Only vendors' boats are allowed in the market area, where hundreds of sampans glide back and forth answering customers' calls. Thai women, dressed in blue tunics and trousers and shaded from the sun by conical straw hats, sell a diverse array of fresh fruits, vegetables, fish, poultry, and meats. Many vendors leave their homes before dawn, paddling several miles to reach the market.

You can visit a smaller market on Ton Tan Canal, about 20 minutes from Damnern Saduak. On this excursion you'll observe a life style still centered on the water—Thai houses clustered along the klong,

Floating Market *at Damnern Saduak, outside Bangkok, often has traffic problems as sampan vendors sell vegetables, fruit, and meat to the local villagers.*

THAILAND

Rose Garden, *a recreation and resort area, features among its performances Thai classical dancing, a wedding ceremony, and a Buddhist ordination. You can also ride elephants, visit a handicraft village.*

Nakhon Pathom *is the tallest Buddhist monument in the world. Its chedi soars some 380 feet and is visible for miles. Here Buddhism was introduced to Thailand before the birth of Christ.*

people in traditional dress, housewives doing laundry at the water's edge, vendors selling produce, young and old bathing or brushing their teeth in the murky canal.

Nakhon Pathom. After the floating market, most visitors return to Bangkok through Nakhon Pathom, 30 miles west of the capital. The town's main attraction is Thailand's highest and largest pagoda, the 380-foot Phra Pathom Chedi. Resembling a huge inverted golden bowl and visible for miles, the chedi is covered with thousands of pieces of broken china.

Dating from 150 B.C., Nakhon Pathom is historically important because here Buddhism was first introduced to Thailand. During the November Fair, the grounds are packed with Thai pilgrims, monks draped in their saffron robes, vendors, and the ever-present fortune tellers. About a mile east of the chedi you can see the former palace where King Mongkut stayed whenever he visited the city (now government offices).

Rose Garden. About 10 minutes east of Nakhon Pathom, on the road to Bangkok, this 50-acre resort features a "Thai Village," where visitors can enjoy a comprehensive cultural show every afternoon. If you time your arrival for lunch, you can dine in one of the resort's two floating pavilions. The Thai village offers a showcase of crafts, cultural, and floral displays.

The 90-minute show, presented in a large thatch-roofed, open-air theater, includes portions of a monk's ordination and a wedding ceremony, Thai dances, and demonstrations of cockfighting, Thai-style boxing, pole and sword fighting, Thai-style bull fighting, and elephants moving teak logs.

Visitors can stay overnight at Rose Garden Hotel; surrounded by gardens, it has two restaurants, a lounge, swimming pool, and shopping facilities.

A brand new "ancient city"

Rising from former rice fields southeast of Bangkok is a make-believe world of temples, palaces, gardens, and waterways—Thailand's brand new Ancient City, a glittering composite of ancient Siam. The complex is about 20 miles (a 45-minute drive) from Bangkok on the road to the beach resort of Pattaya.

More than 50 major structures have been reproduced here—some copies of existing buildings, others modeled after structures now in ruins or long since destroyed. The 216-acre site is shaped roughly like Thailand, and buildings are situated to correspond with their location in the country. Most are three-fourths of the original size, though some are smaller; a few are full-scale replicas.

Buildings from the 6th to 10th century are recreated along the city's narrow roads. One of the finest —set on an island—is a model of Phra Sri Sanpetchaya, the old throne room in the former royal city of Ayutthaya; its white hall gleams under an ornate molded tin roof. Another popular attraction is the replica of Bangkok's Dusit Mahaprasat Hall, still used as a throne hall on ceremonial occasions. Reproductions are amazing in their detail (one door panel required 10 years to carve).

Throughout the city, massive statues recreate figures from Thai folklore. In the parklike setting, you'll find klongs and even a newly created mountain—a 175-foot manmade hill topped by Khao Phra Viharn castle (the original is in Cambodia).

On the north side of the complex, Thais from various parts of the country live in villages of typical Thai houses. Craftsmen demonstrate such skills as silk weaving, woodcarving, and umbrella making.

Upcountry journeys

Within a day's travel from Bangkok by road or rail are several interesting destinations. In the countryside, the life style is leisurely, and English-speaking visitors receive a wide smile—and a look of puzzlement. Several Bangkok tour companies offer excursions to those areas. In addition, the State Railway of Thailand runs roundtrip train excursions from Bangkok on Sunday.

Bridge on the River Kwai. Made infamous by a movie of the same name, this seldom-used, one-track railroad bridge is located near the town of Kanchanaburi about 80 miles (two hours by road) northwest of Bangkok. Though the film was shot in Sri Lanka (Ceylon), the World War II story was based on the Allied soldiers, prisoners of the Japanese, who perished in building the "Death Railway" bridge across the river.

Major points of interest at Kanchanaburi include the bridge (reconstructed since the war) and nearby Neolithic burial sites anthropologically linking Thailand and Malaysia. You can purchase vases, baskets, bamboo products, and good quality star sapphires at the town market and at souvenir stands near the bridge.

A new hotel, the River Kwai Village, was opened in 1975 on the river about 50 miles from the bridge. An air-conditioned hotel built in traditional Thai style, its amenities include a waterfall-fed swimming pool, tribal dances by Karen and Mon villagers, and aviaries containing jungle birds.

Khao Yai National Park. This jungle resort is a four-hour drive (about 130 miles) north of Bangkok. You cross the broad central plain—marked by miles of padi fields, grazing water buffaloes, farmers' stilt houses, and groups of shy children selling fresh fruit—then climb through wooded green hills toward the distant mountains. The park's southern entrance is located at the small town of Khao Yai, between Lop Buri and Nakhon Ratchasima.

Narrow, jungle-shaded roads twist through the park's 542,000 acres. Dense teak forests cover the mountainsides. Hiking trails follow mountain streams and penetrate the jungle. Often you'll see wild birds and animals.

Park facilities include overnight accommodations, a restaurant, wildlife watchtowers, swimming lagoons, and a golf course.

Pimai Ruins. Thailand's version of Angkor—the Pimai Ruins—is located 185 miles east of Bangkok (five hours by road) near the town of Korat. The famous ruins were built by the Khmers, who occupied this country a hundred years before they started building Angkor Wat. During the Khmer period, Pimai was linked by road to Angkor, the capital of the empire.

You can still see the towers and beautifully carved stone galleries, traces of the stone walls that framed the two-square-mile city, its four gateways, and the restored main temple, a fine example of classical Khmer architecture.

Gulf of Thailand resorts

Along the eastern coastline of the Gulf of Thailand are several scenic beach resorts, along with tiny islands and coral reefs to explore. The sports-oriented resorts offer visitors golfing, fishing, sailing, and water-skiing, combined with plenty of after-dark activity. Accommodations range from international standard hotels to air-cooled, thatched bungalows.

The two best known resorts on the Gulf's east coast are in Cholburi Province, within easy reach of Bangkok: Bangsaen, 65 miles southeast of the capital; and the booming resort of Pattaya beach some 35 miles further south. You can reach either resort by road in one to two hours.

Bangsaen. The calm blue waters of Bangsaen Bay, fringed by white sandy beaches and swaying coconut palms, offer Bangkok residents a holiday resort

Towering spires *and upturned roofs appear outside Bangkok on the grounds of the new "Ancient City," an almost-full-size reproduction of Siam.*

THAILAND 141

Horseback riding along Pattaya beach is just one of many activities to enjoy in this former fishing village.

Islands offshore from Pattaya are sites for swimming, sunbathing, sailing, and water-skiing.

for swimming and sunbathing. The challenging 18-hole Bangphra Golf Course is only a 15-minute drive from Bangsaen and a slightly longer trip from Pattaya.

You can explore the monkey cliff on Sammuk Hill behind the beach, fishermen's villages along the coast, a handicraft center at nearby Angsila, and roadside fruit stands for light lunches.

Most visitors stay at the Bangsaen Hotel, with its fresh-water swimming pool, or in one of its palm-shaded bungalows. Planned as a self-contained village, the hotel is separated from the bay by a palm-lined promenade where you'll find local restaurants serving Thai, Chinese, and western food.

Pattaya. Ten years ago, only Thais and a few European residents of Bangkok knew the fishing village of Pattaya and its wide sweeping bay, rimmed with sandy beaches shaded by coconut palms. Today, Pattaya is a popular resort catering to guests from around the world, with accommodations ranging from first-class hotels and beachfront bungalows to converted fishing boats.

A dozen modern beach hotels offer full resort facilities—swimming pools, tennis courts, horseback riding, golf, boating, fishing, water-skiing, scuba diving, yachting, para-sailing (using a parachute), and water cycling (using small boats equipped with foot-powered paddles). Guests have a wide choice of restaurants, supper clubs, and other night spots. Boutiques feature resort wear and dressmakers fashion custom-made apparel.

Just offshore from Pattaya are several islands, ideal for picnicking, swimming, spear fishing, or coral hunting. You can reach Larn Island and smaller Sak Island in about a half hour by speedboat or a little longer by fishing boat.

From Pattaya you can take a day trip into the teak forests near Sriracha to watch working elephants.

Another excursion from Pattaya is the overland tour to the sapphire mines in Chanthaburi, 110 miles away, with stops en route at waterfalls and botanical gardens.

Exploring southern Thailand

South of Bangkok on the Malay Peninsula—that thin strip of land separating the Andaman Sea and the Gulf of Thailand—lie points of historical interest, more beach resorts, and some little-traveled areas probably of interest only to adventurous travelers. It's an area of rubber plantations and coconut groves, of tin mines and deserted tropical islands, of lush mountain scenery and white sand beaches, of fishing villages and crystal clear waters.

The Malay Peninsula begins just west of Bangkok and extends for a thousand miles south to the Johore Strait, a narrow band of water separating Malaysia from the island nation of Singapore. At its narrowest point, the Isthmus of Kra, the peninsula is only 25 miles across; at its widest part—in Malaysia—it is about 200 miles wide. Thailand, Burma, and Malaysia share the long peninsula.

Although off the main tourist track, southern Thailand is easily accessible. The highway south from Bangkok to the Malaysian border (about 825 miles) is completely paved, Thai Airways has service to several areas of interest, and the express trains of Thai Railways are excellent. A number of tour operators run luxury coach services to Singapore, a six-day trip from Bangkok. If you plan to visit Singapore, you can combine two or more modes of transport for a circle trip.

Though the weather is always warm (averaging 80° F.), the best time to visit southern Thailand is during the dry season from October to February.

Down the peninsula

Thailand's National Route 4 runs along the peninsula's eastern coast, paralleling the Gulf of Thailand for about 200 miles. A string of mountains cuts the center of the peninsula, separating this coastal area from the Burmese border.

Phetchaburi. Located 103 miles south of Bangkok, the town is noted for the palace of King Mongkut (see page 127), built on a hill overlooking the town. A cobbled road, lined with thick tropical foliage, winds up the king's "Palace Hill" to roadside stables, a guardroom, and a hall once used for greeting distinguished visitors. Built in neoclassical style and surrounded by colonnaded arcades, the palace provides a splendid site for viewing the river, the town and temples, and the vast rice fields and sugar palms marching toward the sea.

Other sights worth a visit are the limestone hills pocketed with caves, some of which have Buddhist shrines; Haad Chao Samran, a white sandy beach; and the Suan Sema coconut and cantaloupe plantation. The largest Buddhist shrine is Khao Luang, best visited at midday when a shaft of sunlight illuminates the cave.

Since Phetchaburi has no adequate accommodations, it is best visited en route to destinations further south.

Hua Hin. Some 41 miles south of Phetchaburi is Hua Hin, the oldest and one of the most popular of Thailand's southern beach retreats. Once a small fishing village, Hua Hin became Thailand's summer social center when King Rama VII built his summer palace there in 1920. Thailand's present king still spends part of every year in Hua Hin, and prominent Bangkok families maintain spacious beach bungalows along the shore. Besides miles of white sandy beaches, the town has an 18-hole seaside golf course, tennis courts, and some great fishing opportunities.

Khao Luang Cave, *with its stalactites and Buddhist statues, is a popular shrine near Phetchaburi. A vertical shaft of light creates a cathedral-like effect.*

When night shrouds the port north of town, fishermen explode firecrackers as they head for the sea, hoping to ward off evil spirits and to ensure a good catch. During the day, fishing nets dry in the sun against a colorful backdrop of anchored fishing boats.

Not far from town you can visit a factory where Thai cotton is printed in locally inspired designs. Fabrics are sold here at reasonable prices. Other sightseeing destinations include local Buddhist wats and some of the isolated beaches.

Escape to the Samui Islands

Adventurous travelers have discovered an enchanted group of islands some 400 miles south of Bangkok, a refuge of quiet and solitude, of swaying coconut palms, white sand beaches, and warm blue water.

High islands rather than atolls, the Samui Islands lie off southern Thailand's coast, east of Surat Thani in the Gulf of Thailand. Verdant jungle covers much of the main island of Samui (33,000 population), which rises more than a thousand feet above the sea. Coconut plantations climb the island's lower slopes and border numerous deserted beaches. Dirt tracks reach the best beaches—some small and rock rimmed in tiny coves, others large and undeveloped.

The islands are accessible from Bangkok by a 12½-hour rail trip (on the southern express from Bangkok to Surat Thani) with a ferry ride across the gulf. Three ferries make the crossing daily, a trip taking up to five hours. When you reach Samui's port and main town of Tambon Ankthong, you must transfer from the ferry (because the water is too shallow) to a hang yao—or wade ashore if the tide is out. Of the town's four small hotels, the Sea View is the most popular with visitors.

Overnight guests can stay at the Railway Hotel; some of its rooms overlook the sea, others are bungalows under the trees. The town also has a number of small hotels and bungalows.

Prachuap Khiri Khan. Only 20 miles down the coast from Hua Hin, Prachuap faces a large semi-circular bay edged by at least five miles of unspoiled beaches. Wooded mountains and lacy waterfalls beautify the countryside; offshore, islands jut above the surface of the calm waters. For an idyllic day, hire a boat and cruise to one of the three nearby islands for swimming and sunbathing.

The peninsula's west coast

At the small, provincial town of Chumphon, National Route 4 turns west, twisting across the wooded, grassy hills of the Kra Isthmus to Ranong on the Burmese border. South of Ranong, Thailand occupies the rest of the peninsula all the way to the Malaysian border. Mountains march toward the horizon. The highway is never far from the beaches and offshore islands, but at times it runs inland, paralleling mountain streams and offering glimpses of waterfalls and vast rubber plantations.

Ranong. Situated within a few minutes of the Burma border, Ranong lies about 325 miles south of Bangkok. Separating the two countries is the Kra River, which broadens into a wide and lovely blue inlet west of the town. Marked by an architectural style mixing Chinese and Portuguese influences, the buildings lining Ranong's main street are topped with projecting tile roofs shielding pedestrians from the tropical sun and rain.

The best place to stay is the Hotel Thara, located on a mountain slope a few minutes south of town. From the hotel you can make interesting side trips into the mountains, to nearby beaches, and to offshore islands.

South of Ranong you'll also see the first tin mines —some still active, others long abandoned. Though elephants are fast disappearing in southern Thailand, these work animals are still used to transport huge hardwood logs out of the jungles and mountains to roadside pickup spots.

Phuket Island. Thailand's largest island, this scenic and historic spot is destined to become one of Thailand's major beach areas. Lying off the country's west coast about 570 road miles south of Bangkok, Phuket Island is a 14 to 18-hour drive from the capital. Thai Airways has daily service to the island.

Connected to the mainland by a bridge at its northern end, the island is approximately 27 miles long and about 11 miles wide. You drive south between rows of tall stately rubber trees to Phuket City (population 100,000), located on the southern end of the island. A few miles inland from the Andaman Sea, the city has accommodations and offers good shopping for pearls and shells. Many travelers, however, prefer the Phuket Island Resort on the beach 10½ miles to the southwest.

Crystal clear sea water splashes over offshore coral reefs onto the island's white sand beaches. When you want a change from swimming and sunning, explore the rest of the island. In the lowlands, farmers dressed in conical hats and sarongs cultivate rice fields, and water buffaloes graze alongside roads traveled by Thai trucks and motorscooters.

Among the island's historic sites are three wats: Wat Cha-Long, an ancient temple with a sacred image, five miles from the city; Wat Pra-Thong, with a Buddha image half-buried in the ground; and Wat Monkol, containing a golden Buddha image dating from the 13th century.

Surin, 14 miles from the city, has the island's most beautiful stretch of white sand and heavy surf; it offers bungalows and a nine-hole golf course. Rawai Beach, 10½ miles from town, is the departure point for visits to nearby islands. At many of the beaches, you can have a meal of fresh crabs, quick-fried in deep fat, for about 50 cents.

Phangnga Bay. The most popular sightseeing tour from Phuket visits Phangnga Bay, an area of spectacular mountain scenery, caves, and waterfalls, located on the mainland about 62 miles north of Phuket City.

On the way (about 19 miles north of Phuket's bridge) is Gold Caves, an underground shrine containing gold Buddha statues veiled in incense amid limestone stalactites and stalagmites. Not far from the cave is the village of Phangnga, reached by a dirt road that cuts through dense jungle. Here you can board a hang yao for a ride across the bay, past palm-shaded lagoons and along mangrove-bordered waterways. Unusual rock formations dot Phangnga Bay. Poking up above the sea are small rugged mountains, eroded by the water and covered with

Sunset at Chumphon *finds this lone fisherman rowing toward shore. Hired boats visit Lanka Chio, noted for its birds' nests used in the famous soup.*

trees and thick vegetation. Crescents of white sand edge the bases of colorful stone cliffs. Caves and grottos abound, some cutting deeply into the mountain islands; one cave—Thum Lod—is large enough for boats to penetrate.

You can stop at some of the islands, such as Pinggan, noted for having a cave above the water, or at Khao Tapu, marked by its slender, eroded rock pillar. You can also visit the Muslim village of Panyi, built on stilts in the open sea. Though fishing is its main concern, the village has a small school, open-air shops, and even flocks of quacking ducks swimming beneath the houses.

Southernmost Thailand

Just north of the Malaysia border are the region's two largest cities: Hat Yai, with a population of about 200,000; and Songkhla, a beach resort of 150,000. Waterfalls brighten this mountainous area. You'll find domed mosques rather than Buddhist temples, along with other differences—some of the women wear lace veils and many people speak Malaysian, though the area has been part of Thailand for decades. You can reach the area by road, rail, and air from Phuket, Bangkok, or Penang in Malaysia.

Hat Yai. Only about 50 miles north of the Thai-Malaysian border, Hat Yai is a popular city. Visiting Malaysians are attracted by its mountain scenery, shopping opportunities, bullfights, a nine-hole golf course, and active night life. The city has a larger shopping center than Penang Island.

On sidetrips from Hat Yai you can visit the countryside, the modern Prince Songkhla University, a rubber research plantation, waterfalls, and tin mines. On the last Saturday and Sunday of each month, Thai-style bullfights (between two bulls) are held at 10:30 A.M.

The town has some 50 hotels, but most Western visitors prefer the international standard Sukhontha Hotel.

Songkhla. Although Hat Yai is an important rail and commercial center, it's Songkhla — about 20 miles northeast through rubber, banana, and coconut plantations — that proves more interesting. Facing the Gulf of Thailand, Songkhla abuts Samila Bay and salt-water Songkhla Lake, a body of water covering almost 500 square miles.

Nearby sights include fishing villages and a quaint morning lakeside fish market. Day excursions take visitors to Bird Island, famous for its birds' nests collected for Chinese soup; to the top of 2,000-foot Mount Tang Kuan; offshore to visit Cat and Rat islands; and to a potters' village.

Not far from town are the white sand beaches of Pinetree and Samila, usually deserted except for local picnickers and swimmers — or perhaps a wandering cow or two. Near Samila Beach is Suan Tul Park, one of Thailand's largest plantations, known for its topiary shrubbery. The Samila Hotel is across from the park, facing the beach.

Thum Lod Cave *is a natural arch some 165 feet long with stalactites hanging from its ceiling. Boat trips can be made from Phangnga Bay.*

Fishing family *dries squid on wire screens near Songkhla. You can visit the morning fish market and several tropical offshore islands.*

THAILAND 145

Master carver and youthful apprentice create teak elephants. These and other handicrafts—lacquerware, weaving, pottery, silver work, and paper umbrellas—are sold in many of Chiang Mai's shops.

Chiang Mai woman carries her market purchases suspended from a bamboo pole. Samlor (three-wheeled cab) sits in front of a suburban house with sliding wooden shutters on the windows.

North to Chiang Mai

Chiang Mai, "the Rose of the North," is Thailand's second largest city and the center of the nation's traditional folk arts and crafts. Its charm lies in its antiquity, its mixture of cultures, its friendly people, and its leisurely pace. The city's peaceful streets are interspersed with some 99 wats, many reflecting both Thai and Burmese architectural and religious influences.

Fragrant mountain air

Situated in a mountain valley a thousand feet above sea level, Chiang Mai is sliced in half by the Mae Ping River and surrounded by green mountains and padi fields—a sharp contrast to Bangkok's sizzling heat and congestion.

The city lies in the shelter of 5,500-foot Doi Pui, a mountain on the west; not far away is 8,500-foot Doi Inthanon, Thailand's highest peak. In all, the northern region contains 14 of the country's 18 highest mountains. Panoramic scenery is one of Chiang Mai's most valued commodities.

To get there, you can take a 500-mile, overnight rail trip, go by bus or private car, or take the 1½-hour flight north from Bangkok. Until recently, the city was isolated because of lack of transportation; but today Chiang Mai is serviced daily from the capital by several Thai Airways flights. A number of tour operators provide bus transport from the capital.

The best time to visit is between November and February. April is the hottest month, and rain occurs from May to October.

Hotels, dining, night life

Chiang Mai has some 30 hotels, but those favored by most tourists include the Chiang Inn, Porn Ping, Railway, Rincome, Sri Tokyo, and Suriwongse. Most have dining facilities, and a host of other services.

Diverse cuisine. You'll find a good selection of restaurants in the hotels and around the town, most of them serving western, Chinese, and Thai meals. But don't miss having the *khantoke*, a northern-style Thai dinner served at low tables and featuring a variety of spiced dishes accompanied by glutenous rice.

For western-style meals, try the Pub, on Huey Kaew Road; the Somboon, on San Pa Koi Road; and Pat's Restaurant, on Moon Muang Road. For Chinese cuisine, you might try several restaurants including the Chiangmai Restaurant on Chang Klan Road, or Sriprakas on Lamphun Road. The Rincome Hotel features a northern-style Thai dinner; good Thai food is also available at the Wilai Garden on the main highway and Aroon Rai in the night market. The Srisurang on Huey Kaew Road offers western, Chinese, and Thai meals.

Gastronomically adventurous travelers can try the small, open-air roadside stalls. Scattered throughout the city, they serve favorite Thai foods.

Evening entertainment. Night life possibilities are limited in this northern outpost. At the Old Chiang Mai Cultural Center on Pra Tu Hai Ya, diners are served a northern Thai meal while hill tribe members perform dances in costumes. The Snake Bar at the Prince Hotel is a local gathering spot.

In addition to hotel entertainment, the city has many nightclubs, both popular with the locals: the Blue Moon, in the southeast corner of the walled city, and the Rin Kaew on Huey Kaew Road.

Thai handicrafts

Chiang Mai is the center of traditional Thai handicrafts: silk and cotton weaving, pottery and celadon making, silver working, teak woodcarving, costume doll making, and temple bell and Buddha image casting. Other crafts include the making of lacquerware, paper umbrellas, embroidery, and basketry.

Handspun and handwoven Thai silks and cottons are made here in a variety of designs, weights, and colors. Another fabric from the Chiang Mai area blends silk and cotton; the cloth is noted for its coolness and its resistance to creasing.

Household articles formerly used by northern Thai families can sometimes be found in markets.

Silk shopping *in Chiang Mai can uncover beautiful bolts of handspun and handwoven fabric, dresses, and coats. Custom tailoring is offered.*

Tribesmen of the northern hills

Among the hills and mountains of Chiang Mai live tribesmen who differ from the Thais in culture, costume, language, and tradition. Although the origins of the mountain people are mysterious, anthropologists believe they migrated from southern China down the Indochina peninsula, some arriving in Thailand as recently as a hundred years ago.

The six main tribal groups are the Meo, Karen, Akha, Lisu, Lahu, and Yao; each tribe has its own culture. You can visit a Meo village on a day trip from Chiang Mai.

Until recently, the Meo tribespeople cultivated opium poppies; now they grow rice, corn, coffee, and lichee. They also raise various domestic animals and make hand crafted souvenirs. The Meo people, who believe in spirits, live in primitive, thatched wooden huts.

Everyday Meo costumes are magnificent: black shirts and trousers decorated and trimmed in red or white, colorful headbands, and striped leggings. Tribespeople display their wealth in the form of silver neck rings and silver ornamented clothing.

If you visit a Meo village, you'll see the unusual silver jewelry fashioned by skilled tribal craftsmen. They make handsome bracelets, belts, and neck rings, as well as silver bowls, boxes, and candlesticks. Other crafts include pipes and colorful, embroidered cotton handbags.

Resplendently garbed Akha family *relaxes in the sheltered breezeway of their stilt house.*

Chiang Mai, an ancient city

Though its early history is obscure, ancient records indicate that Chiang Mai was founded in 1296. It was the seat of an independent kingdom called Lanna until the mid-16th century, when Burmese war lords conquered the city. Chiang Mai then became the center of a tug of war between Burma and Thailand.

Built nearly seven centuries ago as a fortress protected by walls and a defensive moat, Chiang Mai still retains intact portions of the original walls. The old walled city stands on the western bank of the Mae Ping, separated by the river from the newer part of the city on the eastern bank.

But Chiang Mai is not old-fashioned, and traffic is becoming a problem. *Samlors* (three-wheeled cabs) fill the streets, competing with taxis, buses, and motorcycles. Modern structures rise up beside wats, most of the latter built in the traditional northern style—colored tile roofs stepped in two or three levels, overhanging low teak side walls. Most of the wats house huge Buddhas covered with gold leaf.

Traveling through the residential areas, you'll see teak houses built on stilts in the northern Thai style. Living quarters are below, sleeping rooms above for better ventilation.

Many houses are surrounded by spacious gardens of temperate climate flowers—roses, hydrangeas, and rhododendrons.

Sightseeing in Chiang Mai

Though the main city sights can be seen in a day, you should allow at least three days to take countryside excursions and visit the hill tribes.

Working elephants *still haul teak logs out of the forest near Chiang Mai as they have for centuries. Watch demonstrations of this at Mae Sa.*

Exploring the city

You can see three ancient wats in the old city, visit the local produce market, the university, and a cultural center.

Wats. Four important wats are located within the walls of the old city:

Wat Phra Singh, built in 1345, is the city's largest temple. An important monastery, it houses the three most venerated Buddha images in the north.

Wat Chiang Man is the oldest temple in Chiang Mai, dating from 1297 and constructed under King Mengrai, the city's founder. Behind the sanctuary, a chedi is decorated with 15 elephant statues.

Wat Chedi Luang, built in 1411, contains a 26-foot-high Buddha. Occupied by monks, this wat has the reputation of being the holiest in the city.

Wat Suan Dork, built in 1383, houses Buddha relics and ashes of members of the Chiang Mai royal family.

Outside the walls are several other important temples: Wat Papao, built in the Burmese style; Wat Mahawan, with fine woodcarvings; and Wat Chiang Yuen, with its chedi decorated with dragons, tigers, and Chinese porcelain motifs.

Other city sights. You also may want to visit the central fruit and vegetable market, the arboretum and zoo, and the Winter Fair and sports arena.

The University of Chiang Mai, the country's largest educational institution, spreads over a 500-acre campus. On the grounds are golden-roofed buildings, a lake, gardens, and trees. A Tribal Research Center and museum are also located on the campus. History buffs can visit the Chiang Mai National Museum.

Laddaland. To learn more about northern Thai life styles, crafts, and dances, you can visit Laddaland (also called the Lanna Cultural Center). In a complex of pavilions and gardens, you view dance performances, a costume museum, hill tribe exhibits, typical huts, and a handicrafts village. Here craftsmen offer handmade umbrellas, lacquerware, handwoven cloth, silver ornaments, and teakwood carvings.

Countryside trips

Though Chiang Mai itself offers many attractions, you should travel into the countryside to experience rural Thai life, visit tribal villages, and see some of the north's industrious craftsmen. Local tour companies conduct half-day and full-day excursions into the surrounding countryside. Take along a sweater; temperatures can be cool at higher elevations. Jungle trips and cruises on the Salween and Mekong rivers are also available from Chiang Mai.

Journeying by mini-bus or jeep, you travel deep into the jungle on the upper slopes of Mount Doi Pui. At the Meo village of Doi Pui, you'll visit the Puping Palace, a winter home of Thailand's first family built amid gardens and spectacular mountain scenery, and the monastery of Doi Suthep.

Akha tribeswomen, *dressed in black outfits trimmed in red or white with silver neck rings, live at the Old Chiang Mai Cultural Center.*

Cigarette piper *of the hill tribe at Doi Pui holds an oversized bong (bamboo water filter). It's used to smoke the local tobacco.*

Intricate designs *in bright colors are handpainted on paper umbrellas at handicraft shops in Borsang, the umbrella village.*

Richly decorated metal parasols, *gifts of the Prince of Siam in 1786, decorate the four corners of Wat Hariphunchai in Lamphoon.*

THAILAND **149**

During Loy Krathong *Thais place candle-lit, lotus-shaped boats in the water to carry away their sins.*

King and Queen *participate in ritual ploughing, sowing of Pramane Ground, Bangkok, during Ploughing Ceremony.*

In Lampang, southeast of Chiang Mai, you can visit an elephant training school. Visitors see elephants being bathed and being trained to drag, push, and stack enormous logs with their trunks and tusks.

East of Chiang Mai, tours stop in the umbrella village of Borsang and the silk and cotton-weaving town of Sankamphaeng. Other possible tours include visits to the Chiang Dao Caves north of the city, and the 300-foot-high Mae Klang waterfalls south of the city.

About 15 miles south of Chiang Mai, you can visit Lamphoon, noted for local silk weaving and old temples. Farther south is Pasang, known for its cotton fabrics and beauty contests.

Festivals and events

Though many of Thailand's festivals are religious in nature, associated with the life of Lord Buddha, they sparkle with fun, color, and gaiety. Nearly every week brings holiday festivities. Many of the colorful events have been celebrated for centuries.

Some of the country's festivals are regulated by the lunar calendar so they occur on different days each year. When you arrive in Thailand, check with the Tourism Authority of Thailand (see page 151) or look in the Bangkok newspapers for current dates.

Here are some annual festivals and events:

January-March

New Year Celebration. The Thais offer gifts to thousands of saffron-robed monks from December 31 to January 2. In Bangkok, bells toll and gongs sound, while games and displays get underway at Pramane Ground. The Chinese New Year is celebrated in February with three days of festivities.

Phra Buddhabaht Festival. This 3-day ceremony is held at the Shrine of the Holy Footprint in Sara Buri in February.

Magha Puja. This event commemorates the meeting of Lord Buddha with 1,250 disciples. Today, his followers perform good deeds and crowd the temples to pray during the full moon in February.

Kite flying contests. From February to April, contests are held on the Pramane Ground in Bangkok. Competitors try to destroy other contestants' kites with barbs attached to kite strings. *Chula* (male kites) compete with *Pakpae* (female kites).

April-June

Chakri Day. Every year on April 6 ceremonies take place honoring the first king of the Chakri Dynasty, Rama I, who established Bangkok as the capital of the country.

Songkran Festival. This 3-day event, April 13-15, is Thailand's New Year holiday. Water and perfume are sprinkled on images of Buddha, and the King receives a ceremonial bath. Bangkok celebrates with a fair of folk dancing, singing, and music. In the rural areas, the water throwing (meant to wash away evil spirits) becomes very energetic, often drenching bystanders. In Chiang Mai a water festival queen is chosen to reign over the festivities.

Ploughing Ceremony. A traditional May ritual, this ceremony begins the rice planting season. The King and Queen preside at Pramane Ground for the

Practical information for visitors to Thailand

Here are some practical details to help you plan your trip to Thailand:

Entry requirements. You may visit Thailand for up to 15 days without a visa, but you need a valid passport and proof of onward passage. For longer stays, apply for a visa at the nearest Thailand consulate or embassy. The visa requires three photos, costs $5.00, and is good for 90 days. Thailand consulates are located in Montgomery, AL; Los Angeles; Miami; Chicago; Honolulu; Grosse Point, MI; Kansas City, MO; Elkins Park, PA; El Paso, TX; and Richmond, VA.

You will need an international health certificate showing inoculation against smallpox, cholera, and yellow fever if you are coming from an infected area. The U.S. Public Health Service recommends you have typhoid, paratyphoid, tetanus, and gamma globulin shots.

On departure, you pay an airport tax of $2.

Customs. Visitors are allowed to bring in personal effects including sports equipment, cameras, film (5 rolls and 40 pieces of film pack). You may also bring in 200 cigarettes and one quart of wine or liquor.

Currency. The rate of exchange of the Thailand baht ("baat") is B 20 to U.S. $1. Thailand has no limit on the amount of travelers' checks or foreign currency, providing the amount you take out of the country does not exceed the original amount brought in. You are limited to B 500 for import or export, and local currency can be reexchanged upon departure. Officials recommend you change money at a bank or an authorized money changer.

Health conditions. Bangkok, Chiang Mai, and other major centers have adequate medical facilities. Most hotels have drug stores where you can purchase everyday medicines and toiletries.

Tipping. Light tipping is the rule in Bangkok—most hotels and restaurants add a 10 percent service charge. However, visitors usually tip even with a service charge: B 2-5 for porters or bell boys, no standard tip for chambermaids or roomboys, and 10 percent tip for waiters.

At air and rail terminals rates are fixed: airport porters B 5 a bag, railway porters B 1 for two bags. At restaurants with or without a service charge, a 10 percent tip is customary. Taxi drivers do not expect tips but may be given one if the driver helps with luggage. At beauty and barber shops, tips are not expected, but B 5-10 is acceptable.

Climate. Thailand's weather is tropical—with cool, hot, and wet seasons. But persistently high humidity is the greatest climatic reality. In Bangkok, the best time to visit is November to February, the so-called "cool" season, when daytime temperatures average 84°F.

The hot and humid weather lasts from March to May, when temperatures soar to 100°F. Bangkok usually has smog during this season because of its location on a flat plain, the filled-in klongs, and the heavy traffic.

The rainy season starts in June and lasts until September, the wettest month in most parts of upper Thailand. During this period, monsoon rains are sporadic, often torrential, and usually occur in the afternoon and evening.

Chiang Mai, at a higher elevation than Bangkok, is cooler and a little less humid during the hot season. Sea breezes temper the heat and humidity at the beach resorts.

For more information. Get in touch with the Tourism Authority of Thailand (TAT), Ratchadamnoen Avenue, Bangkok, or their U.S. offices: 3440 Wilshire Boulevard, Suite 1101, Los Angeles 90010, and 5 World Trade Center, New York 10048.

---

ritual ploughing and sowing of the furrows (see page 12).

Visakha Puja. Held on the full moon day in May, this commemorates Buddha's birth, enlightenment, and nirvana (see page 13).

July-September

Asalha Puja. Commemorating the first sermon delivered by Lord Buddha, this Buddhist retreat precedes Buddhist Lent. At this time, young men who wish to become monks have their heads and eyebrows shaved before entering the temple.

October-December

Tod Kathin. Each November the people take gifts of food and clothing to Buddhist monks at the temples.

Phra Chedi Klang Nam Festival. This fair, held in connection with Loy Krathong, is celebrated with boat races and a pilgrimage to the island temple in the river at Paknam, 14 miles south of Bangkok.

Loy Krathong. In November the rivers streams, lakes, and canals of Thailand glitter with thousands of tiny floating *krathongs*, which represent prayers. Made of banana leaves, they are decorated with flowers and shaped like birds, boats, and other intricate designs.

Golden Mount Festival. This countryside fair is celebrated in November; in Bangkok, bazaars are held at Wat Sraket amid general merriment.

Elephant round-up. Each November an elephant round-up is staged at Surin (see page 138).

King's Birthday. December 5 is a national holiday; public buildings are illuminated and full dress ceremonies occur at the Grand Palace.

Sule Pagoda (top) *marks the center of Rangoon's commercial district.* **Gawdawpalin Temple (right)** *rises beside the Irrawaddy River at Pagan. Stalls in Mandalay's Zegyo Market* **(far right)** *offer Burmese household articles.*

152 BURMA

Burma

Pagodas, ancient ruins, and fabled Mandalay

(See page 126 for map)

Until recently, Burma was one of the most isolated countries in Southeast Asia—not because of geography or war but because of an intense desire to shut itself off from the rest of the world. Now, following a decade of tight military control, Burma is taking its first tentative steps to reestablish relations with other Southeast Asian countries and the rest of the world.

This has resulted in increasingly relaxed restrictions for travelers to Burma. In the 1960s visitors could only stay 24 hours in the country. At present you can obtain a seven-day, non-renewable visa. And, although accommodations are limited, you can travel freely through the rolling, lowland country along the Irrawaddy River as far north as Mandalay. Unfortunately, the equally fascinating mountain country fringing the lowlands in the north is still closed to tourists because of frequent unrest among the hill tribes and an insurgent movement by the Chinese-supported Burmese Communist Party.

But despite difficulties in the hills, government tourist officials speculate that 15-day visas may be issued within the next few years.

Burma—then and now

The second largest country in Southeast Asia (behind Indonesia), Burma covers an area of about 262,000 square miles. It stretches some 1,200 miles from the peaks of the Himalayas to the Bay of Bengal and Andaman Sea, with a maximum width of 575 miles. Bordered by China on the north, India and Bangladesh on the northwest, and Thailand on the southeast, Burma occupies a strategic location in Southeast Asia.

The old colonial city of Rangoon is Burma's capital, main port, and business center. Other important cities are Mandalay, the country's second

Basket maker, *wearing a checkered* longyi, *assembles baskets, bags, and bird cages at Rangoon's Bogyoke Market. At nearby stalls you can purchase the colorful cotton cloth used by Burmese for clothing.*

Barefooted schoolboy *offers his bouquet of flowers at the sacred, golden-spired Shwedagon Pagoda in Rangoon. In a few years, he'll be old enough to become a Buddhist monk.*

largest city—noted for its silk weaving and its historic role as former capital of the Burmese kingdom—and Moulmein, on the Salween River, a trading center for teak, rice, and rubber. The fascinating ruins of Pagan, southwest of Mandalay, are a goal of most visitors.

Mountains and deltas

The dry, rolling hills of northern Burma contrast sharply with the flat and tropical southern delta. Jungle, interspersed with rubber plantations and teak forests, covers mountain slopes and valleys.

Burma's main artery is the Irrawaddy River, navigable for 900 miles of its 1,300-mile length. Rising high in Tibet's mountains, it flows from the rolling hills of the north down through the broad central plain, emptying into the Gulf of Martaban near Rangoon. The Irrawaddy serves as the country's economic lifeline and major highway. *Padis* (rice fields) in the valleys and dry rice cultivation on the hills form Burma's rice bowl.

History and government

Although Burma's history dates back to about the 9th century B.C., the Burmese people were not unified until 1044 A.D., when the warrior-king Anawratha conquered the Mon people, beginning a dynasty at Pagan that lasted until 1287. Pressured by the Mongols on the north and the Shan tribe on the east, the Pagan empire collapsed, and general disunity prevailed for nearly five hundred years. A new Burmese dynasty reunited much of Burma in the late 18th century, and in 1885 the country was annexed by the British.

During the Japanese occupation of 1942-45, a group of nationalists known as the Thirty Comrades gained control of the ragtag Burmese army; after the war, they negotiated the independence of Burma in 1948.

In 1962 a military coup led by General Ne Win (one of the "Thirty") seized the government and has since guided Burma along "the Burmese Road to Socialism," a unique blend of Marxism and Theravada Buddhism.

Now the winds of change are breathing through the country. The government is gradually coming under civilian control, and a new constitution is being drafted that hopefully will strengthen Burmese unity.

The Burmese people

Burma embraces some 126 racial, tribal, and ethnic groups totaling almost 27 million inhabitants.

About three-fourths of the people are Burmese, graceful and small in stature, a kind and fun-loving race descended from Mongoloid stock. Minorities with strong representation are the Shans, Karens, Kachines, Chin Akha, Bre Kayah, and Yinbaw. In addition, many Chinese, Pakistani, and Indo-Burman people have settled in the country.

In Burma, the Burmese are named after the day of their birth and have no family name. On marriage, the Burmese woman does not change her name. Married and single women are addressed as "Daw"; for men, the Burmese form of address "U" is equivalent to "Mr."

Sarongs and collars of brass. Both men and women wear the Burmese sarong, called the *longyi* when worn by a man and the *htamein* when worn by a woman. Though the sarongs appear similar, the woman's comes in all patterns and colors, but the man's is usually a plain color with a checkered pattern. Many Burmese women rub a gold paste makeup over cheeks and nose "to keep the skin tight"; the paste is made primarily from finely ground powder of the chenakat tree.

Among the non-Burmese hill tribes, the cultural patterns and modes of dress are diverse. Many tribal people wear brilliant costumes with distinctive features. The "giraffe-necked" women of the Padaung Tribe ornament themselves with high collars of coiled brass. Other groups wear feather bonnets, bright beads, elaborate silver jewelry, turbans, or cloth leggings.

Language. Burmese is the official language of government and language of instruction in elementary schools. English is the second language, studied in secondary schools.

Religion. Nearly all Burmese are Buddhists, and most of their cultural activities are related to Buddhism. The country's main pagodas are not only places of worship but also often commercial and social centers. Burmese men and boys spend part of their lives as ordained novices in a Buddhist monastery, wearing the saffron robes of the monks. The Burmese express a deep respect for their religion by removing footwear in pagodas and other religious places, and visitors should follow suit.

The temple experience

In Burma, perhaps more than in any other Southeast Asian country, temples are the religious and social centers of the people. For the Western visitor, a casual stroll through a busy city temple—such as Rangoon's Shwedagon or Mandalay's Arakan pagodas—can offer a rewarding glimpse into the Burmese way of life.

Entering the temple is an experience in itself. Carrying your shoes, you are funneled toward the pagoda's main temple through a long arcade jammed with dozens of tiny stalls. Vendors, selling everything from soup to shoes, call out as you pass. Small children dash through the crowd, dodging yellow-draped Buddhist monks clutching alms bowls, who seem serenely apart from the confusion.

Suddenly you're in the main temple, and activity ceases. Bronze urns picketed with sticks of incense send thin clouds of aromatic smoke toward the rafters, where small doves murmur and coo. As you wander, cool tiles soothing your feet, you can almost feel the soft vibrations of low gongs that occasionally pulse through the halls. Devout worshippers place offerings of flowers and incense at the shrines and then, on bended knees or prone on the floor, pray to Buddha.

Planning your trip

Burma lies some 8,500 air miles west of the United States—a trip taking about 19 hours from California. The time difference between the west coast of the U.S. and Burma is 14½ hours. When it is noon Tuesday in Burma, it's 9:30 P.M. Monday in California.

Visitors can enter Burma at Rangoon either by plane or ship. Four international airlines and the national Burma Airlines land at Mingaladon International Airport, about 12 miles north of Rangoon. Steamship companies dock at Rangoon on the Gulf of Martaban. Overland travel into Burma is forbidden.

Japanese taxis and trishaws

Apart from Rangoon's bus system, transportation in the city is largely provided by bright orange, Japanese-made, three-wheeled taxis (seating four or five), buses for transfers, a few jeep taxis, and trishaws (known as sidecars) for short trips. Meters are required but usually out of order—so settle the price first. A short ride in the city costs about 2 Ks. (about U.S. 50 cents). For all-day sightseeing in Rangoon, hire a taxi with an English-speaking driver at a flat rate. If you bargain first, prices should range from U.S. $10 to $15.

No rental cars are available, and train travel is not recommended because the countryside is unsettled and dangerous.

Because of the seven-day limit for tourists, most visitors prefer to fly Burma Airlines to Mandalay and Pagan. However, from Rangoon you can reach both places by steamer on the Irrawaddy River; the river trip to Mandalay takes about 24 hours.

Limited accommodations

Hotels in Burma range from spartan to comfortable but are adequate for adventurous travelers. With only about a thousand hotel beds in the whole country and with more than ten thousand yearly visitors, confirmed reservations are a must. Hotels add a 10 percent service charge and 10 percent tax.

Few restaurants

Travelers find it difficult to sample native foods because the country has few restaurants—Burmese rarely eat outside their homes except for snacks or an occasional Chinese meal. Hotels serve Continental and Chinese meals; occasionally Burmese dishes appear on the menu.

Burma has an interesting cuisine, less spicy than food in some neighboring countries but seasoned liberally with onions, garlic, chilies, ginger, and a highly flavored shrimp paste. Burmese eat two meals a day, one around midmorning, the other in early evening; both meals are similar.

A typical meal includes boiled white rice; a thin, clear, bland soup with vegetables known as *hingyo;* raw vegetables to dip into a spicy hot relish called *ngapi;* fried vegetables or a salad called *lethok* or *thanat,* garnished with fried onions and garlic; and a meat or fish curry. (Often the cooking oil floats to the surface of the curry; Burmese spoon it over their rice.) Dishes should all be eaten at the same time, though some hotels serve in courses. Dessert, if served, is usually fruit.

Two national dishes of Burma you might try are *khaukswe* (chicken in coconut gravy over egg noodles) and *mohinga* (rice noodles in fish soup). These noodle dishes are often eaten as snacks, accompanied by condiments of lime, chilies, onions, and eggs.

Local soft drinks, beer (the local brand is Mandalay), coffee, and tea are all safe to drink. Water should be bottled or boiled.

Shopping in Burma

The outstanding buys in Burma include hand-forged silverware, with some good buys available in goblets, bowls, and trays. Other good buys are lacquerware and cotton goods.

Tourists are allowed to purchase these items only at approved stores, such as hotel shops or the Diplomatic Shop in Rangoon. All goods bought at these shops must be paid in foreign currency. (Tourists carrying American dollars will not encounter problems in Rangoon, but not all foreign money is accepted.)

Other objects representative of Burmese craftsmanship are handwoven fabrics, teak and ivory carvings, mother-of-pearl objects, pipes, and tobacco products.

Large shops are open from 9 A.M. to 5 P.M.; smaller shops extend their hours, opening at 8 A.M., and closing at 7 or 8 P.M.

Rangoon, city of golden pagodas

An old colonial city of lakes and parks, Rangoon lies on the Hlaing (or Rangoon) River, 21 miles inland from the Gulf of Martaban. Linked to the earliest Burmese history by golden-spired temples built six centuries before Christ, Rangoon today remains the gracious city laid out by the British around the turn of the century, though it now shows signs of wear and neglect. Burma's capital since 1885, it has a population of 1,800,000.

The name Rangoon derives from *Yangon,* meaning "end of strife"; it was the name bestowed on the small fishing village and religious center in 1755 by the Burmese King Alaungpaya to mark his victory over the Mons.

But it was not until the British occupation (1852-1948) that Rangoon became Burma's major port and economic center. With the riverfront as a base and the golden Sule Pagoda marking the city center, the British planned Rangoon's business section in the "colonial grid" pattern of wide streets and tree-lined boulevards running in straight, even blocks from the traffic circle around the Sule Pagoda. This early commercial district now houses most of the principal shops, the Strand Hotel, transportation and business offices, and government buildings.

Rangoon's colonial aura and the absence of high-rise buildings contribute to an atmosphere reminiscent of the quieter days before World War II. Motor traffic is light, consisting primarily of trucks, buses, and small three-wheeled taxis painted bright orange. Most people you see on the street are wearing the national dress, the colorfully printed cotton *longyis.*

Although more western travelers visit Rangoon now than a few years ago, western tourists are still rare enough to be conspicuous. Burmese are friendly and talkative people; and since English is the second language, usually the visitor can find assistance when he needs it. For a street map of Rangoon, inquire at the Tourist Burma office, 34 Strand Road, near the Burma Airlines office.

Rangoon's hotels and restaurants

Rangoon has four hotels and several government rest houses. The Inya Lake Hotel is located near

Leafy trees *line many of the streets in the old colonial city of Rangoon. Motor traffic is relatively light in Burma's leisurely paced capital.*

Shwedagon Pagoda, *described by Kipling as a "golden wonder," towers 326 feet above the city. Bamboo framework encircles the upper spire.*

the airport. The Strand and Railway hotels are in downtown Rangoon, and Kanbawza Palace is midway between the city and airport.

Both the Inya Lake and Strand hotels are air-conditioned and offer dining rooms, bar, and entertainment; the Inya Lake has a swimming pool.

Look for Burma's best western-style restaurant at the Inya Lake Hotel. Other restaurants are the Strand Hotel dining room and the Continental, at the corner of Sule Pagoda Road and Bogyoke Street. Light snacks are available at Nanthida, opposite the Strand Hotel, and the People's Patisserie on Sule Pagoda Road.

For Chinese cuisine try the Kwan Lock, 67-22nd Street, for elaborate Chinese dishes; the Golden Palace, 84-37th Street, specializing in Shanghai and Szechuan cooking; and the Nam Sin at 8th Mile Prome Road, for Peking or Shanghai specialties.

Handicraft shopping

Burmese handicrafts are available in government shops at the Strand and Inya Lake hotels, at the airport, and at the large Diplomatic Shop on Sule Pagoda Road. In these stores you can find silver and lacquerware, ivory and teak carvings, hand-woven silk and cotton, and mother-of-pearl items.

Other places to browse are the Pagan Shop Moonlite and Burma Handicrafts on Sule Pagoda Road and the numerous shops on Edward Street producing lacquerwork items for Buddhist ceremonies.

Shwedagon Pagoda, a landmark shrine

Towering above Rangoon, the bell-shaped Shwedagon Pagoda—Rudyard Kipling's "golden wonder" —forms a landmark that has dominated the city since the first shrine was built almost 2,600 years ago. Of the thousands of Buddhist temples in Burma, it is probably the most revered by Buddhist pilgrims and tourists because of the eight sacred hairs of Gautama Buddha enshrined here.

You may be unprepared for the size and brilliance of the pagoda. Its spire soars 326 feet, the entire surface shimmering with gold plate. Atop the spire is the *hti* (umbrella), encrusted with more than 5,000 rubies, diamonds, and other precious stones. Numerous ornate smaller pagodas cluster around the base of the spire.

You reach the main part of the pagoda by covered stairways; be prepared for a steep climb. Each roofed aisle is an elongated market where you can buy flowers and other temple offerings, souvenirs, household goods—even soups and sandals. Elevators to the top of the shrine are located near the east, west, and south entrances.

As a mark of respect, visitors are requested to go barefooted—no shoes or stockings. Best time to visit the pagoda is early morning or late afternoon, when the flagstones are cooler under bare feet.

Other Rangoon highlights

As you explore the city, you'll see many of these colorful sights:

Sule Pagoda. Situated in the heart of the city, the octagonal Sule Pagoda equals the Shwedagon in beauty but not in size. Built in Burmese style, it has four main entrances leading to an open platform ringed with lesser pagodas. Built about 2,250 years ago, the Sule Pagoda contains relics of Buddha brought from India. If you can, visit in early evening when floodlights illuminate the complex.

Bogyoke Market. "What is your country?" and "Change money for a good price?" are two questions you'll probably be asked in this shopping area where the Burmese themselves shop. Located on Bogyoke Street, about a mile west of the Railway Station, the Bogyoke Market's stalls offer yards of colorful cotton fabrics, hand-carved ivory, and other handicrafts—as well as the multitude of everyday items needed by city residents.

Rangoon River. Warehouses and shops line the riverfront, where dock workers load rice and teak on black-hulled ships and boatmen propel their brightly-painted sampans across the river. Near the Strand Hotel you can hire a sampan water taxi for a better look at life along the river. The waterfront rivals Bombay and Calcutta in volume of traffic.

Botataung Pagoda. The gilded Botataung Pagoda, one of the few pagodas that you can walk into, is near Strand Road. Typical of the earlier Mon temple architecture, it consists of a single enclosed temple and has only one entrance. Inside are six chambers whose walls and ceilings are covered with semiprecious stones, interspersed with small, square mirrors.

Chinatown. Rangoon's Chinatown centers about a half mile west of the Sule Pagoda, bordered on the north by Fraser Street and on the south by Dalhousie Street. Here, you'll see shops where families work on handicrafts and tailors sew new suits. The Chinese have their own schools, temples, and cultural activities in areas similar to Chinatowns throughout Southeast Asia.

Cultural Institute. Located on Shwedagon Road, this complex includes the National Museum, National Gallery of Art, National Library, and National Academy of Music, Drama, and Dancing.

The small National Museum features possessions of the last king of Burma and furnishings from the Royal Palace in Mandalay. The museum is open Monday through Thursday from 10 A.M. to 3 P.M., closed on Fridays and national holidays, and open on Saturday from 1 to 3 P.M.

You can attend performances of Burmese classical dancing and music—played on traditional instruments—at the National Academy of Music, Drama, and Dancing. Ask at your hotel for information on performances.

Sidetrips out of Rangoon

Within 5 to 10 miles of the city are a variety of sights you can see on day or half-day trips.

Royal Lake. One of the most popular scenic destinations around Rangoon is Royal Lake. A palm-lined road encircles the lake, tropical islands and floating gardens dot its waters, and lotus blossoms float on its placid surface. Along the shore is the Museum of Natural History. The glittering image of the golden Shwedagon is reflected in lake waters.

If you visit Burma during a holiday or festival, visit Bogyoke Gardens on Royal Lake. Stalls and amusements are set up, and the Burmese wear their finest apparel to celebrate.

Kabe Aye (World Peace) Pagoda. About 8 miles north of Rangoon along Kokine Road (the airport road), you can see the site where the 6th Buddhist Synod was held in 1954-56, a period also marking the anniversary of Buddha's enlightenment. Nearby, the Great Cave has an Assembly Hall with room for 10,000 people.

Inya Lakes district. A favorite relaxing spot for the Burmese, the Inya Lakes can be seen on your return trip to Rangoon. From Kabe Aye, take Prome Road and follow the western lake shore back to the city.

Day trip to Pegu. Pegu is the site of Burma's serene-faced Reclining Buddha, largest and most lifelike in Southeast Asia, and the Shwemawdaw (Great Golden God) Pagoda. The 50-mile trip northeast from the capital takes approximately 2 hours either by road or rail.

During the days of the Mon dynasty, Pegu was the site of a great city and seaport. Founded in 573, the town was destroyed by one Burmese King in 1757 and rebuilt by another in 1782-1819. In the 16th and 17th century, travelers were awed by its size and magnificence, but after a change in the river's course, Pegu never regained its former splendor.

The Reclining Buddha, known as Shwethalyaung, stretches 181 feet and rises 46 feet at the shoulder from mosaic glass cushions. Its site is a mile west of the railway station. Believed to have been built in A.D. 994, it disappeared under jungle growth after Pegu's destruction in 1757. Railway workers rediscovered it in 1881. Now fully restored to its former greatness, the Reclining Buddha attracts scores of Burmese and tourists.

A mile east of the railway station lies the Shwemawdaw Pagoda, rising 288 feet above its platform. According to legend it contains two of Buddha's hairs—making it one of the most venerated shrines in Burma. When you pass through the main entrance and climb the steps to the platform, you'll see murals recording the destruction of the pagoda by earthquake in 1930 and the subsequent states of reconstruction.

Colorful winged sampans *do a brisk business transporting Rangoon's citizens across the wide river. You can also hire a sampan taxi for harbor trips.*

Massive white Ananda Temple, *most impressive and most venerated of Pagan's remaining monuments, is one of several open to the public. Its golden spire, damaged in the 1975 earthquake, is being rebuilt*

Sandoway (Ngapali) Beach. With miles of swaying palms and white sand beaches, this seaside resort on Burma's western coast is a popular retreat for Rangoon's diplomatic families. Ngapali is not a Burmese name—folklore attributes it to Italian visitors; they thought it resembled their seaside town of Naples.

Relaxation is the keynote. Daytime activities include golf on the six-hole course at Mazin, 2 miles from Sandoway, and mackerel fishing in Andrew Bay, about 6 miles south.

Sandoway's palm-fringed beach slopes gently down to the sea. A half mile offshore, submerged rocks make a breakwater, creating a placid, lagoon-like setting at low tide, perfect for swimming.

One hotel, the Sandoway, has 10 simple but comfortable *basha*-type bungalows situated on the beach (open October to May).

Tourist Burma and Burma Airlines both have overnight tours and special roundtrip Sunday flights to Sandoway. Since accommodations are limited, confirmed reservations are essential.

The lost world of Pagan

Nestled in a broad curve along the east bank of the Irrawaddy River, the ancient ruins of Pagan (rhymes with "anon") seem to meditate beneath the tropical sun. Slowly crumbling walls, rain-eroded shrines, and an occasional broken stupa mark the passage of time in this former center of Buddhist learning. Pagan lies about 400 miles north of Rangoon—a 2-hour flight.

From the air the size of the complex is startling —roughly 16 square miles, containing the remains of almost 5,000 temples. Stretched along an 8-mile bend of the Irrawaddy on a parched plain, the ruins are the survivors of an estimated 30,000 pagodas and temples that once blanketed the Pagan landscape. Centuries ago, 3 million people lived on this plain; now the village of Nyaung-U stands alone among Pagan's ruins, its 3,000 people still living in woven bamboo and thatch houses as their ancestors did.

Some historians believe the armies of Kublai Khan destroyed Pagan when they swept down from the north in 1287. Many archeologists think Pagan's enemies were time, negligence, and ignorance.

Although many of Pagan's temples and pagodas suffered damage in July 1975 when the area was hit by a severe earthquake, the character and general view of Pagan and its attractions have not changed. You can still wander among thousands of temples and pagodas. Some are small and have exquisitely carved designs; others are great hulking masses of stone. All the best-known structures are still standing in their original form, though many have damaged roofs and cracked walls.

Pagan's history

A magnificent center of Buddhist learning almost a thousand years ago, Pagan may have lost its luster, but it remains one of the most impressive collections of ruins in Southeast Asia, second only to Cambodia's Angkor Wat (now closed).

Folklore asserts that Pagan began as a cluster of 19 villages whose royal dynasty ruled from the 2nd century A.D. But it was not until the reign of Anawrahta in 1044 that Pagan came to flower.

Anawrahta was a military leader with a knack for administration and a zealot's energy to convert his people to Theravada Buddhism. After conquering the Mon kingdom of Thaton, he began a feverish program of temple construction and religious conversion lasting more than two hundred years.

Visiting Pagan

With the opening of the Thiripyitsaya Hotel in 1973, Pagan finally has adequate visitor accommodations. The hotel has 25 modern, air-conditioned rooms, and additional rooms are being built. The only other tourist accommodation is the modest Burma Airways Guest House, a clean but esthetically unappealing building.

Upon arrival at Nyaung-U Airport, a free Burma Airways bus may meet you, or you can take a taxi jeep to your hotel. For visitors who are not members of tour groups, the best way to see Pagan is to hire a jeep—ask your hotel desk clerk for a driver who speaks English. Arrange this in advance.

The most interesting time to visit Pagan is during the March festival period when thousands of pilgrims—laymen, monks, and nuns—arrive from all over the country. Unfortunately, this is also the dry season, an uncomfortably hot time for visitors.

Temple-viewing

Over the years, only about a hundred of Pagan's monuments have escaped destruction by decay and ruin. You won't want to visit all of them, but your sightseeing should include some of these outstanding temples:

Shwezigon Pagoda. Dominating the countryside with its massive golden dome, the Shwezigon Pagoda draws a steady stream of pilgrims. Built by King Anawrahta, it is one of Pagan's most active religious centers. The sacred golden, bell-shaped stupa at the center of the complex is thought to contain the collarbone and a tooth of Buddha. One of the oldest of the typically Burmese stupas found at Pagan, it is the prototype upon which later stupas—including Rangoon's Shwedagon Pagoda—were modeled.

Located in the village of Nyaung-U, the Shwezigon Pagoda and the colorful market nearby are the first attractions most visitors see.

Ananda Temple. The most impressive of Pagan's remaining monuments is undoubtedly the Ananda Temple. Built in 1091, the whitewashed building is roughly 200 feet square and was originally 168 feet tall; its crowning gold spire was toppled during the 1975 earthquake. It is currently being rebuilt. Visitors enter under a sign stating "No Foot Wearing," a reminder that this temple and even the muddiest ruins at Pagan are places of worship in which all visitors must remove shoes and socks.

Walking inside, bare feet refreshed by the cool floor, you will come to an enormous statue of Buddha. Note the position of the hands. This is the Blessing Buddha; on the remaining three inside walls of the temple, you see the Preaching Buddha, Departing Buddha, and Teaching Buddha, all distinguished by the position of the hands. The inner walls are decorated with stone Buddhas, bas-reliefs, and glazed terra cotta tiles which illustrate ancient legends.

Gold foil for Buddha

Throughout Burma, temples, pagodas, and images glitter with gold—frequently tiny squares of gold foil pressed and molded on by worshippers. Some statues have been gilded so often that the original shapes are indistinct. Temple devotees buy the small, filmlike squares at temple approaches.

In the southeastern part of Mandalay, you can visit a workshop and see gold foil produced by men of the goldbeaters' guild, carrying on an ancient craft much as their fathers did. In small charcoal furnaces, gold bullion is melted and purified in crucibles. Then the lumps of gold are pounded into flat rods about a foot long. Hand-cranked rollers flatten and stretch the rods, followed by repeated hammering and beating, until the gold ribbons measure ¾-inch thick and 55 feet long.

The ribbon is cut into small squares that are placed between layers of bamboo paper beaten with a sledge hammer. With repeated pounding and turning, each package eventually measures about two inches square; this is then divided and beaten again. The final product measures five inches square and an incredible 1/200,000 of an inch thick.

Women transfer the gold leafs to paper, cutting them in 2½-inch squares and placing them inside protective folders. In Mandalay a single gold leaf sells for about 4¢.

In a side wing of the Ananda Temple, the small Archeological Museum contains exhibits illustrating the economic, architectural, and religious history of Pagan. Along the museum's verandahs, you'll find inscribed stones recording religious endowments of the Pagan period.

Thatbyinnyu Temple. The best overall views of Pagan are obtained from the Thatbyinnyu Temple, not far from the Ananda Temple. Through narrow passageways and up steep flights of stairs, you can climb almost to the top of the 201-foot-high temple for a panorama well worth the effort.

From your perch you watch swallows swoop and turn among pagodas stretching toward the horizon. The wind rolls over twisting rows of acacia trees to comb through fields of corn, and far below, Burmese go about their daily life as they have for generations.

Other temples. Pieces of glazed green limestone decorate the two-story Htilominlo Temple, built in 1211 A.D. Rows of stone sculptures flank the interior corridor, and four Buddhas guard the central room.

Largest building of its kind in Burma, the uncompleted Dhammayangyi Temple symbolizes Buddha's rays of truth. Built in 1183 A.D., the Sulamani Temple closely resembles the Thatbyinnyu Temple in layout; traces of its original frescoes remain.

The pyramidlike Manuha Temple was built by the captive Mon king Manuha in 1059 A.D. Nearby Manpaya Temple served as his residence; built of brick and surfaced with stone, the square-shaped temple has perforated stone windows as did the earlier temples of Pagan.

Brick walls enclose the rectangular Upali Thein (Ordination Hall), named after the celebrated monk Upali. Frescoes on its walls and ceilings remain well preserved.

Lacquerware—a local craft

Like a scene out of the past, Burmese women walk gracefully to the market, huge baskets of finished lacquerware balanced on their heads. Though Pagan's greatness has disappeared, its legacy of artistic excellence survives.

In the marketplace of Nyaung-U, visitors can choose lacquered items—cylindrical cigarette boxes, round bowls, and compartmented boxes. The tiny hamlet of Mynaka, not far from Nyaung-U, is Burma's lacquerware center. Many of the pieces sold in Rangoon's finest shops are made here, and visitors can pick up some good bargains. Your tour guide or taxi driver can take you to the village, where you can shop and see various pieces made.

Artisans of all ages work at the local craft. The specialty is black lacquerware, decorated with intricate and abstract designs in gold leaf. Less expensive items include non-gold leaf work—lacquer decorated with yellows, greens, and reds. The entire process, from weaving the bamboo-horsehair

Lacquerware *requires time, patience, and a steady hand to produce beautiful and lasting works of art. You can buy lacquerware at shops throughout Burma.*

framework to final polish, may take a full year; between layers of lacquer, the pieces rest in a damp cellar for several weeks.

Fabled Mandalay

The name Mandalay evokes exotic images of the mysterious East, though today visitors find a curious mixture of old and new Burma. Mandalay appears to be ancient—wide, tree-lined streets exude a timeless aura, and the Burmese wooden buildings hint at antiquity.

For hundreds of years a large village stood on the site; then, in 1857, King Mindon built the royal capital city of Mandalay. It was the heart of Burma until 1885, when the British annexed the country and deposed Burma's last king. During World War II more than a third of the city was destroyed by Japanese and Allied bombing. Though the city is only a fragment of its once grand past, enough older monuments have survived to provide a vivid contrast to the modern era.

Mandalay sprawls over a 25-square-mile area on the east bank of the Irrawaddy River, 430 miles north of Rangoon. By air, it's a half hour's flight from Pagan. Only 248 feet above sea level, Mandalay is hot, dry, and dusty—receiving only 30 inches of rain annually.

From the air you can see Mandalay Hill rising out of the plains to the northeast, and you notice the almost perfect geometrical pattern of the city, the mile-square site of the Royal Palace and the roads cut at right angles.

Enormous white lions *dwarf visitors at the base of Mandalay Hill. It takes an hour to climb the 1,729 steps to the viewpoint that overlooks this ancient city and the Irrawaddy River.*

Getting settled in Mandalay

Most visitors prefer the Mandalay Hotel near the moat of the Royal Palace, though the city has several other hotels. Reservations should be made in advance through your travel agent or the Burma Airways tourist information service in Rangoon.

Local transportation relies heavily on pony carts to get around the city and bullock carts for moving goods. Although you can easily get to most of the sights on foot, the taxis (World War II jeeps) are cheap and save time in getting to specific destinations. Private automobiles are scarce. Wide, pug-nosed buses convey passengers, and overloaded antique trucks transport teak logs.

Mandalay is surprisingly clean for a city with such a large population of horses and bullocks. From the outside, buildings show less wear and tear than those in central Rangoon, and Mandalay's main streets are all paved.

Burma's cultural center

Constructed by Burmese kings rather than by British colonial governors, Mandalay is the most Burmese city in the country.

With its saffron-clad monks, monasteries, and famous pagoda, Mandalay is the center of Burmese Buddhism and learning. Buddhism enters all aspects of Burmese life—festivals, birth, marriage, family, and death. Here you'll find all the elements of Burma's ancient system—educational, social, and political.

If you are in the city between July and March, try to attend a performance at the National School of Dance and Music here.

A town to explore

Mandalay centers on the Diamond Jubilee clock tower, designed by an Italian count in 1903, and the nearby Zegyo Market. Bordered on the north by B Road, the market operates indoors by day and outdoors at night.

In the evening the street is barricaded to vehicular traffic, providing the site for an open-air bazaar that lasts from 6 to 9 P.M. Flickering kerosene lamps illuminate the wares, spread on tables and pieces of cloth on the street; sellers squat next to their merchandise. Here you can buy Burmese food, fancy bars of soap, medicines, and yards of cloth from the vendors. If you plan to do any shopping in the marketplace, remember that bargaining is a way of life.

During the day, wander down side streets near the market, looking into homes and small shops that form part of Burma's massive cottage industries. In the space of a few blocks, you can see numerous artisans at work—rolling cigars, carving ivory pieces, weaving silk, or carving a harp. Don't enter a house unless you're sure it's a workshop or you're invited in.

Mandalay Hill. Standing at the northeast corner of the city, Mandalay Hill rises 774 feet from the river plain. No Burmese would visit Mandalay without making a pilgrimage up this sacred hill. Two enormous white lions guard the entrance to the temple stairs; it's a long and strenuous climb—1,729 steps—taking an hour to reach the top. At dusk, the most dramatic time, you have an unobstructed view of the sunset over the Irrawaddy River.

The chief attraction of Mandalay Hill's pagodas is the Shwe Nandow Monastery, a magnificent example of 19th century carved and gilded timber buildings. It contains a replica of the royal throne, glass mosaics, and some outstanding Burmese woodcarvings.

At the southern approach to the hill is the Kyauk Tawgyi Pagoda. Legends relate it took 10,000 men 13 days to haul this huge marble Buddha from a canal to the pagoda site. Around the shrine stand figures of Buddha's 80 disciples.

Below the hill the Kuthodaw Pagoda is notable for its army of small white *chedis* (small shrines) lined up in rows. Each of these 729 temples contains a marble slab, upon which is inscribed a portion of the Buddhist *Tripitaka* (canon) formulated by the 5th Buddhist Synod in the 1860s.

The Golden Palace. All that remains of the Royal Palace is the massive, rose-colored wall that enclosed the palace grounds—27 feet high, 10 feet thick, and a mile square. It is edged by a broad moat, 225 feet wide and 11 feet deep.

Located on the north side of Mandalay, in the shadow of Mandalay Hill, the palace once housed the royal family. Its interior included some fine examples of Burmese woodcarvings. The palace was destroyed during a Japanese bombing attack in 1945.

You can enter the palace grounds, however, and view modern Burma's Independence Monument in the center of the palace square. The palace museum contains furniture from the royal household. English-speaking guides relate historic details.

Shwekyimyint Pagoda. Far older than Mandalay, the pagoda was built in 1167 by King Minshinsaw. You'll find it in the center of the city, midway between B and C roads. The shrine is noted for its original Buddha figure and the many gold and silver images adorned with precious stones.

Mahamuni (Arakan) Pagoda. One of Mandalay's most venerated shrines, this pagoda contains the Mahamuni image of Buddha, a 12-foot-tall statue covered with thousands of tiny squares of gold leaf. Believed to be an ancient statue from another part of Burma, the image attracts thousands of devout pilgrims who place offerings of flowers and incense at the shrine. Tiny stalls line the long arcade leading into the main temple. The shrine lies south of the city.

Aywezun. One place you shouldn't miss is Aywezun (or "place of the buffaloes"), located at the edge of town on the Mandalay River. It is difficult to find on your own, so take a taxi. At this miniature port,

Water buffalo teams *haul burdensome loads up the muddy banks of the miniature river port of Aywezun, located just outside Mandalay.*

merchandise is unloaded from small boats and carted into town. Rickety old trucks back deep into the water and teak logs are floated onto the truck bed. Teams of water buffalo are then harnessed to the truck, hauling it up to the road. Along a dike near the river, houses built on high stilts cluster over the water. Families of river workers crowd into these precarious structures.

Outside of Mandalay

North and south of Mandalay along the Irrawaddy River, green belts of land mark the sites of three former Burmese capitals. Today, these grand cities are in ruins, and Burmese farmers plant tobacco, yams, and truck vegetables on the river lands. You can reach the deserted capitals on a day trip from Mandalay by taxi.

Amarapura. A few miles south of Mandalay, Amarapura was founded by King Bodawpaya in 1781. All that remains of the old City of the Immortals are worn walls, pagodas, and tombs.

Most of the weaving of Mandalay silk or cotton is done here by Kathe villagers; the material is used for the beautifully patterned open skirts, *acheik htamens*, worn by Burmese women.

Ava. A little further downstream from Amarapura stands Ava, the capital from 1364 to 1781. Access is difficult, and inquiries should be made in Mandalay.

At the northern gate facing the Irrawaddy, the city walls remain almost intact. Farmers have cultivated the area within the walls and around the 90-foot-high watchtower. A nearby monastery contains excellent examples of Burmese masonry art and architecture.

Sagaing. Burma's capital from 1322 to 1364, Sagaing lies on a peninsula on the west bank of the Irrawaddy; you reach it along the mile-long Ava road and rail bridge, the only span across the river. One of the most unusual of the city's temples is Kaung Hun Daw Pagoda. Modeled after the Mahaceti in Sri Lanka, it has a solid stone hemisphere that rises 151 feet with a 400-foot circumference.

The Shan Hills

Famed for cool, year-round temperatures, the Shan Hills of central Burma are a mountain retreat for officials and families wishing to escape Rangoon's heat and humidity. The Salween River carves deep gorges through the vast plateau country. Cupped amid pine-covered hills is Inle Lake, home of the leg-rowing lake people.

From Rangoon, it's a 1¾-hour flight to Kalaw's Heho Airport. In the Shan Hills, you can make your base at Kalaw or Taunggyi, seat of the Shan state government.

Mountain excursions

Cool, fresh air and pleasant walks among sweet-smelling pines are attractions at Kalaw, situated at an elevation of 4,340 feet. Modest accommodations are available at the Kalaw Hotel. You can arrange day trips to Pindaya Caves, with its carvings and Buddha figures, or to Inle Lake. Box lunches can be ordered from the hotel for excursions.

Further up the winding road at 4,675 feet is Taunggyi, capital of the Shan state. It's a 40-minute bus ride from the airport; during the wet season the road is frequently closed. In Taunggyi you can walk among the pines or climb the Crag, a rocky outcrop. Every five days, hill people in colorful dress congregate here for the local market.

Tourists stay in the 44-room Taunggyi Hotel. Bring a jacket, for evening temperatures are cool.

Inle Lake's leg-rowers

A favorite destination is a visit to Inle Lake, home of the leg-rowers. For generations, lake-dwelling villagers have fished and farmed from long, narrow boats. Group tours usually include a visit to Inle Lake, or you can make arrangements in Taunggyi.

Standing on a small platform on the stern, one leg wrapped around an oar, the boatman propels his shallow craft amid floating vegetable gardens and stilt villages. During the annual water festival in October, teams of leg-rowers race on the lake.

Surrounded by high mountains, 20-mile-long Inle Lake is fringed with dozens of tiny villages. Largest of these is Inbawhkon, site of the local market. Small houses, topped by reed-thatched roofs, are built on stilts above the water. The lake people—called *Intha*, sons of the lake—farm floating island gardens (mud built up on matted reeds and planted with vegetables) and stilt-supported arbors. Fishermen row and fish at the same time, balanced on

Reed-thatched roofs *top stilt houses in villages bordering Inle Lake. Marshy land is cut by watery channels. Shallow boats provide transport.*

their shell-like boats; large, conical bamboo fish traps are used to net the fish.

On the lake you travel by motorized *hlay*, a long, narrow boat. It has no seats, so passengers must squat on the floor. You'll stop at the *yma-ma*, a miniature floating market, where you see the leg-rowers up close.

Skilled weavers in the Inle region turn out intricately patterned, handwoven silks and cotton cloth; if you wish, you can visit one of the weaving villages to see weavers at work.

In the village of Nam-Hu, you can see the Paung-Daw-U Pagoda and its three heavily-gilded Buddhas. Centuries old, the statues have been gilded so many times they resemble balls of gold. An annual festival honors these sacred figures.

Festivals and events

Throughout Burma, colorful festivals and celebrations occur during the year. Each ethnic group—the Karens, Shan, Arkanese, Mons, and Kayah—has its own festival. Burma's foreign groups—Indians, Pakistanis, Nepalese, and Chinese—each observe special national days.

Burmese Buddhist families celebrate weddings, name-giving for newborns, ordination of boys as monks, and the ear-boring ceremony for young girls. Since many of the festivals are based on the lunar calendar, dates change from year to year.

Here are a few of the festivals and events occurring about the same time annually:

Independence Day. A countrywide celebration comes on January 4, with parades, sports, dancing,

Practical information for visitors to Burma

To help you plan your trip, here are some practical details you will want to know:

Entry requirements. Seven-day tourist visas are currently being issued for sightseeing in and around Rangoon and for places of historical and cultural interest, such as Mandalay, Pagan, Nyaung-U, Taunggyi, and Pegu. To apply for a visa, you will need a passport, three application forms, a detailed itinerary, and four photos (1½ x 2 inches).

Apply at either the Union of Burma Embassy, 2300 'S' Street N.W., Washington, D.C. 20008; or the Consulate-General of the Union of Burma, 10 E. 77th Street, New York, N.Y. 10021. A visa fee of $6.25 should be sent with passport and completed forms. If you apply by mail, allow about 3 weeks for processing. Carry extra passport photos; immigration officials require one on arrival at Rangoon. A return or onward ticket is required.

Newspaper writers, publishers, priests, and "hippies" need special visas obtained directly from the Burma Government.

You will need an international health certificate showing inoculation against smallpox; cholera and yellow fever shots are also required if you are coming from an infected area. The U.S. Public Health Service recommends that you have cholera, typhoid, paratyphoid, tetanus, and gamma globulin shots.

Customs. Along with your personal items, you can bring in 200 cigarettes, 8 ounces of tobacco, or 50 cigars; one bottle of liquor; one bottle of perfume; one still camera with two rolls of film; and one movie camera with one roll of film. Register your camera and similar equipment when you enter the country.

Currency. The kyat (pronounced chat) is the Burmese unit of currency; at the official exchange rate, U.S. $1 equals Ks. 6.8. All foreign currency must be declared upon entry, and you will be given an official form to record all currency exchanges with authorized money changers. When you leave the country, this form must be returned to customs officers. Upon departure, you can reconvert up to 25 percent of the total amount that you have cashed into kyats. It is illegal to bring Burmese currency or undeclared foreign currency into Burma or to change money with an unauthorized dealer.

Tipping. Light tipping is the rule. In hotels and restaurants, a service charge is added to the bill. However, on departure you may wish to tip 1 or 2 kyats for good service and leave your room boy 2 to 5 kyats, depending on length of stay. Any price you bargain on, including taxi fares, includes the tip.

Health conditions. Don't drink tap water and don't use ice cubes. Also avoid milk, ice cream, green salads, and uncooked foods.

Climate. Burma's cool season—from November through February—is the best time to visit. Year-round temperatures vary from an average low of 65°F. in January to an average high of 97°F. in April. Monsoon rains occur from late May through October, coinciding with the hot season. During this steamy period, humidity averages about 98 percent. Even during the dry season, mornings in January and February are often cloudy and misty with humidity from 96 to 100 percent.

Local customs. In Burma all Buddhist temples are sacred, including the ruins at Pagan, and all visitors must remove both shoes and socks as a sign of respect. Sandals or thongs are convenient footgear between temples.

For more information. The best source of information in Burma is the Tourist Information Service, Burma Airways Corporation, 104 Strand Road, Rangoon. You can also request information from the Union of Burma Consulate General or the Union of Burma Embassy (see 'Entry requirements").

In Burma, the U.S. Embassy is located at 581 Merchant Street, Rangoon.

---

and carnivals. It is followed by the week-long Independence Day fair, when a circuslike atmosphere prevails.

Union Day. Celebrating the unity of Burma's various ethnic states on February 12, this holiday is similar to Independence Day. It features boat racing and other events.

Thingyan, or Water Festival. This is a time of merrymaking, with scented water for Buddha images and buckets of water for participants and spectators (see page 12).

Festival of the Full Moon of Kason. This celebration commemorates important events in Buddha's life (see page 13).

Thadingyut, or Festival of Light. Marking the end of Buddhist Lent, Thadingyut is usually held during the full moon in September or October (see page 12).

Inle Festival. The most famous and colorful festival of the hill tribes occurs in late September or early October at Inle Lake. A golden barge, towed by leg-rowers, transports gilded images from the Paung-Daw-U Pagoda to each lakeside village.

Tazaungdaing. Another festival of lights is held in November, marked by great processions, music, and dancing. The night before the full moon, unmarried girls gather to weave robes for Buddhist monks.

Forested hills surround the Laotian city of Luang Prabang **(top).** Towers of a Khmer temple **(right)** loom above Cambodia's war-damaged Angkor complex. **(Far right),** Vietnamese shoppers gather at colorful Saigon market.

166 INDOCHINA

Indochina

History and culture of Vietnam, Laos, Cambodia

(See page 126 for map)

This chapter deals with Vietnam, Laos, and Cambodia (Democratic Republic of Kampuchea). All three of these countries were closed to normal tourism following their takeover by Communist forces. Only recently has there been any indication of renewed interest in limited tourism. However, the future of such tourism is still uncertain.

The history and traditions of these countries form an important part of the history and people of Southeast Asia. Therefore, despite the uncertainty of tourism, basic information on the geography, history, people, and culture of Indochina has been retained in this book.

Vietnam

With the Communist takeover of South Vietnam in April 1975, the country of Vietnam was closed to tourism. As of late 1977, Vietnam (formerly North and South Vietnam) appeared to be the first Indochinese country reopening its doors to limited tourism.

Rail and road links are being restored in the country, and limited air service is available. Visas are very difficult for Americans to obtain, though, and accommodations are limited.

The information within this section will encompass both the northern and southern parts of Vietnam.

Mountains and deltas

Vietnam stretches along the eastern coast of the Indochina peninsula, from the border of China south to the Gulf of Thailand. Laos and Cambodia border the country on the west, while Vietnam's east coast faces the Gulf of Tonkin and the South China Sea.

Vietnam's 127,000 square miles encompass forested hill country and the fertile Red River Valley and delta in the north. To the south are the lush rice lands of the Mekong River delta. The two areas are joined by the Truong-Son mountain chain in central Vietnam.

Vietnam is warm and humid with a tropical monsoon climate. The driest months are November to April. Temperatures average 77°F. to 86°F. in Saigon (Ho Chi Minh City) and 63°F. to 86°F. in Hanoi. The average annual rainfall is about 59 inches.

Centuries of conflict

Vietnam's early history was closely entwined with that of China; Vietnam was a province of its vast northern neighbor for a thousand years. The Vietnamese gained their independence in 939 A.D. In the 13th century, Vietnam was reconquered by Chinese Mongol invaders, but the country soon regained its independence. Conquered by the French in the mid-19th century, Vietnam became part of French Indochina, along with Laos and Cambodia.

The Japanese gained control of the Indochina peninsula in 1941 but left the Vichy French in command. In 1945, with Japanese defeat inevitable, Japan removed the French rulers and granted independence to Vietnam.

Communist troops under Ho Chi Minh took brief but effective control of Vietnam until driven out by Chinese and British troops. Then France again took charge, and the protracted struggle began—the Communists fighting against the French, and later against the Americans, for control of all Vietnam.

Officially the 1954 Geneva Convention ended the civil war, temporarily dividing the country along a "demilitarized zone"—the 17th parallel—into North and South Vietnam. The treaty provided for later elections to reunite the country.

But, the Vietnamese did not recognize the Geneva Convention. The Communists in the North, under Ho Chi Minh, and anti-Communists in the South, under Bao Dai and later Ngo Dinh Diem, continued the struggle.

In 1955 the government of Diem proclaimed the Republic of Vietnam. During the next 8 years, the government turned more and more dictatorial, and Diem was assassinated during a military revolt in 1963. After elections in 1967, Nguyen Van Thieu became president and Nguyen Cao Ky (who served in the interim) became vice-president. At a second election held in 1971, President Thieu was re-elected with Tran Van Huong as vice-president.

United States involvement in Vietnam began in the early 1950s, reaching a peak in 1968-69 with some 500,000 troops being stationed in the country. In 1969 the U.S. began a gradual withdrawal of troops under the "Vietnamization" policy. The 1973 Paris Agreement ended the armed conflict for the United States, but Vietnam's internal struggles continued.

In 1975 the South Vietnamese government collapsed and the pro-Communist North Vietnamese took control. The new capital of the country of Vietnam is Hanoi in the north.

Most are rice farmers

The great majority of the 45 million people in Vietnam are ethnic Vietnamese, mostly plains dwellers and rice farmers. Racial minorities account for about 15 percent of the population. These minorities include about 1 million mainly urban Chinese and about 400,000 Khmers, mostly farmers. The highlands are inhabited by some tribespeople of non-Vietnamese racial background known as Montagnards (highland peoples).

A reserved and courteous people, the Vietnamese are small in stature and of southern Mongoloid stock. Despite the deep imprint of Chinese rule, they have developed a distinctive national culture.

Vietnamese is the language of the people, government, and business. However, both the Chinese and Khmer have tended to retain their own languages. In Saigon, English and French are spoken by many people, due to the extensive earlier influence from abroad. Foreign languages are not widely known in the north, but some people are now learning Russian.

Confucianism, Taoism, Buddhism, and Christianity have influenced Vietnam. The pro-Communist Vietnamese government has declared itself against these "old" religions. Several Vietnamese Buddhist sects, involved with nationalistic politics prior to the Communist takeover, have been discouraged. However, no major repressive measures have been applied to the practice of the basic religions.

Prior to 1975, fewer than half the Vietnamese

Hundreds of sampan houseboats line the banks of Perfume River at Hue. This quiet city was formerly imperial capital of Vietnam.

were nominal Buddhists, and many followed a Vietnamese form of Buddhism often combined with elements of Confucianism, Taoism, and ancestor worship. Roman Catholics and Protestants comprised about 10 percent of the population; Cao Dai and Hoa Hao, both reformed sects of Buddhism, each had more than a million adherents.

Though discouraged by the government, Vietnamese men still wear western-style clothing. The women dress more traditionally in the *ao dai*—a high-collared, form-fitting silk garment worn over trousers.

Vietnamese cuisine is light, imaginative, and not too highly seasoned. Most of the dishes are based on seafood, beef, rice, and a variety of vegetables. Some well-known dishes are *cha gio* (fried rolls), rice paper rolls filled with crabmeat, pork, mushrooms, vegetables, and noodles; *bo bay mon* (beef in seven dishes), each dish prepared differently with special ingredients and sauces; and *pho*, a typical Vietnamese soup with beef and noodles.

The Vietnamese people are known for such local craft products as lacquerware, ceramics, embroidered wooden sandals, delicate fabrics, pottery, ivory, and shellcraft. However, craft items made of imported materials such as ivory are scarcer since the Communist takeover.

Towns and regions

Vietnam's towns and regions offer history, culture, and scenic beauty.

Saigon. Now officially named Ho Chi Minh City, Saigon lies in the southernmost quarter of the country, along the west bank of the Saigon River near the Canal of Ben Nghe. Fairly young as a city, it dates back some 200 years to when it was a fishing village of thatched huts. Its population hovers near 3 million. The government is seeking to reduce this by encouraging people to move to rural, agricultural communities, but this relocation effort has not been too successful.

In pre-war days, Saigon was often called the Paris of the East. Its tree-lined streets, French language, and late 19th-century architecture kindled expatriate reminiscences of turn-of-the-century France. Decades of French control were evident in the architecture of public buildings, as well as in civic administration, and cuisine.

Today, the city is quieter. The main boulevard, Dong Khoi (formerly Tu Do), is no longer bustling with the traffic of ancient cars and thousands of Japanese motorcycles. The lack of gasoline has taken its toll, making bicycles the main source of transportation for many.

Saigon's three and four-story buildings and shady boulevards remain, but many of the open-air cafes and bars popular with GIs are now closed and boarded up. Most of the major hotels are still open—many of them official guest houses now, and some used by tourists.

The central market, marked by its tile-roofed clock tower, still sprawls near the railway stations.

Lush tropical vegetation *and palm trees border a quiet bay near Qui Nhon. Miles of this spectacular coastline front the South China Sea.*

Vietnamese shop here at stalls offering fresh fruit and vegetables, fattened pigs, scrawny chickens, and buckets filled with squid, shrimp, crab, fish, and giant green lobsters.

Near Saigon. The southern part of Vietnam has many miles of spectacular coastline fronting the South China Sea. Two hours south of the city is the once-popular, traditional beach resort of Vung Tau (formerly Cap St. Jacques). Several hours north are Nha Trang and Dai Lanh beaches. Nha Trang has beach bungalows that are used by foreign tourists.

Vietnam's charming old hill resort of Dalat is located 180 miles north of Saigon. Situated some 4,000 feet above sea level, the town overlooks lakes surrounded by pine-clad hills. The Dalat region is noted for its waterfalls, hillside viewpoints, profusion of flowers, and bracing, springlike air.

Hue. Once Vietnam's imperial capital, Hue lies 658 miles north of Saigon in the central part of the country. Cutting through the city is the Perfume River, its banks lined with hundreds of sampan houseboats.

Though badly damaged during the 1968 Tet Offensive, Hue exudes a timeless quality, its mood influenced by the six Imperial Tombs on the edge of the city. Though in need of restoration, these remote and quiet mausoleums reflect the grandeur of Vietnam's past.

Hanoi. Capital of Vietnam, Hanoi is located on the Red River in the northern part of the country 60 miles from the major port of Haiphong. Until the 18th century, Hanoi was the capital of the Annamite Empire.

The Red River delta region is one of the most heavily populated areas in Vietnam with about 390 people per square mile.

Haiphong. One of Vietnam's principal industrial cities is Haiphong, an inland port 25 miles from the Gulf of Tonkin. Built in 1874, it is an important transit port. Industrial development has been aided in the area by the nearness of coal mines.

Laos

Since the Communist takeover of Laos, tourist traffic has depended on the current political relationship between Laos and Thailand. The border has been closed and reopened repeatedly. Even when the border is open, it is difficult to obtain a visa, especially for Americans.

A landlocked kingdom

Laos is a landlocked kingdom in the heart of Southeast Asia. Burma and China border it on the north, Vietnam on the east, Cambodia on the south, and Thailand on the west.

The country covers an area of 91,428 square miles, with a shape similar to Italy minus the toe. The landscape is dominated by jungle-covered mountains and deep river valleys. Many of the country's inhabitants live in the fertile valley of the Mekong River, a waterway that functions as a main transportation route. Laos has no railroads, and many of the country's roads become impassable during the monsoon months.

Laos has a tropical climate with wet and dry seasons. The most pleasant period is from October through March, when temperatures average 70°F. The monsoon season lasts from June to September, averaging 10 to 12 inches of rainfall a month. April is the hottest month, with temperatures reaching 100°F.

Kingdom of Lan Xang

Until the 13th century, Laos was part of the Angkor Indo-Khmer civilization. In the middle of the 14th century, Laos became a unified kingdom called Lan Xang, the "Kingdom of a Million Elephants," extending from south China to north Thailand.

Lan Xang endured for about 350 "golden age" years, finally succumbing to internal and external pressures. The territory was split into three kingdoms: Luang Prabang, Vientiane, and Champassak. Vulnerable to invaders from Vietnam and Thailand, the weakened Laotian kingdoms came under French control in 1893. The French governed the region for the next half century.

In 1947 unified Laos became a constitutional monarchy with the King of Luang Prabang, a direct descendant of the Lan Xang royal line, recognized as king of all Laos. In 1949 the Kingdom of Laos became an independent state within the French union, receiving full independence from France in 1954.

After a dissident group, the pro-Communist Pathet Lao, reverted to armed rebellion, an attempt was made to form a government of national unity representing pro-West, pro-Communist, and neutralist factions. This led to the formation in 1962 of a triumvirate government of Lao princes under Premier Souvanna Phouma, a neutralist. It also called for a Declaration of Protocol on the neutrality of Laos and the withdrawal of foreign military personnel.

The action of 1962 did not settle the political or military difficulties of Lao factions or of Laos. In the next dozen years, Laos became the battleground for the Pathet Lao and the neutralist and rightest forces of the Vientiane government. After the fall of South Vietnam in 1975, the pro-Communist Pathet Lao took control of the Laos government.

A cultural mix

Laos has a fascinating cultural mixture influenced by the Indo-Khmer, French, Burmese, and Khmer people. The dominant ethnic group, the Lao, is of Thai stock. Other segments of the population include the Black, Red, and White Thai; the Meo; the Yao; and a variety of tribal groups. The country also has large groups of Chinese, Pakistani, Indian, and Vietnamese inhabitants.

The gentle-mannered and tolerant Lao are lighter skinned than the Thai people, are small in stature, and have delicate facial features.

Wet-rice farming in the lowlands and some dry-rice farming in the hills provide a major portion of the Laotian diet. This is supplemented with hunting and fishing.

Laotian food, often hot and spicy, is eaten with sticky rice. One of the most famous dishes is *orlam;* a bit like cabbage stew, it contains buffalo skin, pork, grouse, chili, wood mushrooms, lemon grass, sandalwood (for flavoring), eggplant, and jungle herbs.

The official language of the country is Lao, though French was formerly used in government and business. Similar to Thai, the Lao language has six tones, only three of which translate directly to Bangkok Thai. Lao script is based on Pali—the religious language of Buddhism and an offshoot of Sanskrit.

Prior to the Pathet Lao regime, Theravada Buddhism was the state religion. However, the new government has sought to abolish traditional religion and substitute a socialist doctrine.

Before 1975, a team of United Nations and French experts worked with the Laotians to revive crafts that were in danger of dying out. These skills included weaving, ceramics, basketry, and silversmithing. The Meo tribeswomen are known

Early shoppers *browse through Vientiane's morning market. Bright-colored umbrellas shield produce vendors from hot sun.*

Shaded *from sun by a stilt house, three generations process and sell sugar in a village north of Luang Prabang.*

for embroidered collars, belts, and decorations for cloth turbans. Members of both the Meo and Yao tribes make beautifully crafted silver jewelry.

Ancient capitals

The history and culture of Laos are reflected in the country's towns and villages.

Vientiane. Overlooking the Mekong River, Vientiane was built by the French on the site of the ancient capital of Lan Xang.

Pagodas with upturned tile roofs and smiling *nagas* (serpents) dot the skyline of Vientiane. Along the quiet residential streets, corrugated-metal and thatch-roofed houses on stilts peep through groves of mangoes, coconut palms, and flamboyant trees.

It was once a city of some 150,000 people, but many inhabitants have now left. The tree-lined streets are no longer filled with automobiles and trucks. Instead, due to a fuel shortage, bicycles have become the main source of transportation.

In the early morning hours, the market is still the center of Vientiane activity. Sarong-clad women peddle their items, which vary from slippery eels to bolts of Laotian silk and handwoven *sinhs* (the national dress for Laotian women).

Luang Prabang. As the royal, religious, and social capital of Laos before the Communist takeover, Luang Prabang reflected the traditions and dress of the ancient Kingdom of Lan Xang.

The city lies approximately 100 miles northwest of Vientiane. Surrounded by forested hills, it rests about a thousand feet above sea level where the Nam Khan joins the Mekong River.

Ban Ha Ngum. About a 90-minute drive southeast of Luang Prabang is Ban Ha Ngum, a Meo village of wooden huts perched on a bald hilltop. The nomad Meo tribes practice slash-and-burn agriculture, wandering from hilltop to hilltop, farming and hunting the mountainous terrain of northern Laos.

Ecologically disastrous, this form of agriculture involves cutting the underbrush and burning it away to plant crops on hilltops. As a result of this practice, much of the rich topsoil erodes away during the rainy season.

The migration path of the earlier Meos, from southern China to Laos, is still visible. Traveling through thickly forested land, they left a swath a hundred miles wide across the mountains of central and northern Thailand.

Cambodia

Of the three countries discussed in this chapter, Cambodia seems the least likely to reopen for tourism for many years to come. The borders are sealed and the English language has been banned.

The political leaders are seeking to create a "pure" socialist state. Reports indicate that they feel this will be accomplished through the ruthless repression of established religion and traditional social patterns. With this current political regime, there is no way of knowing what actual changes will occur in the country and its people.

Mountains ring a flat plain

Part of a once-powerful empire, Cambodia (currently called the Democratic Republic of Kampuchea) occupies a southeastern portion of the Indochina peninsula. Generally characterized as a flat plain ringed by low, densely forested mountains, it is bordered by Thailand on the west and north, Laos on the northeast, Vietnam on the east and south, and the Gulf of Thailand on the southwest.

Covering 69,898 square miles, Cambodia is roughly the size of Washington state. Most of the people live in thatched huts built on stilts along the Mekong River and in the tributary lake basin of the Tonle Sap, or Great Lake, which drains the alluvial central plain.

Cambodia has a milder and drier climate than its neighbors, but it is still hot. The most pleasant period is from November to May, when the northeast monsoon blows. December is the coolest month. April through July are the hot months, and the rainy season lasts from April to October. Temperatures in Phnom Penh average 81°F. to 90°F. with high humidity, but light breezes moderate the heat.

A once powerful Khmer empire

Cambodia traces its history back to the once-powerful Hindu states of Funan and Chienla, finally overthrown by the Khmers after several hundred years of rivalry and war. From the 9th to the 15th century, a united Khmer empire stretched from the Gulf of Thailand to the Chinese border; it was the leading power on the southeast Asian peninsula. The Khmer capital was at Angkor Thom—then a great center of culture and learning, today a major monument among the Angkor ruins.

Impressive achievements in artistic and social development came during the period of Khmer rule. But continued struggles with neighboring states finally resulted in the abandonment of Angkor sometime before 1450. In subsequent centuries, the jungle took over the city, and it was not until 1861 that Angkor was rediscovered by the French. Restoration work continued for the next 90 years.

In 1846, the country came under joint Thai-Vietnamese control; then in 1863, it became a French protectorate. Shortly thereafter, the French joined Cambodia with Vietnam and Laos, administering the three countries as French Indochina until the Japanese occupation during World War II.

King Norodom Sihanouk, placed on the throne by the French in 1941, worked for complete independence, which he finally achieved in 1953. Two years later the king abdicated in favor of his father, becoming chief of state. From 1955 to 1970, Prince

Fishermen reap *a bountiful harvest from Tonle Sap in Cambodia. During the rainy season, the lake increases its size tenfold.*

Sihanouk favored a policy of neutralism toward the Indochina war between North and South Vietnamese, at times criticizing the United States' Vietnam policy.

In March 1970, the Parliament voted unanimously to replace Prince Sihanouk as chief of state. The change of government occurred because the Prince had allowed the "Viet Cong" to use the eastern half of Cambodia as a corridor from North Vietnam and Laos into South Vietnam. The government remained intact under General Lon Nol, the prime minister. In the June 1972 presidential elections, Lon Nol was elected the first president.

In early May 1970, thousands of United States and South Vietnamese troops crossed into Cambodia in an attempt to destroy the National Liberation Forces and North Vietnamese troops. Though the Americans stayed less than 60 days, the South Vietnamese remained. Racial clashes resulted between the two peoples, who had been traditional enemies for centuries.

Despite the military moves, the North Vietnamese pushed westward across the republic, aided by Khmers loyal to Sihanouk, who had formed a government-in-exile in Peking.

In October 1970 the country's legislature abolished the monarchy, and Cambodia's name was changed to the Khmer Republic.

Following the fall of South Vietnam in 1975, a new regime took over power in Cambodia. This new government's apparent objective is to destroy all western influence and traditional cultural and social patterns. Cambodia has been renamed Democratic Republic of Kampuchea.

Khmer people in majority

In Cambodia, the Khmer people dominate the ethnic groups by comprising more than 85 percent

172 INDOCHINA

of the country's population. Minority groups include Chinese, Vietnamese, and smaller groups of Cham-Malays (a Muslim group) and scattered hill tribes.

Before the outbreak of war in 1970-71, about two-thirds of the Khmers lived in villages on the central plain. Here they cultivated rice, the country's main crop and chief export. During the war many people migrated to Phnom Penh in an effort to escape the warfare and establish new homes, a move that disrupted the rice economy. The war also destroyed thousands of acres of rubber plantations in the east and northeast, areas that once had the highest yields of rubber per acre in the world. The economic upheaval changed the life style of many Khmers from one of rural isolation to an urban existence.

This situation is now being reversed by the current government. Much of the population of Phnom Penh has been forced to evacuate into rural areas to form new agricultural communes.

Khmer, or Cambodian, is the most widely used language among the people of the country. Chinese and Vietnamese have been the major languages of business and trade in the past. French was the former language of government. English has been banned.

All traditional religions have been rigorously repressed in this country where Theravada Buddhism used to condition many aspects of everyday Cambodian life.

A town, lake, and temples

Important historical sites in Cambodia include Phnom Penh and Angkor.

Phnom Penh. Once a city of over 2 million people, today Phnom Penh (pronounced *P'nom pen*—the first "P" is hard) is a quiet town of only 20,000. Most of the population has been sent back into the rural areas by the government.

Phnom Penh spreads along the western bank of the Tonle Sap River near its union with the Mekong River. Constructed on a compact and orderly scale, the town reflects both French and Khmer architecture.

The city took its name from the Phnom, a 90-foot manmade hill at the northern edge of the city. Crowning the hill, a stupa-ringed pagoda was built in the 1880s on the ruins of shrines dating back to 1370.

Prior to the war, Phnom Penh was the jumping-off place for visitors to Angkor.

Angkor. The ancient cities and temples of the Angkor complex cover some 60 square miles. Most of this area, located 200 miles northwest of Phnom Penh, is engulfed in jungle.

Except for Angkor Wat, this entire region was abandoned by the Khmers in the 15th century when the Thais sacked the city. Most of Angkor was neglected and virtually forgotten during the following centuries until it was rediscovered by the French in 1861.

Angkor Wat, the largest and most magnificent monument, was built in the 12th century. Both Hinduism and Buddhism influenced the royal Khmer builders, and they succeeded in blending the two concepts. Although many of the nearby temples were abandoned after the Thai invasion, Angkor Wat was not; Buddhist monks lived in Angkor Wat for some time.

Located a short distance north of Angkor Wat, Angkor Thom was once a city of a million people covering an area of 6 square miles. Much of the area had been excavated before the war, but the full extent of the ruins is still a mystery.

A short distance west of Angkor Wat and Angkor Thom are the ruins of Ta Pnohm. Huge banyan trees have so overgrown the area that no effort has been made to clear it. If the enormous roots of these trees were removed, most of the Ta Pnohm structure would crumble.

About 18 miles north of Angkor is Banteay, the Citadel of Women. Rediscovered in 1914, this temple has unusual carvings cut deep into its pink limestone structure.

Tonle Sap. Also called the Great Lake, Tonle Sap is a most unusual body of water. It is generally recognized as the world's richest fresh-water fishing grounds, but it has another unique characteristic. During the dry season—November to May—the lake empties (by way of the Tonle Sap River) into the Mekong River; by May it covers a mere 1,000 square miles. But when the rainy season begins in June, the Tonle Sap River reverses its flow and the lake becomes enormous—covering about one-seventh (10,000 square miles) of the country.

The Phnom *towers above the northern edge of Phnom Penh. The Cambodian city took its name from this 90-foot, manmade hill.*

INDOCHINA

Suggested Reading List

A Concise History of Southeast Asia, by Nicholas Tarling. Singapore: Donald Moore Press Ltd., 1967. This book traces the common and diverse historical and geographical factors that have affected this region since prehistoric times.

All-Asia Guide, edited by William Knox. Hong Kong: Far Eastern Economic Review Ltd., 1974. A tightly written handbook which presents basic facts and travel information for a trip from Bangladesh to the Philippines.

Angkor, by Malcolm MacDonald. London: Jonathan Cape, 1961. Easy to read, this book traces Khmer history—their kings, statues, and life today—with 80 pages of black and white photographs.

The Arts of Thailand, edited by Theodore Bowie. Bloomington: Indiana University Press, 1960. The treasures of Bangkok's National Museum — architecture, sculpture, and paintings—are illustrated and briefly described.

Bali and Beyond, by Colin Simpson. Sydney: Angus and Robertson Pty., Ltd., 1972. A detailed, personal journey through Bali—explaining dances, trances, food, and festivals—with additional observations on Jakarta and north Sumatra.

Bangkok-Biography of a City, by Alec Waugh. Boston/Toronto: Little Brown and Company, 1971. Presenting an intimate look at the city's history, this book covers the temples, wars, and people.

Common Birds of the Malay Peninsula, by M. W. F. Tweedie. Kuala Lumpur/Singapore: Longman Malaysia SDN., Berhad, 1970. This book tells where and when to find some 150 Malaysian birds.

The Flavour of Singapore, edited by John Hitchcock. London: Four Corners Publishing Co., 1973. The gourmet, at home or abroad, will find information on Singapore's restaurants and recipes for Chinese, Malay/Indonesian, Nonya, Indian, and European dishes.

Fodor's South-East Asia, by Eugene Fodor and Robert C. Fisher. New York: David McKay Company Inc., 1976. A definitive handbook on where to stay, how to enjoy, and what to see in the countries of Southeast Asia.

Guide to Bali, by Star Black, Hans Hoefer, and Werner Hahn. Hong Kong: APA Publications (HK) Ltd., 1973. This beautifully photographed guide reveals the inside story of Bali, its origins, religion, customs, and culture.

Guide to Java, by Peter Hutton and Hans Hoefer. Hong Kong: APA Publications Ltd., 1974. Text and color photos in this guidebook reveal the cities, sights, and people on Indonesia's largest island.

Guide to Malaysia, by Hans Hoefer, Star Black, and Harold Stephens. Singapore: Straits Times Press (M) Bhd., 1972. With color photos and an interesting text, the authors take you on a tour of Malaysia —its people, customs, mosques, cities, and villages.

Guide to Singapore, by Hans Hoefer and Star Black. Singapore: Straits Times Press (M) Bhd., 1973. Mood-evoking color photos and concise text put the island nation in perspective by covering its history, people, and sights.

Longhouse and Jungle, by Guy Arnold. Singapore: Donald Moore Press Ltd., 1967. This book covers an expedition to Sarawak in Insular Malaysia which studied the nomadic Penans.

Morning of the World, Bali, by Hubert Sieben and Jan Grant. Vermont/Tokyo: Charles E. Tuttle Co., 1970. This picture book, with numerous color photos, illustrates Bali's people and natural beauty.

Orient Travel Guide, by John C. Caldwell. New York: The John Day Company, 1971. A practical guide with suggested Asian tours, including travel in Thailand, Malaysia, Singapore, Philippines, Cambodia, and Indonesia.

Papineau's Guide to Malaysia, by Aristide J. G. Papineau. Singapore: Andre Publications, 1976. This tourist guide to Malaysia covers points of interest in the cities, towns, and jungles; it also includes practical details on local transportation.

Penang, by Robert C. Crock and Margaretha Ratman. Petaling Jaya (Malaysia): Walter D. Andreae, 1973. The island and people of Penang are revealed with color photos and brief text.

The Philippines, by John Cockcroft. Sydney: Angus and Robertson Ltd., 1968. The author covers the nation's geography, people, and places to see, in photographs and brief text.

The Philippines, by Keith Lightfoot. New York/Washington: Praeger Publishers, 1974. This book looks at the nation's history, economy, and people —especially the population explosion—and western misconceptions about the Philippines.

Singapore, by Sally Backhouse. Harrisburg (Pa.): Stackpole Books, 1973. This is one of the few books which considers all aspects of Singapore: its history, economy, living conditions, geography, plant and animal life, and the exotic beauty of its land and people.

Thailand and Angkor, a Nagel's Encyclopedia-Guide, by Johanna Dittmar. Geneva: Nagel Publishers, 1973. This book covers Thailand's geography, history, people, religion, culture, main destinations. Appendix covers ruins of Angkor, Cambodia.

Index

Airport taxes (see Practical information)

Bibliography, 174
Brunei, 90
Burma, 152-165
   art and craft centers, 161, 162
   beach resort, 159
   boat trip, 164
   climate, 161, 164, 165
   colonial influences, 156, 161
   cultural influences, 155, 162
   cultural centers, 158, 162
   entertainment, traditional, 158
   entry requirements, 165
   festivals and events, 160, 164-165
   food and drink, 155-156
   geography, 153, 154
   government, 154
   handicrafts, 156, 157, 161, 162, 164
   hill resorts, 164
   historic sites, 157, 158, 159-161, 163-164
   history, 154, 156, 158, 159, 160-161
   hotels, 155, 156-157, 160, 162, 164
   Inle Lake, 164
   Kalaw, 164
   language, 155, 156
   Mandalay, 161-164
   map, 126
   museums, 158, 161
   Pagan, 159-161
   Pegu, 158
   people, 154-155
   Pindaya Caves, 164
   practical information, 165
   Rangoon, 156-158
      excursions, 158-159
   religion, 155, 157, 160, 162, 163, 164
   Sandoway Beach, 159
   Shan Hills, 164
   shopping, 156, 157, 161
   Taunggyi, 164
   tourist information, 165
   transportation, 155, 159, 160, 162

Cambodia, 171-173
   Angkor ruins, 173
   climate, 172
   cultural influences, 173
   geography, 172
   historic sites, 173
   history, 172
   Khmer ruins, 173
   language, 173
   map, 126
   people, 172-173
   Phnom Penh, 173
   religion, 173
   Tonle Sap, 173
Cham empire, 9
Colonial influences, 10
Cultural influences, 9

Customs allowances (see Practical information)

Entry requirements (see Practical information)

Festivals and events, 11-13 (also see individual countries)

Geography and geology, 5-7 (also see individual countries)

Health conditions (see Practical information)
Historical influences, 9-10

Indochina (Cambodia, Laos, Vietnam) 166-173

Indonesia, 44-73
   art and craft centers, 50, 54, 56, 58, 62, 64
   Bali, 61-64
   Bandung, 55
   beach resorts, 54, 56, 62, 64
   Belawan, 66
   Bogor, 55
   Borobudur, 56, 58
   Brastagi, 66
   Bukittinggi, 67, 68
   climate, 55, 73
   colonial influences, 47, 50, 53, 59, 65, 70
   cultural centers, 55, 64
   cultural influences, 47, 56, 59, 65
   Denpasar (Bali), 62
   entertainment, 48, 51-52
      traditional, 48, 51-52, 55-56, 58, 59, 60, 64, 65, 67
   entry requirements, 73
   festivals and events, 58, 60, 61, 65, 70, 72-73
   food and drink, 49
   gardens, 55, 67
   geography, 45, 47, 65, 70
   government, 47
   handicrafts, 49, 50, 52, 56, 58, 62, 64, 67, 72
   hill resorts, 55, 60, 66
   historic sites, 53, 55, 56, 58, 64, 66
   history, 47, 50
   hotels, 48-49, 51, 62, 66, 68
   Irian Jaya, 70-71
   Jakarta, 49-54
      excursions, 54-56
   Java, 49-61
   Kalimantan (Borneo) 69-70
   Komodo dragon, 72
   Lake Toba, 66-67
   language, 47-48
   Lesser Sunda Islands, 72
   Madura Island bull races, 61
   Majapahit ruins, 61
   Maluku Islands, 72
   maps, 46, 59, 62
   Medan, 65-66
   Mount Agung, 62, 64
   Mount Batur, 64
   Mount Bromo, 60
   museums, 53, 56, 58, 61, 62, 67
   Nias Island, 68
   Padang, 67, 68
   Palembang, 68-69
   Pandaan, 60
   people, 47, 61, 65, 66, 67, 68, 70
   plants and animals, 47, 65, 67, 69, 70
   practical information, 73
   Prambanan, 58
   religion, 48, 61-62, 66, 68, 70
   Samudra, 56
   shopping, 49, 52, 60
   Sibolga, 67

Indonesia (continued)
   sports, 54
   Sulawesi (Celebes), 70
   Sumatra, 65-69
   Surabaya, 59-60
   Surakarta, 58-59
   Thousand Islands, 54
   tourist information, 73
   transportation, 11, 48, 50, 54, 59, 63, 64, 65, 66, 68, 69, 70
   Tretes, 60
   tribal villages, 61, 66, 67, 68
   turtle farm, 65
   Ujung Pandang, 70
   volcanoes, 45, 56, 59, 60, 62, 64, 65, 70
   Yogyakarta, 56

Inoculations (see Practical information)

Khmer empire, 9, 141, 172

Laos, 170-171
   climate, 170
   cultural influences, 170
   food, 170
   geography, 170
   government, 170
   handicrafts, 170-171
   historic sites, 171
   history, 170
   language, 170
   Luang Prabang, 171
   map, 126
   people, 170, 171
   religion, 170
   shopping (see handicrafts)
   transportation, 171
   tribal villages, 171
   Vientiane, 171

Majapahit empire, 61, 105

Malaysia, 74-101
   art and craft centers, 84, 88, 96, 100
   Batu Caves, 85
   beach resorts, 86, 89, 90-91, 95, 96
   boat trips, 100
   Cameron Highlands, 78
   climate, 86, 95, 97, 101
   colonial influences, 75, 77-78, 86, 87, 93
   cultural centers, 85, 88, 100
   cultural influences, 75, 77-78, 93
   east coast, 94-96
      offshore islands, 96
   entertainment, 81, 82
      traditional, 81, 82, 85, 95, 98, 100
   entry requirements, 101
   festivals and events, 85, 100-101
   food and drink, 80-81, 82, 86
   Fraser's Hill, 78
   gardens, 88, 94
   Genting Highlands, 78
   geography, 77
   George Town (Penang), 86, 87-88
      excursions, 88-89
   government, 79
   handicrafts, 81, 82, 85, 87, 89, 95, 96, 97, 100
   hill resorts, 78
   historic sites, 81, 83, 87, 93, 94, 98

Malaysia (continued)
   history, 77, 79, 81, 86, 87, 93
   hotels, 80, 81-82, 86, 93, 95, 96, 97, 98
   Insular Malaysia, 96-101
   Johore Bahru, 94
   Kota Belud, 98
   Kota Bharu, 95, 96
   Kota Kinabalu, 97-98
   Kuala Lumpur, 81-84
      excursions, 84-85
   Kuala Trengganu, 95-96
   Kuantan, 95
   Kuching, 98, 100
   Langkawi Islands, 90
   language, 79
   longhouses, 100
   Malacca, 93-94
   map, 76
   Mount Kinabalu, 98
   Mount Ophir, 94
   museums, 84, 88, 93, 98, 100
   national parks, 85, 96, 98
   Pangkor Island, 90-91
   Penang Island, 86-89
   people, 75, 79, 93-94, 97, 98, 100
   plants and animals, 77, 95, 96
   Port Dickson, 91
   practical information, 101
   religion, 79, 83, 85, 87, 88, 94
   rubber plantations, 85-86, 91, 94, 100
   Seremban, 91
   shopping, 81, 82-83, 87, 93
   sports, 81, 85, 94, 95, 96, 98
   tin mines, 86
   tourist information, 101
   transportation, 79-80, 86-87, 91, 95, 96, 97, 93
   white rajahs, 98, 100

Philippines, 14-43
   art and craft centers, 26, 27, 32, 37, 41, 42
   Baguio, 30-32
   Banaue, rice terraces, 33
   Batang, 34
   beach resorts, 30, 34, 37, 38, 42
   boat trips, 28, 29, 36, 41
   climate, 30, 43
   colonial influences, 17, 37-38, 39
   Corregidor, 27
   cultural centers, 20, 26, 38, 39
   cultural influences, 17, 34, 36, 37, 38, 40, 41, 42
   Davao, 42
   entertainment, 20, 22, 31
      traditional, 20, 22, 26, 42
   entry requirements, 43
   festivals and events, 24, 38, 42-43
   food and drink, 19-20
   gardens and parks, 23, 31, 32, 41, 42
   geography and geology, 15, 17, 23
   government, 17-18
   handicrafts, 20, 22, 24, 26, 29, 32-33, 37, 41
   hill resorts, 28, 30
   historic sites, 17, 23, 24, 25, 27, 34, 37, 38, 39, 41
   history, 17, 20, 23, 33, 38
   hotels, 19, 21, 31, 34, 36, 37, 38, 39, 42
   Iloilo, 37
   jeepneys, 15
   language, 18

INDEX   **175**

Philippines (continued)
  Legazpi City, 29
  Mactan Island, 38
  Manila, 20–27
    excursions, 27–30
  map, 16
  Mayon Volcano, 29
  Mindanao Island, 39–42
  museums, 26, 27, 37
  national parks, 36, 42
  Pagsanjan Falls, 29
  Panay Island, 37–38
  people, 18, 34, 36, 39, 41, 42
  plants and animals, 18
  practical information, 43
  religion, 18
  rice terraces, 33–34
  Samal Island, 42
  Santa Cruz Island, 41
  shopping, 20
  sports, 18, 32, 34, 36, 41, 42
  Taal Lake and Volcano, 28
  Tagaytay, 28
  tourist information, 43
  transportation, 19, 20, 25, 30, 33–34, 36, 39
  Vigan, 34
  volcanoes, 17, 28, 29
  Zamboanga, 39, 41
Plants and animals, 7 (also see individual countries)
Practical information
  Burma, 165
  Indonesia, 73
  Malaysia, 101
  Philippines, 43
  Singapore, 123
  Thailand, 151

Reading list, 174
Religious customs (see individual countries)
Rice cultivation, 7–8, 11–12, 33–34, 61
Ruins
  Angkor (Cambodia), 173
  Ayutthaya (Thailand), 138
  Majapahit (Indonesia), 61, 105
  Pagan (Burma), 159–160
  Pimai (Thailand), 141

Singapore, 102–123
  art, 117
  boat trips, 108
  climate, 123
  colonial influences, 103, 105
  cultural influences, 103, 105, 106
  dining, 108, 118–121
  entertainment, 108, 121
    traditional, 121
  entry requirements, 123
  festivals and events, 110, 122–123
  food and drink, ll8–121
  gardens and parks, 106, 109, 110, 115, 117
  geography, 104
  government, 105–106
  handicrafts, 113
  historic sites, 110, 112, 113
  history, 105
  hotels, 108, 110
  language, 106
  map, 104
  museums, 110
  nature reserve, 106, 115
  night markets, 112,
  people, 103, 105, 106, 110, 112, 113, 114, 118
  plants and animals, 106, 115, 117–118
  practical information, 123
  Raffles, Sir Stamford, 105, 107
  religion, 106, 110, 114
  restaurants, 118–121
  Sentosa Island, 116
  shopping, 108–109, 112, 113–114
  sightseeing, 109–118
  sports, 110, 115, 116, 118, 121–122
  tourist information, 123
  transportation, 107–108

Southeast Asia
  climate, 7
  cultural influences, 9–10
  ethnic groups, 8
  festivals and events, 11–13
  geography, and geology, 5–7

Southeast Asia (continued)
  plants and animals, 7
  religions, 9
  rice cultivation and rites, 7

Vietnam, 167-170
  climate, 168
  cultural influences, 168
  Dalat, 169
  food, 169
  geography, 167-168
  Haiphong, 170
  handicrafts, 169
  Hanoi, 169-170
  history and government, 168
  Hue, 169
  language, 168
  map, 126
  people, 168-169
  religion, 168-169
  Saigon, 169
  transportation, 169

Thailand, 124–151
  Ancient City, 140–141
  art and craft centers, 140, 142, 143, 145, 147, 148, 150
  Ayutthaya, 138
  Bangkok, 132–137
    excursions, 137–142
  Bang Pa-In, 138
  Bangsaen, 141–142
  beach resorts, 141–142, 143–145
  boat trips, 137–138, 139, 148
  Bridge on the River Kwai, 141
  caves, 143, 144–145
  Chanthaburi, 142
  Chiang Mai, 146–148
  climate, 146, 151,
  cultural influences, 127, 129, 130, 147
  Damnern Saduak, 139–140
  Doi Pui, 148
  elephants, 140, 142, 148, 150
  entertainment, 131, 133–134
    traditional, 131, 134, 140, 147, 148

Thailand (continued)
  entry requirements, 151
  festivals and events, 150–151
  floating markets, 137, 139–140
  food and drink, 131
  geography, 127
  government, 127
  handicrafts, 131, 134, 143, 147, 150
  Hat Yai, 145
  historic sites, 135, 136, 138, 140, 143, 148
  history, 127, 132, 138, 148
  hotels, 131, 133, 142, 143, 144, 145, 146
  Hua Hin, 143
  Kanchanaburi, 141
  Khmer ruins, Pimai, 141
  language, 129
  map, 126
  museums, 137
  Nakhon Pathom, 140
  national parks, 141
  Pattaya, 142
  people, 129, 147, 148
  Phangnga Bay, 144–145
  Phetchaburi, 143
  Phuket Island, 144
  Pimai ruins, 141
  plants and animals, 127–128
  Prachuap Khiri Khan, 144
  practical information, 151
  Ranong, 144
  religion, 129–130, 135
  Rose Garden, 140
  Samui Islands, 143
  shopping, 131, 134, 143, 144
  snake farm, 137
  Songkhla, 145
  sports, 130, 132, 141, 143, 144, 145
  Surin elephant roundup, 138
  Surin (southern Thailand), 144
  Thompson, Jim, 131, 136–137
  tourist information, 151
  transportation, 130, 137–138, 142, 143, 145, 146, 148

Visas (see Practical information)

PHOTOGRAPHERS

Air Vietnam: 167, 168. **American President Lines:** 28. **Reg Butler:** 39 (left), **146** (right), **149** (bottom right). **Jack Cannon:** back cover (left). **Lawrence A. Clancy:** 9 (right), 18, 23 (left), 25, 26, 27 (left), 29, 40 (top right, bottom left), 78, 80 (left), 83 (left), 88 (left), 89, 92 (bottom right), 111 (bottom left), 116 (bottom), 121, 124 (top), 128 (top left), 133, 136, 139. **Robin Dannhorn:** 171 (right). **Phyllis Elving:** 14 (bottom), 15, 23 (right), 24, 27 (right), 30 (right), 33 (left), 35 (top right, bottom left), 36, 37, 40 (top left). **Jack Fields:** 71 (top left, top right, center left, bottom left), 72 (left). **Shirley Fockler:** 48, 52 (right), 57 (top left, bottom right), 64, 66, 67 (right), 96, 99 (bottom right), 113 (left), 128 (bottom right), 142 (left), 149 (bottom left), 153, 164, 166 (top), 171 (left), 172, 173. **James C. Gebbie:** 58 (right), 63 (top left), 130, 140, 142 (right), 145 (bottom), 148. **Hadmoko:** 72 (right). **David Hartley:** 128 (bottom left). **Hilton Hotels:** 21 (right). **Walter Houk:** 141. **Indonesian Tourist Board:** 71 (bottom right). **Paul Johnston:** 116 (top). **Khmer Republic Ministry of Tourism:** 166 (bottom). **David Lampton:** 44 (top), 52 (left), 54, 55 (right), 65. **Antonio S. Lopez Jr.:** 32. **William Marken:** 10, 137. **Le Anh Tai:** 169. **Leslie McReynolds:** back cover (center). **Pacific Area Travel Association:** 58 (left), 61, 63 (bottom right), 68, 69 (left), 79, 81, 92 (top right), 99 (top right), 125. **Pacific Travel News:** 129. **Pan American Airlines:** 132. **Dionisio Paoner:** 39 (right). **Philippine Airlines:** 21 (left). **Philippine Department of Tourism:** 14 (top), 19, 20, 22, 30 (left), 31, 33 (right), 35 (top left, bottom right), 38, 40 (bottom right), 41, 42. **Jeff Phillips:** 8 (top), 9 (left), 75, 82, 83 (right), 84, 87, 92 (top left, bottom right), 95 (right), 97, 103, 128 (top right), 149 (top right), 152 (bottom), 154, 156, 157, 158, 159, 161, 162, 163, back cover (right). **Qantas Airways:** 111 (top left). **Frederic M. Rea:** 11, 53, 67 (left), 69 (right). **Mary Ann Reese:** 4 (top), 5, 44 (bottom), 45, 49, 50, 55 (left), 57 (top right, bottom left), 60, 63 (top right). **Diane Rose:** 63 (bottom left). **Singapore Tourism Promotion Board:** 102, 105, 106, 108, 109, 111 (top right, bottom right), 112, 113 (right), 114, 115, 117, 118, 119, 120, 122. **Tops Metropolitan Studio Productions:** 51. **Tourist Development Corporation of Malaysia:** 12 (bottom), 13, 74, 80 (right), 85, 86, 88 (right), 90, 91, 95 (left), 98, 99 (top left, bottom left), 100. **Tourist Organization of Thailand:** 4 (bottom), 7, 8 (bottom), 12 (top left, right), 124 (bottom), 131, 134, 135, 138, 143, 144, 145 (top), 146 (left), 147, 149 (top left), 150. **U.S. Information Service:** 152 (top).

Art work by JoAnn Bowen.